The Student Edition of MATLAB®

Version 5

User's Guide

The
MATH
WORKS
Inc.

by Duane Hanselman
and Bruce Littlefield

The MATLAB®
Curriculum Series

PRENTICE HALL, Upper Saddle River, NJ 07458

Library of Congress Cataloging-in-Publication Data

The student edition of MATLAB : version 5, user's guide / The
   MathWorks, Inc. :   by Duane Hanselman and Bruce
   Littlefield.
       p.   cm. — (The MATLAB curriculum series)
   Includes bibliographical references (p.   –   ) and index.
   ISBN 0–13–272550–9 (user's guide)
    1. MATLAB.   2. Numerical analysis—Data processing.
 I. MatWorks, Inc.   II. Series.
 QA297.58436   1997
 519.4′1285′53042—dc21   97–11102
                                               CIP

Publisher: Tom Robbins
Editorial / Production Supervision: Rose Kernan
Editor-in-Chief: Marcia Horton
Managing Editor: Bayani Mendoza de Leon
Vice President of Production and Manufacturing:
   David W. Riccardi
Manufacturing Buyer: Donna Sullivan
Manufacturing Manager: Trudy Pisciotti
Copy Editor: Marjorie Schustak
Marketing Manager: Joe Hayton
Editorial Assistant: Nancy Garcia
Book Cover and Box Design: The MathWorks, Inc.
Color Insert Design: Joe Sengotta
CD-Holder Design: Paul Gourhan
Composition: BookMasters, Inc.

RESTRICTED RIGHTS LEGEND

Use, duplication, or disclosure by the Government is subject to
restrictions as set forth in subdivision (b)(3)(ii) of the Rights in
Technical Data and Computer Software clause at 52.227-7013

The software described in this document is furnished under a license
agreement. The software may be used or copied only under the terms
of the license agreement.

MATLAB and SIMULINK are registered trademarks of
The MathWorks, Inc. Other product and company names mentioned
are trademarks or trade names of their respective companies.

The author and publisher of this book have used their best efforts in preparing this book. These efforts
include the development, research, and testing of the theories and programs to determine their effectiveness.
The author and publisher make no warranty of any kind, expressed or implied, with regard to these programs
or the documentation contained in this book. The author and publisher shall not be liable in any event for
incidental or consequential damages in connection with, or arising out of, the furnishing, performance, or use
of these programs.

Printed in the United States of America

10 9 8 7 6 5 4 3 2 1

ISBN 0-13-272550-9

Prentice-Hall International (UK) Limited, London
Prentice-Hall of Australia Pty. Limited, Sydney
Prentice-Hall Canada Inc., Toronto
Prentice-Hall Hispanoamericana, S.A., Mexico
Prentice-Hall of India Private Limited, New Delhi
Prentice-Hall of Japan, Inc., Tokyo
Simon & Schuster Asia Pte. Ltd., Singapore
Editora Prentice-Hall do Brasil, Ltda., Rio de Janeiro

The MathWorks, Inc.
24 Prime Park Way
Natick, Massachusetts 01760
Phone: (508) 647-7000
Fax: (508) 647-7001
E-mail: info@mathworks.com
http://www.mathworks.com

Contents

A Quick Overview   xxvii

Introduction   1

1

Scientific Features   13

2

Command Window Features   23

3

18 Three-Dimensional Graphics 213

19 Cell Arrays and Structures 239

20

21 | Control System Toolbox — 319

22 | Signal Processing Toolbox — 335

23 | Help! — 349

M-File List of Student Edition   **361**

Preface to the Instructor

For hundreds of thousands of industrial, government, and academic users spanning a broad range of engineering, scientific, and other applications, MATLAB has become the premier technical computing environment. Now students can affordably use this powerful computation, data analysis, and visualization software in their undergraduate and graduate studies, while getting acquainted with a tool that will prove invaluable throughout their careers.

As computers have become indispensable for creative work in science and engineering, academic institutions are increasingly aware of the importance of computer use and promoting software "literacy." However, the high cost of commercial-quality software and the challenge of integrating it into the curriculum have made it difficult to turn that awareness into positive results. In response, we created *The Student Edition of MATLAB* and its *User's Guide* so students can be introduced to this powerful tool early in their academic careers. *The Student Edition of MATLAB* encapsulates algorithmic mathematics in a form that can be easily applied to a wide range of disciplines, in courses such as Digital Signal Processing, Control Theory, Linear Algebra, Signals and Systems, Numerical Methods, Applied Mathematics, and Advanced Engineering Mathematics. By itself or when coupled with other texts, MATLAB can be incorporated effectively into the curriculum to enhance the understanding of both fundamental and advanced topics, while enabling the student actively to put theory into practice.

This latest version introduces *The Student Edition of MATLAB 5,* with significant enhancements spanning all of MATLAB—math, data visualization, presentation graphics, arrays and data structures, language constructs, and application development. The availability of this student edition coincides with the availability of the professional MATLAB 5, so you can keep both students' home copies and on-campus computer lab licenses of the professional version synchronized.

We are pleased to see how widespread this movement has become. As we visit colleges and universities from Stanford to MIT and travel on to the leading institutions throughout Europe and the Pacific Rim, we are consistently rewarded by the sight of students using MATLAB, not simply to get the answers, but rather to understand how to get the answers. It is happening across departments at schools, large and small, around the world. We sincerely hope that you enjoy taking part.

Technical Support for Instructors

The MathWorks provides technical support to registered instructors who have adopted *The Student Edition of MATLAB* for use in their courses. For technical support questions, instructors may direct inquiries:

via Web: http://www.mathworks.com/support.html
via e-mail: support@mathworks.com
via telephone: (508) 647-7000
via fax: (508) 647-7201

Other Information Sources for Instructors and Students

Consult the comprehensive tutorials and reference information in the online MATLAB Help Desk by typing helpdesk at the MATLAB prompt. (You must have either Netscape Navigator or Internet Explorer to use this facility, but do not need an Internet connection.)

Use the MATLAB online help facility by typing help <command> at the MATLAB prompt (where <command> is the name of the function about which you would like information). Even better, access help from the menu.

Students and instructors with access to Usenet newsgroups can participate in the MATLAB newsgroup, comp.soft-sys.MATLAB. Here an active community of MATLAB users—spanning industries, countries, applications, and schools—exchange ideas, help with each other's questions and problems, share user-written functions and tools, and generally talk MATLAB. Members of the MathWorks staff also participate, and the newsgroup has become a stimulating, open, and free-flowing forum that embodies the spirit of MATLAB.

On the World Wide Web (WWW), use your favorite browser to reach the Math-Works educational Web site at http://education.mathworks.com. This site offers tips and tools for MATLAB and SIMULINK, pointers to educational sites, and information about support resources. Additional information can be found at the MathWorks Home Page at http://www.mathworks.com.

The MathWorks maintains an electronic archive of user-contributed routines, product information, and other useful things. It can be reached using anonymous ftp to ftp.mathworks.com, or from The MathWorks Home Page on the WWW.

The quarterly MathWorks newsletter *MATLAB News & Notes* provides information on new products, technical notes and tips, application articles, a calendar of trade shows and conferences, and other useful information. *MATLAB News & Notes* is free for registered users of *The Student Edition of MATLAB*.

MATLAB-Based Books

A wide selection of texts may be used with *The Student Edition of MATLAB*, many featuring MATLAB based exercises, problem sets, and supplemental M-files. These include standard texts or supplemental workbooks in a broad range of courses, such as Digital Signal Processing, Control Theory, Linear Algebra, Signals and Systems, Linear Systems, Numerical Methods, Applied Mathematics, Advanced Engineering Mathematics, Probability and Statistics, and Calculus.

For a current list of MATLAB based books, consult the MathWorks Home Page on the WWW at http://www.mathworks.com or the MathWorks anonymous ftp server at ftp.mathworks.com in pub/books/booklist/. Or contact your MathWorks educational account representative at (508) 647-7000 (email: info@mathworks.com).

Acknowledgments

The Student Edition of MATLAB is the product of a collaborative effort between The MathWorks and Prentice Hall. Many people contributed to the development of *The Student Edition of MATLAB*. At MathWorks, we especially want to acknowledge Cleve Moler, Liz Callanan, Jim Tung, Sharon Reposa, Helen Paret, Bob Gilmore, Marjorie Berman, Anthony Urrico, Greg Bartlett, Michael Thornton, Surekha Iyer and Lela Skoufaki. At Prentice Hall, Tom Robbins, Nancy García, Rose Kernan, Bayani DeLeon, Donna Sullivan, Joe Hayton, Marcia Horton, Meghan Dacey, Joe Sengotta, and Paul Gourhan.

We would also like to thank the countless individuals who have provided feedback on the earlier versions of *The Student Edition of MATLAB*. The shape of MATLAB 5 has, in many respects, been influenced by such feedback.

Part One: Introduction

To the Student

The Student Edition of MATLAB brings us back to our roots. The very first version of MATLAB, written at the University of New Mexico and Stanford University in the late 1970s, was intended for use in courses in Matrix Theory, Linear Algebra, and Numerical Analysis. We had been involved in the development of LINPACK and EISPACK, which were FORTRAN subroutine packages for matrix manipulation, and we wanted our students to be able to use these packages without writing FORTRAN programs.

Today MATLAB's capabilities extend far beyond the original "Matrix Laboratory." MATLAB is a high-performance language for technical computing. It integrates computation, visualization, and programming in an easy-to-use environment where problems and solutions are expressed in familiar mathematical notation. Typical uses include:

- Math and computation
- Algorithm development
- Modeling, simulation, and prototyping
- Data analysis, exploration, and visualization
- Scientific and engineering graphics
- Application development, including graphical user interface building

MATLAB is an interactive system whose basic data element is an array that does not require dimensioning. This allows you to solve many technical computing problems, especially those with matrix and vector formulations, in a fraction of the time it would take to write a program in a scalar non-interactive language such as C or FORTRAN.

MATLAB has evolved over the period of years with input from many users. With *The Student Edition of MATLAB 5,* you have the latest state of our art. This new version includes significant enhancements in every part of MATLAB from core mathematical routines and programming language constructs, to data structures and object-oriented methods, to visualization and GUI building tools.

We've continued to maintain close ties to the academic community and have offered academic discounts and classroom licensing arrangements. We have been pleased with the popularity of MATLAB in the computer labs on campus. *The Student Edition of MATLAB* makes it practical for students to use MATLAB on their own personal computers in their homes, dorms, or wherever they study.

Mathematics is the common language of much science and engineering. Matrices, differential equations, arrays of data, plots, and graphs are the basic building blocks of both applied mathematics and MATLAB. It is the underlying mathematical base that makes MATLAB accessible and powerful. One professor. who is a MATLAB fan, told us, "The reason why MATLAB is so useful for signal processing is that it wasn't designed specifically for signal processing, but for mathematics." MATLAB has been used in many different fields:

A physics grad student analyzing and visualizing data from her experiments with magnetic fields of superconductors.

An internationally known amusement park modeling the control systems for its water rides.

A large food company analyzing how microwave ovens cook pizzas.

A cable television company investigating encoding and compression schemes for digital TV.

A sports equipment manufacturer modeling golf swings.

A third grader learning her multiplication tables.

In all of these cases, and thousands more, MATLAB's mathematical foundation made it useful in places and applications far beyond those we contemplated originally.

About the Cover

The cover of this guide depicts a solution to a problem that has played a small, but interesting, role in the history of numerical methods during the last 30 years. The problem involves finding the modes of vibration of a membrane supported by an L-shaped domain consisting of three unit squares. The nonconvex corner in the domain generates singularities in the solutions, thereby providing challenges for both the underlying mathematical theory and the computational algorithms. There are important applications, including wave guides, structures, and semiconductors.

Two of the founders of modern numerical analysis, George Forsythe and J.H. Wilkinson, worked on the problem in the 1950s. (See G.E. Forsythe and W.R. Wasow, *Finite-Difference Methods for Partial Differential Equations*, Wiley, 1960.) One of the authors of MATLAB (Moler) used finite difference techniques to compute solutions in 1965. Typical computer runs took up to half an hour of dedicated computer time on what were then Stanford University's primary computers, an IBM 7090 and Burroughs B5000. The first version of the approach we now use was published in 1967 by L. Fox , P. Henrici, and C. Moler (*SIAM J. Numer. Anal.* 4, 1967, pp. 89-102). It replaced finite differences by combinations of distinguished fundamental solutions to the underlying differential equation formed from Bessel and trigonometric functions. The idea is a generalization of the fact that the real and imaginary parts of complex analytic functions are solutions to Laplace's equation. In the early 1970s, new matrix algorithms, particularly Gene Golub's orthogonalization techniques for least square problems, provided further algorithmic improvements. Today, MATLAB allows you to express the entire algorithm in a few dozen lines, to compute the solution with great accuracy in about a second on a computer at home, and to manipulate color three-dimensional displays of the results. We have included our MATLAB program, membrane.m and logo.m with the M-files supplied with this *Student Edition of MATLAB.*

The Student Edition of MATLAB vs. Professional MATLAB

The Student Edition of MATLAB 5 provides full support of all language, graphics, external interfacing, and other functionality of the professional version of MATLAB 5.0. The maximum matrix size has been expanded to 16,384 elements—twice as large as the previous version, and large enough to process 128-by-128 images or manipulate sound data or other signals for coursework.

Three toolboxes are included with *The Student Edition of MATLAB 5:* Signal Processing Toolbox, Control System Toolbox, and Symbolic Math Toolbox. No other MathWorks toolboxes may be used with *The Student Edition.*

How to Upgrade to Professional MATLAB

You can obtain a professional version of MATLAB 5 for Microsoft Windows 95 and NT, Macintosh, and Linux personal computers; UNIX workstations from Sun, Hewlett-Packard, IBM, Silicon Graphics, and Digital; and Open VMS computers.

In addition, a comprehensive set of toolboxes is available for use with professional MATLAB, covering areas such as neural networks, fuzzy logic, wavelets, statistics, image processing, and optimization. Blocksets are add-ins to professional SIMULINK that provide additional libraries of block for specialized applications like communications, DSP design, and fixed-point simulation. Real-Time Workshop is a program that allows you to generate C code from SIMULINK block diagrams and to run it on a variety of real-time systems. For product information or to learn about our educational discount options, call or write to your educational account representative at The Math-Works at:

The MathWorks, Inc.
University Sales Department
24 Prime Park Way
Natick, MA 01760-1500
Phone: (508) 647-7000
E-mail: info@mathworks.com

Support, Registration, and Warranty

Student Support Policy

Neither Prentice Hall, Inc. nor The MathWorks, Inc. provides technical support to student users of *The Student Edition of MATLAB*. If you encounter difficulty while using *The Student Edition* software:

1. Read the relevant section of this *User's Guide* containing tutorial and/or reference information on the commands or procedures you are trying to execute.

2. Use the software's online help facility by typing help <command> at the MATLAB prompt where <command> is the name of the function you are executing.

3. Consult the comprehensive online reference documentation by typing helpdesk at the MATLAB prompt.

4. Write down the sequence of procedures you were executing so that you can explain to your instructor the nature of the problem. Be certain to note the exact error message you encountered.

5. If you have consulted this *User's Guide* and the online help system and are still stymied, you may post your question to the comp.soft-sys.matlab newsgroup, if you have access to Usenet newsgroups. Many active MATLAB users participate in the newsgroups, and they are a good resource for answers or tips about MATLAB usage.

Student User Registration

Students who have purchased the software package will find a card in the package for registering as a user of *The Student Edition of MATLAB*. Take a moment now to complete and return this card to us. Registered student users:

Are entitled to replace defective CDs at no charge.

Quality for a discount on upgrades to professional versions of MATLAB.

Become active members of the worldwide MATLAB user community.

It is very important that you return this card. Otherwise you will not be on our mailing list and you will not qualify for student upgrades and other promotions.

Defective CD Replacement

Contact Prentice Hall at matlab@prenhall.com for CD replacement. You must send us your damaged or defective CD, and we will provide you with a new one.

Limited Warranty

No warranties, express or implied, are made by The MathWorks, Inc. that the program or documentation is free of error. Further, The MathWorks, Inc. does not warrant the program for correctness, accuracy, or fitness for a task. You rely on the results of the program solely at your own risk. The program should not be relied on as the sole basis to solve a problem whose incorrect solution could result in injury to person or property. If the program is employed in such a manner, it is at the user's own risk, and The MathWorks, Inc. disclaims all liability for such misuse. Neither The MathWorks, Inc. nor anyone less who has been involved in the creation, production, or delivery of this program shall be liable for any direct or indirect damages.

Toolboxes

MATLAB is both an environment and a programming language, and one of its great strengths is the fact that the MATLAB language allows you to build your own reusable tools. You can easily create your own special functions and programs (known as M-files) in MATLAB code. As you write more and more MATLAB functions to deal with certain problems, you might be tempted to group related functions together into special directories for inconvenience. This leads directly to the concept of a *Toolbox*: a specialized collection of M-files for working on particular classes of problems.

Toolboxes are more than just collections of useful functions; they represent the efforts of some of the world's top researchers in fields such as controls, signal processing, system identification, and others. Because of this, the MATLAB Application Toolboxes let you "stand on the shoulders" of world class scientists to learn and apply their tools.

The Student Edition of MATLAB contains three toolboxes, bundled free with the software: the *Signal Processing Toolbox, Control System Toolbox,* and *Symbolic Math Toolbox.*

All toolboxes are built directly on top of MATLAB. This has some very important implications for you:

Every toolbox builds on the robust numerics, rock-solid accuracy, and years of experience in MATLAB.

Netscape Navigator 2.0 or later or Microsoft Internet Explorer version 3.0 (to run the MATLAB Help Desk)

The MATLAB Notebook for Windows

The MATLAB Notebook for Windows is a dynamic integration of MATLAB and Microsoft Word, which allows you to construct interactive word processing documents containing live MATLAB commands and graphics.

Using the Notebook, you can create an M-book, a standard Microsoft Word document that contains not only text, but also MATLAB commands and the output from those commands. You can think of an M-book as MATLAB running within word, with a full set of powerful word processing capabilities available to annotate and document your MATLAB work. If you are a Microsoft Word user, you will find the Notebook to be a natural environment that combines a familiar and powerful word processor with the computational and graphing capabilities of MATLAB. The MATLAB Notebook benefits any MATLAB user who needs to create interactive, technical documents, such as:

Electronic textbooks

Electronic handbooks

Interactive MATLAB sessions

Technical reports and project design logbooks

Interactive product specifications

Electronic class notes and homeworks

The enabling technology of the MATLAB Notebook is Dynamic Data Exchange (DDE), which provides the communication between MATLAB and Word. With a single keystroke, MATLAB commands entered in the Notebook are formatted and sent via DDE to MATLAB for evaluation. The result of the command is returned to the Notebook and inserted in the Word document. The Notebook handles both text and graphic output from MATLAB.

To use the Notebook, first make sure that you have installed Word for Windows version 6.0 or 7.0, then follow instructions below. After you have installed the Notebook, double-click on the M-book titled MATLAB Notebook README in the Student Edition Startup Folder for more information. Other example M-books are included with *The Student Edition of MATLAB;* they are described in the README M-book.

PC Installation Procedure

1. Place the CD-ROM distribution disk into the CD-ROM drive. On Windows 95, the Setup program begins to run automatically if MATLAB was not pre-

viously installed. Otherwise, double-click the **setup.exe** icon to begin the installation procedure.

2. Accept or reject the software licensing agreement displayed. If you accept the terms of the agreement, you may proceed with the installation.

3. On the **Customer Information** screen, enter your name and your school's name. Press the **Next** button.

4. Click in the box beside a component name to indicate which products you want to install. Click on a check mark to deselect any component you do not want to install at this time. You can add any deselected component to your installation at a later time. This screen assumes C:\MATLAB is the destination directory for installation of MATLAB and any selected toolboxes. Press **Browse** if you want to install into a different directory.

MATLAB for Macintosh

System Requirements

MATLAB for the Macintosh runs on:

Any Power Macintosh

Any Macintosh equipped with a 68020 or 68030 microprocessor and a 68881 or 68882 math coprocessor

Any Macintosh equipped with a 68040 microprocessor (math coprocessor is built in).

MATLAB will not run on a Macintosh with a 68LC040 microprocessor.

MATLAB requires the following minimum configuration:

26 MB of free space on your hard drive. An additional 60 MB is required for the optional online Help system.

16 MB memory partition

CD-ROM drive

Color QuickDraw

System 7.1 or later; System 7.5 or later is preferred.

Note

Suggested total system memory assumes a reasonably large System Folder. Your memory requirements may vary depending upon the exact size of your System Folder.

Macintosh Installation Procedure

1. Place the CD-ROM distribution disk into the CD-ROM drive. Double-click the **Install MATLAB** icon.

- Search path browser/editor
- Workspace browser
- Web-based online Help Desk/documentation viewer
- GUI builder
- Handle Graphics® property editor
- Preparsed P-code files (P-files)
- Enhanced, self-diagnosing Application Program Interface (API)

New Data Types, Structures, and Language Features

MATLAB 5 introduces new data types and language improvements. These new features make it easy to build much larger and more complex MATLAB applications.

- Multidimensional arrays
- User-definable data structures
- Cell arrays: multitype data arrays
- Character arrays: two bytes per character
- Single byte data type for images
- Object-oriented programming
- Variable-length argument lists
- Multifunction and private M-files
- Function and operator overloading
- `switch`/`case` statements

Faster, Better Graphics and Visualization

MATLAB 5 adds powerful new visualization techniques and significantly faster graphics using the Z-buffer algorithm. Presentation graphics are also improved to give you more options and control over how you present your data.

- Visualization
  - Truecolor (RGB) support
  - Fast and accurate Z-buffer display algorithm
  - Flat, Gouraud, and Phong lighting
  - Vectorized patches for three dimensional modeling
  - Camera view model, perspective
  - Efficient 8-bit image display
  - Image file import/export
- Presentation graphics
  - Greek symbols, sub/superscripts, multiline text

- Dual axis plots
- Three-dimensional quiver, ribbon, and stem plots
- Pie charts, three-dimensional bar charts
- Extended curve marker symbol family

More Mathematical and Data Analysis Tools

With more than 500 mathematical, statistical, and engineering functions, MATLAB gives you immediate access to the numeric computing tools you need. New features with MATLAB 5 include:

- New ordinary differential equation solvers (ODEs)
- Delaunay triangulation
- Gridding for irregularly sampled data
- Set theory functions
- Two-dimensional quadrature
- Time and date handling functions
- Multidimensional interpolation, convolution, and FFT's
- Bit-wise operators
- Iterative sparse methods
- Sparse matrix eigenvalues and singular values

About *The Student Edition of MATLAB 5*

The Student Edition of MATLAB 5 is a full-featured version of MATLAB 5. The sole difference is that *The Student Edition* limits each matrix to 16,384 elements, large enough to study image processing algorithms on 128-by-128 images or manipulate speech data or other signals for coursework.

Application Toolboxes

MATLAB toolboxes are libraries of functions that customize MATLAB for solving particular classes of problems. They're written in the MATLAB language, so you can view the source algorithms, and add new ones. The large selection of toolboxes lets you compare techniques and choose the right approach for your particular application.

Three toolboxes are bundled with *The Student Edition of MATLAB 5*:

- Signal Processing Toolbox
- Control System Toolbox
- Symbolic Math Toolbox

For information about these toolboxes, consult the corresponding chapters in this book or the online toolbox documentation.

The MATLAB Notebook allows you to access MATLAB's numeric computation and visualization software from within a word processing environment (Microsoft Word). The MATLAB Notebook is included with the Student Edition of MATLAB 5.

Using the Notebook, you can create a document that contains text, MATLAB commands, and the output from MATLAB commands. You can think of this document as a record of an interactive MATLAB session annotated with text or as a document embedded with live MATLAB commands and output.

- The Notebook is useful for creating electronic or printed:
- Documents
- Records of MATLAB sessions
- Class notes
- Textbooks and handbooks
- Technical reports

You will have the option to install the MATLAB Notebook when you install MATLAB. For more information on using it, consult the *MATLAB Notebook User's Guide* in the online documentation.

The Student Edition of SIMULINK 2

SIMULINK is an add-on to MATLAB that adds a block diagram interface and live simulation capabilities to the core numeric, graphics, and language functionality of MATLAB. *The Student Edition of SIMULINK 2* is designed for use with *The Student Edition of MATLAB 5,* and is available from Prentice-Hall.

Upgrading from MATLAB 4 to MATLAB 5

MATLAB 5 is a major upgrade to MATLAB. Although The MathWorks endeavors to maintain full upward compatibility between subsequent releases of MATLAB, inevitably there are situations where this is not possible. In the case of MATLAB 5, there are a number of changes that you need to know about in order to migrate your code from MATLAB 4 to MATLAB 5.

For a complete description of these changes, and how to address them in your MATLAB code, consult Chapter 2 of the online *MATLAB 5 New Features Guide*.

Symbolic Math Toolbox Changes

The Symbolic Math Toolbox has changed dramatically from its initial release to version 2 which is bundled with this *Student Edition*. The syntax for symbolic operations is now significantly easier and more natural to use, improvements that were made possible by MATLAB 5's architecture. Unfortunately, this new syntax of the Symbolic Math Toolbox is, as a result, quite different from the syntax of the toolbox's first version. To help you with the transition, functions have been added to support the old syntax, so your code will continue to run. However, this is a temporary solution. Since these "grandfathered" functions will be phased out over time, you should learn and utilize the new syntax described in this book and the online documentation as quickly as possible.

New Platform-Specific Features

MS Windows

Path Browser

The Path Browser lets you view and modify the MATLAB search path. All changes take effect in MATLAB immediately.

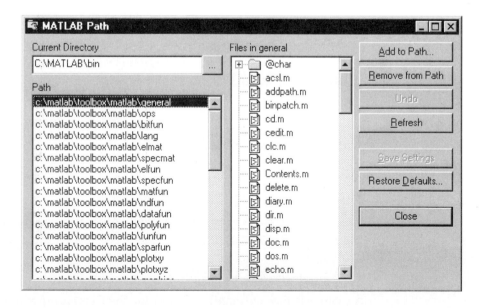

Workspace Browser

The Workspace Browser lets you view the contents of the current MATLAB workspace. It provides a graphical representation of the traditional whos output. In addition, you can clear workspace variables and rename them.

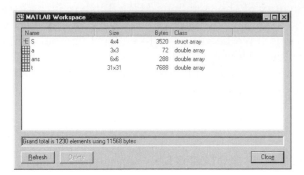

M-File Editor/Debugger

The graphical M-file editor/debugger allows you to set breakpoints and single-step through M-code. The M-file editor/debugger starts automatically when a breakpoint is hit. When MATLAB is installed, this program becomes the default editor.

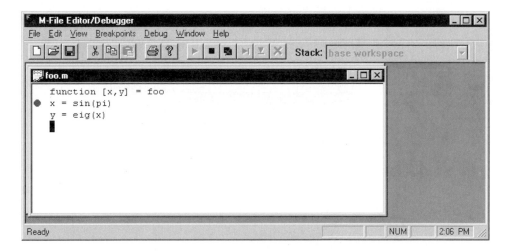

Command Window Toolbar

A toolbar is now optionally present for the *Command* window. The toolbar provides single-click access to several commonly used operations:

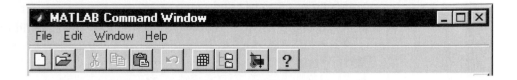

- Open a new editor window
- Open a file for editing
- Cut, copy, paste, and undo
- Open the Workspace Browser
- Open the Path Browser
- Create new SIMULINK model (if SIMULINK is installed)
- Access the Help facility

New Dialog Boxes

New **Preferences** dialog boxes are accessible through the **File** menu. Some of these were previously available through the **Options** menu in MATLAB 4. There are three categories of preferences:

- General
- Command Window Font
- Copying Options

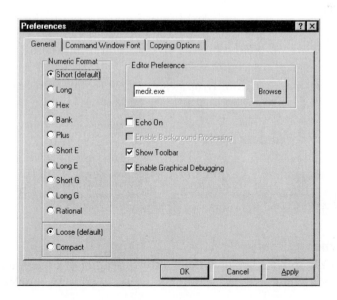

16-bit Stereo Sound

MATLAB 5 now supports 16-bit stereo sound on the Windows platform.

Macintosh

Two new features available on the Macintosh platform are:

- Japanese characters

  It is now possible to generate annotation and string constants that use Japanese characters.

- 16-bit stereo sound

  MATLAB 5 now supports 16-bit stereo sound.

User Interface Enhancements

- Optional toolbars in the *Command* window, *Editor* windows, and M-file debugger allow rapid access to commonly used features.

- Color syntax highlighting in the *Command* window, *Editor* windows, and M-file debugger provides visual cues for identifying blocks of code, comments, and strings.

- Almost all lists and text items in the Command Window, Editor, Path Browser, Workspace Browser, M-file debugger, and Command History Window have optional dynamic or "live" scrolling; the display is scrolled as the scroll box of a scrollbar is moved.

- Macintosh Drag and Drop is supported throughout MATLAB for rapid and easy exchange of text between windows.

Command Window Features

- Typing on the current command line can now be undone and redone. This includes cutting, clearing, overtyping, dragging, and dropping.

- Placing the caret on an error message and pressing **Enter** opens the M-file in the Editor, positioned to the offending line.

Command History Window

The *Command History* window contains a list of all commands executed from the *Command* window. Commands are saved between MATLAB sessions, so you can select and execute a group of commands from a previous day's work to continue quickly from where you left off.

```
▤▦▦▦▦▦▦▦ Command History ▦▦▦▦▦▦▦▤
%----- Starting MATLAB at 10:12 AM 3/1/96 -----%
edit why
dir
help why
surf(peaks(20))
close
cd ..
dir
```

Path Browser

The Path Browser provides an intuitive, easy-to-use graphical interface for viewing and modifying the MATLAB search path. You can reorder or modify the search path simply by dragging items in the path list. Similarly, you can change the current MATLAB directory by dragging any folder into the current MATLAB directory area.

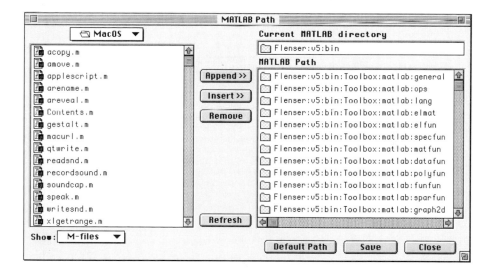

Workspace Browser

The Workspace Browser allows you to view the contents of the current MATLAB workspace. It provides a graphic representation of the traditional whos output. You can delete variables from the workspace and sort the workspace by various criteria. Double-clicking on a workspace variable displays that variable's contents in the *Command* window.

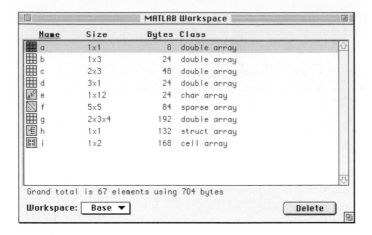

M-File Debugger

MATLAB 5 includes a graphical M-file debugger, which allows you to set breakpoints and single-step through M-code. Selecting text in the debugger window and pressing the **Enter** (not the **Return**) key evaluates that text in the *Command* window.

```
                        why.m

1      function reason = why
2      %WHY Provides succinct answers to any questions.
3      %    WHY displays a succinct answer.
4      %
5      %    S = WHY returns the reason in the string S.
6
7      %    Copyright (c) 1984-96 by The MathWorks, Inc.
8      %    $Revision: 5.4 $  $Date: 1996/04/24 20:24:53 $
9
10  ●   Y = ['How the hell should I know?'
11  -       'Why not?                   '
12  -       'It feels good.             '
13  -       'R.T.F.M.                   '
14  -       'Why? Because we like you!  '
15  -       'Stupid question.           '
16  -       'Jack made me do it.        '
17  -       'Because it''s there.        '
18  -       'For people like you.       '
19  -       'Time to get back to work.  '];
20  - ◆ rsn = Y(fix(10*rand)+1,:);
21  -   if nargout
22  -     reason = rsn;
23  -   else
24  -     disp(' ')
25        ...
```

Stack: why

Editor Features

- Command-clicking in the title of an *Editor* window displays a pop-up menu containing the full path to the M-file. Selecting a folder from the pop-up menu opens that folder in the Finder.

- Selecting text in an *Editor* window and pressing **Enter** evaluates that text in the *Command* window.

- Typing a close parenthesis, bracket, or brace briefly highlights the matching open parenthesis, bracket, or brace.

```
why.m

20      'For people like you.        '
21      'Time to get back to work.   '];
22
23 rsn = Y(fix(10*rand)+1,:);
24 if nargout
25   reason = rsn;
26 else
27   disp(' ')
28   disp(rsn)
```

- Double-clicking a parenthesis, bracket, or brace selects all text within the matching parenthesis, bracket, or brace.

- Line numbers may be optionally displayed.

Introduction

1

1

Now that you've installed MATLAB, it's time to see what it can do. In this tutorial you will be shown some of its capabilities; to show all of what MATLAB can do would simply take too much time. As you follow this tutorial, you will begin to see the power of MATLAB to solve a wide variety of problems important to you. You may find it beneficial to go through this tutorial while running MATLAB. In doing so, you will be able to enter the MATLAB statements as described, confirm the results presented, and develop a hands-on understanding of MATLAB.

Perhaps the easiest way to visualize MATLAB is to think of it as a full-featured calculator. Like a basic calculator, it does simple math such as addition, subtraction, multiplication, and division. Like a scientific calculator, it handles complex numbers, square roots and powers, logarithms, and trigonometric operations such as sine, cosine, and tangent. Like a programmable calculator, it can be used to store and retrieve data; you can create, execute, and save sequences of commands to automate the computation of important equations; you can make logical comparisons and control the order in which commands are executed. Like the most powerful calculators available, it allows you to plot data in a wide variety of ways, perform matrix algebra, manipulate polynomials, integrate functions, manipulate equations symbolically, and so on.

In reality, MATLAB offers many more features and is more multifaceted than any calculator. MATLAB is a tool for making mathematical calculations. It is a user-friendly programming language with features more advanced and much easier to use than computer languages such as BASIC, Pascal, or C. It provides a rich environment for data visualization through its powerful graphics capabilities. MATLAB is an application development platform, where you can create graphical user interfaces (GUIs) that offer a visual approach to solving specific problems. In addition, MATLAB offers sets of problem-solving tools for specific application areas, called **Toolboxes**. For example, this Student Edition of MATLAB includes the *Control System Toolbox,* the *Signal Processing Toolbox,* and the *Symbolic Math Toolbox*. In addition, you can create toolboxes of your own.

Because of the vast power of MATLAB, it is important to start with the basics. That is, rather than taking in everything at once and hoping that you understand some of it, in the beginning it is helpful to think of MATLAB as a calculator. First, as a basic calculator; next, as a scientific calculator; then, as a programmable calculator; then, finally, as a top-of-the-line calculator. By using this calculator analogy, you will see the ease with which MATLAB solves everyday problems, and will begin to see how MATLAB can be used to solve complex problems in a flexible, straightforward manner.

Depending on your background, you may find parts of this tutorial boring, or some of it may be over your head. In either case, find a point in the tutorial where you're comfortable, start up MATLAB, and begin. To assist you while learning, the following conventions are used throughout this text:

Bold	Important terms and facts
Bold italics	New terms
Bold initial caps	Keyboard key names, menu names, and menu items
`Constant width`	User input, function and file names, commands, and screen displays
Italics	Window names, book titles, toolbox names, company names, example text, and mathematical notation

Running MATLAB creates one or more windows on your monitor. Of these, the *Command* window is the primary place where you interact with MATLAB. This window has an appearance as shown below. The character string `EDU»` is the MATLAB prompt in the Student Edition. In other versions of MATLAB, the prompt is simply ». When the *Command* window is active, a cursor (most likely blinking) should appear to the right of the prompt, as shown in the figure. This

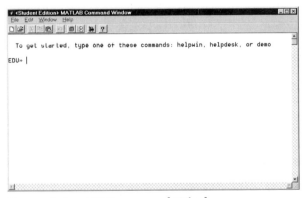

Figure 1.1   PC Command Window

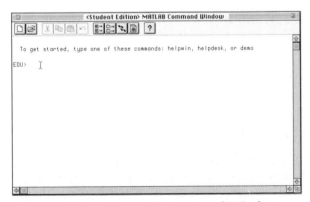

Figure 1.2   Mac Initial Command Window

cursor and the MATLAB prompt signify that MATLAB is waiting to answer a mathematical question.

1.1 Simple Math

Just like a calculator, MATLAB can do simple math. Consider the following simple example: Mary goes to the office-supply store and buys 4 erasers at 25 cents each, 6 memo pads at 52 cents each, and 2 rolls of tape at 99 cents each. How many items did Mary buy, and how much did they cost?

To solve this using your calculator, you enter:

$$4 + 6 + 2 = 12 \text{ items} \qquad 4 \cdot 25 + 6 \cdot 52 + 2 \cdot 99 = 610 \text{ cents}$$

In MATLAB, this can be solved in a number of different ways. First, the above-mentioned calculator approach can be taken:

```
EDU» 4+6+2
ans =
    12

EDU» 4*25 + 6*52 + 2*99
ans =
   610
```

Note that MATLAB doesn't care about spaces, for the most part, and that multiplication takes precedence over addition. Note also that MATLAB calls the result ans (short for *answer*) for both computations.

As an alternative, the above problem can be solved by storing information in **MATLAB variables**:

```
EDU» erasers=4
erasers =
    4

EDU» pads=6
pads =
    6

EDU» tape=2;
```

```
EDU» items=erasers+pads+tape
items =
    12
EDU» cost=erasers*25+pads*52+tape*99
cost =
    610
```

Here we created three MATLAB variables—erasers, pads, and tape—to store the number of each items. After entering each statement, MATLAB displayed the results, except in the case of tape. The semicolon at the end of the line EDU» tape=2; tells MATLAB to evaluate the line but not tell us the answer. Finally, rather than calling the results ans, we told MATLAB to call the number of items purchased items and the total price paid cost. At each step, MATLAB remembered past information. Because MATLAB remembers things, let's ask what the average cost per item was.

```
EDU» average_cost=cost/items
average_cost =
    50.8333
```

Because *average cost* is two words and MATLAB variable names must be one word, the underscore was used to create the single MATLAB variable average_cost.

In addition to addition and multiplication, MATLAB offers the following basic arithmetic operations:

Operation	Symbol	Example
addition, $a + b$	+	5+3
subtraction, $a - b$	–	23–12
multiplication, $a \cdot b$	*	3.14*0.85
division, $a \div b$	/ or \	56/8 = 8\56
exponentiation, a^b	^	5^2

The order in which these operations are evaluated in a given expression is given by the usual rules of precedence, which can be summarized as follows: **Expressions are evaluated from left to right, with the exponentiation operation having the highest order of precedence, followed by both multiplication and division having equal precedence, followed by both**

addition and subtraction having equal precedence. Parentheses can be used to alter this usual ordering, in which case evaluation initiates within the innermost parentheses and proceeds outward.

1.2   The MATLAB Workspace

As you work in the *Command* window, MATLAB remembers the commands you enter as well as the values of any variables you create. These commands and variables are said to reside in the ***MATLAB Workspace,*** and may be recalled whenever you wish. For example, to check the value of tape, all you have to do is ask MATLAB for it by entering its name at the prompt:

```
EDU» tape
tape =
       2
```

If you can't remember the name of a variable, you can ask MATLAB for a list of the variables it knows by using the MATLAB command who:

```
EDU»who
Your variables are:

ans              cost            items          tape
average_cost     erasers         pads
```

Note that MATLAB doesn't tell you the value of all the variables; it merely gives you their names. To find their values, you must enter their names at the MATLAB prompt. Just like a calculator, there's only so much room to store variables.

To recall previous commands, MATLAB uses the **Cursor** keys (←→↑↓) on your keyboard. For example, pressing the ↑ key once recalls the most recent command to the MATLAB prompt. Repeated pressing scrolls back through prior commands one at a time. In a similar manner, pressing the ↓ key scrolls forward through commands. Moreover, entering the first few characters of a known previous command at the prompt and then pressing the ↑ key immediately recalls the most recent command having those initial characters. At any time, the ← and → keys can be used to move the cursor within the command at the MATLAB prompt. In this manner, the command can be edited. Alternatively, the **Mouse** can be used along with the **Clipboard** to cut, copy, paste, and edit the text at the command prompt.

1.3   About Variables

Like any other computer language, MATLAB has rules about variable names. Earlier it was noted that variable names must be a single word containing no spaces. More specifically, MATLAB variable-naming rules are:

Variable Naming Rules	Comments/Examples
Variable names are case sensitive.	`Items`, `items`, `itEms`, and `ITEMS` are all different **MATLAB** variables
Variable names can contain up to 31 characters, and characters beyond the thirty-first are ignored.	`howaboutthisvariablename`

Variable names must start with a letter, followed by any number of letters, digits, or underscores. Punctuation characters are not allowed, since many of them have special meaning to MATLAB.	`how_about_this_variable_name`
	`X51483`
	`a_b_c_d_e`

In addition to these naming rules, MATLAB has several special variables. They are:

Special Variables	Value
`ans`	The default variable name used for results
`pi`	The ratio of the circumference of a circle to its diameter
`eps`	The smallest number such that, when added to one, creates a number greater than one on the computer
`flops`	Count of floating point operations
`inf`	Stands for infinity, e.g., 1/0
`NaN` (or) `nan`	Stands for Not-a-Number, e.g., 0/0
`i` (and) `j`	$i=j=\sqrt{-1}$
`nargin`	Number of function input arguments used
`nargout`	Number of function output arguments used
`realmin`	The smallest usable positive real number
`realmax`	The largest usable positive real number

As you create variables in MATLAB, there may be instances where you wish to redefine one or more variables. For example:

```
EDU» erasers=4;

EDU» pads=6;

EDU» tape=2;

EDU» items=erasers+pads+tape
items =
     12

EDU» erasers=6
erasers =
      6

EDU» items
items =
     12
```

Here, using the first example again, we found the number of items Mary purchased. Afterward, we changed the number of erasers to 6, overwriting its prior value of 4. In doing so, the value of items has not changed. Unlike a spreadsheet, MATLAB **does not** recalculate the number of items based on the new value of erasers. **When MATLAB performs a calculation, it does so using the values it knows at the time the requested command is evaluated.** In the above-mentioned example, if you wish to recalculate the number of items, the total cost, and the average cost, it is necessary to recall the appropriate MATLAB commands and ask MATLAB to evaluate them again.

The special variables given above follow this guideline also. When you start MATLAB, they have the values given above; if you change their values, the original special values are lost until you clear the variables or restart MATLAB. With this in mind, avoid redefining special variables unless absolutely necessary.

Variables in the MATLAB workspace can be unconditionally deleted by using the command clear. For example:

```
EDU» clear erasers
```

deletes just the variable erasers.

```
EDU» clear cost items
```

deletes both cost and items.

```
EDU» clear cl*
```

uses the wildcard * to delete all variables that start with the letters cl.

```
EDU» clear
```

deletes all variables in the workspace! You are not asked to confirm this command. All variables are cleared and cannot be retrieved!

Needless to say, the `clear` command is dangerous and should be used with caution. Thankfully, there is seldom a need to clear variables from the workspace.

1.4 Comments and Punctuation

All text after a percent sign (%) is taken as a comment statement, e.g.:

```
EDU» erasers=4  % Number of erasers.
erasers =
      4
```

The variable `erasers` is given the value 4, and MATLAB simply ignores the percent sign and all text following it. This feature makes it easy to document what you are doing.

Multiple commands can be placed on one line if they are separated by commas or semicolons, e.g.:

```
EDU» erasers=4, pads=6; tape=2
erasers =
      4
tape =
      2
```

Commas tell MATLAB to display results; **semicolons suppress printing**.

```
EDU» average_cost=cost/...
   items
average_cost =
   50.8333
```

As shown above, a succession of three periods tells MATLAB that the rest of a statement appears on the next line. Statement continuation, as shown above, works if the succession of three periods occurs between variable names or operators. That is, a variable name cannot be split between two lines:

```
EDU» average_cost=cost/it...
ems
??? age_cost=cost/items
                  |
Missing operator, comma, or semicolon.
```

Likewise, comment statements cannot be continued:

```
EDU» % Comments cannot be continued ...
EDU» either
??? Undefined function or variable either.
```

You can interrupt MATLAB at any time by pressing **Ctrl-C** (pressing the **Ctrl** and **C** keys simultaneously) on a PC. Pressing ⌘–. (pressing the ⌘ and . keys simultaneously) on a Macintosh does the same thing.

1.5   Complex Numbers

One of the most powerful features of MATLAB is that it does not require any special handling for complex numbers. Complex numbers are formed in MATLAB in several ways. Examples of complex numbers include:

```
EDU» c1=1−2i   % the appended i signifies the imaginary part
c1 =
    1.0000 − 2.0000i

EDU» c1=1−2j   % j also works
c1 =
    1.0000 − 2.0000i

EDU» c2=3*(2−sqrt(−1)*3)
c2 =
    6.0000 − 9.0000i

EDU» c3=sqrt(−2)
c3 =
         0 + 1.4142i

EDU» c4=6+sin(.5)*i
c4 =
    6.0000 + 0.4794i

EDU» c5=6+sin(.5)*j
c5 =
    6.0000 + 0.4794i
```

In the last two examples, the MATLAB default values of $i=j=\sqrt{-1}$ are used to form the imaginary part. Multiplication by i or j is required in these cases since $sin(.5)i$ and $sin(.5)j$ mean nothing to MATLAB. Termination with the characters i and j, as shown in the first two examples above, works only for numerical constants, not for expressions.

Some programming languages require special handling for complex numbers wherever they appear. In MATLAB, no special handling is required. Mathematical operations on complex numbers are written the same as those for real numbers:

```
EDU» c6=(c1+c2)/c3   % from the above data
c6 =
   −7.7782 − 4.9497i
```

```
EDU» check_it_out=i^2   % sqrt(-1) squared must be -1!
check_it_out =
    -1.0000 + 0.0000i
```

In general, operations on complex numbers lead to complex numbers. In those cases where a negligible real or imaginary part remains, you can use the functions `real` and `imag` to extract the real and imaginary parts, respectively.

As a final example of complex arithmetic, consider the Euler (sounds like *Oiler*) identity, which relates the **polar** form of a complex number to its **rectangular** form:

$$M\angle\theta \equiv M \cdot e^{j\theta} = a + bi$$

where the polar form is given by a **magnitude** M and an **angle** θ, and the rectangular form is given by $a + bi$. The relationships among these forms are:

$$M = \sqrt{a^2 + b^2}$$

$$\theta = \tan^{-1}(b/a)$$

$$a = M\cos\theta$$

$$b = M\sin\theta$$

In MATLAB, the conversion between polar and rectangular forms makes use of the functions `real`, `imag`, `abs`, and `angle`:

```
EDU» c1
c1 =
    1.0000 - 2.0000i

EDU» mag_c1=abs(c1)
mag_c1 =
    2.2361

EDU» angle_c1=angle(c1)
angle_c1 =
    -1.1071

EDU» deg_c1=angle_c1*180/pi
deg_c1 =
    -63.4349

EDU» real_c1=real(c1)
real_c1 =
    1

EDU» imag_c1=imag(c1)
imag_c1 =
    -2
```

The MATLAB function abs computes the magnitude of complex numbers or the absolute value of real numbers, depending upon which one you give it. Likewise, the MATLAB function angle computes the angle of a complex number in radians.

Scientific Features

2.1 Common Mathematical Functions

Like most scientific calculators, MATLAB offers many common functions important to mathematics, engineering, and the sciences. In addition to common functions, MATLAB offers hundreds of specialized functions and algorithms that are useful to solve specific problems. All of these functions and algorithms (as well as all other MATLAB features) are listed in the reference tables in Chapter 24. In addition, more comprehensive help is available by consulting on-line help, which is thoroughly discussed in Chapter 23.

2.1 Common Mathematical Functions

A partial list of the common functions that MATLAB supports is shown in the following table. Most of these functions are used in the same way you would write them mathematically:

```
EDU» x=sqrt(2)/2
x =
    0.7071

EDU» y=asin(x)
y =
    0.7854

EDU» y_deg=y*180/pi
y_deg =
   45.0000
```

These commands find the angle where the sine function has a value of $\sqrt{2}/2$. While your calculator may work in degrees or radians, MATLAB works only in radians, where 2π radians is equal to 360 degrees. Other examples include:

Common Functions	
abs(x)	Absolute value or magnitude of complex number
acos(x)	Inverse cosine
acosh(x)	Inverse hyperbolic cosine
angle(x)	Four-quadrant angle of complex
asin(x)	Inverse sine
asinh(x)	Inverse hyperbolic sine
atan(x)	Inverse tangent
atan2(x,y)	Four-quadrant inverse tangent
atanh(x)	Inverse hyperbolic tangent
ceil(x)	Round toward plus infinity
conj(x)	Complex conjugate
cos(x)	Cosine
cosh(x)	Hyperbolic cosine
exp(x)	Exponential: e^x
fix(x)	Round toward zero
floor(x)	Round toward minus infinity
gcd(x,y)	Greatest common divisor of integers x and y
imag(x)	Complex imaginary part
lcm(x,y)	Least common multiple of integers x and y
log(x)	Natural logarithm
log10(x)	Common logarithm
real(x)	Complex real part
rem(x,y)	Remainder after division: rem(x,y) gives the remainder of x/y
round(x)	Round toward nearest integer
sign(x)	Signum function: return sign of argument, e.g., sign(1.2)=1, sign(−23.4)=−1, sign(0)=0
sin(x)	Sine
sinh(x)	Hyperbolic sine
sqrt(x)	Square root
tan(x)	Tangent
tanh(x)	Hyperbolic tangent

```
EDU» 4*atan(1) % one way to approximate pi
ans =
        3.1416

EDU» help atan2 % asks for help on the function atan2

 ATAN2 Four-quadrant inverse tangent.
    ATAN2(Y,X) is the four-quadrant arctangent of the real
    parts of the elements of X and Y.
    -pi <= ATAN2(Y,X) <= pi.

    See also ATAN.

EDU» help atan % see the difference between atan2 and atan?

 ATAN  Inverse tangent.
    ATAN(X) is the arctangent of the elements of X.

    See also ATAN2.

EDU» 180/pi*atan(-2/3) % atan2 uses vector sign information
ans =
        -33.69

EDU» 180/pi*atan2(2,-3)
ans =
        146.31

EDU» 180/pi*atan2(-2,3)
ans =
        -33.69

EDU» 180/pi*atan2(2,3)
ans =
         33.69

EDU» 180/pi*atan2(-2,-3) % 180/pi converts angle to degrees
ans =
        -146.31
```

Yet more examples include:

```
EDU» y=sqrt(3^2 + 4^2) % show 3-4-5 right triangle relationship
y =
     5

EDU» y=rem(23,4) % 23/4 has a remainder of 3
y =
     3
```

```
EDU» x=2.6, y1=fix(x), y2=floor(x), y3=ceil(x), y4=round(x)
x =
     2.6000
y1 =
     2
y2 =
     2
y3 =
     3
y4 =
     3

EDU» gcd(18,81) % 9 is the largest factor common to 18 and 81
ans =
     9

EDU» lcm(18,81) % 162 is the least common multiple of 18 and 81
ans =
     162
```

Example: Estimating the Height of a Building

Problem: Consider the problem of estimating the height of a building, as illustrated in Fig. 2.1. If the observer is a distance D from the building, the angle from the observer to the top of the building is θ, and the height of the observer is h, what is the building height?

Solution: Draw a simple diagram as shown in Fig. 2.1. The building height is h + H, where H is the length of the triangle side opposite the observer. This length can be found from the triangle relationship

$$\tan(\theta) = \frac{H}{D}$$

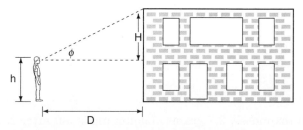

Figure 2.1   Estimating Building Height

Therefore, the building height is h + H = h + D · tan(θ).

If h = 2 meters, D = 50 meters, and θ is 60 degrees, MATLAB gives a solution of:

```
EDU» h=2
h =
     2
EDU» theta=60
theta =
    60
EDU» D=50
D =
    50
EDU» building_height=h+D*tan(theta*pi/180)
building_height =
       88.603
```

Note that since MATLAB always uses radians, θ was converted to radians by multiplying by pi/180 before being passed to the tangent function.

Example: Radioactive Decay Example

Problem: The radioactive element polonium has a half-life of 140 days, which means that because of radioactive decay the amount of polonium remaining after 140 days is one-half of the original amount. Starting with 10 grams of polonium today, how much is left after 250 days?

Solution: After one half-life, or 140 days, 10 · 0.5 = 5 grams remain. After two half-lives or 280 days, 5 · 0.5 = 10 · 0.5 · 0.5 = 10 · (0.5)^2 = 2.5 grams remain. Therefore, the correct solution should be between 5 and 2.5 grams, and the amount remaining after any period of time is given by

$$\text{amount remaining} = \text{initial amount} \cdot (0.5)^{\text{time/half-time}}$$

For this example, time = 250, and the MATLAB solution is

```
EDU» initial_amount=10;
EDU» half_life=140;
EDU» time=250;
EDU» amount_left=initial_amount*0.5^(time/half_life)
amount_left =
       2.9003
```

Thus, approximately 2.9 grams of polonium is left after 250 days. Note that exponentiation ^ takes precedence over multiplication *. Therefore, `0.5^(time/half_life)` is computed before multiplying by `initial_amount`.

Example: Acid Concentration Problem

Problem: As part of the manufacturing process for cast parts at an automotive plant, parts are dipped in water to cool them, then dipped in an acid–water bath to clean them. Over time, the concentration of the acid–water solution decreases because of the water introduced at immersion and the solution removed when the parts are taken from the acid–water bath. To maintain quality, the acid–water solution's acidity must not fall below some minimum. Start with a 90% acid–water concentration. If the minimum concentration is 50%, the water introduced into the acid–water bath is equal to 1% of the bath's volume, and 1% of the solution is removed when the part is removed, how many parts can be dipped into the acid–water bath before it drops below the minimum acidity?

Solution: Initially, the acid concentration is initial_con = 90% = acid/(acid + water). When the first part is dipped in the acid–water bath, the concentration is reduced to

$$\text{con} = \frac{\text{acid}}{(\text{acid} + \text{water}) + \text{water added}}$$

$$= \frac{\text{acid}}{(\text{acid} + \text{water}) + \text{lost}(\text{acid} + \text{water})}$$

$$= \frac{\text{acid}}{(1 + \text{lost})(\text{acid} + \text{water})}$$

$$= \frac{\text{initial\_con}}{(1 + \text{lost})}$$

where "acid" is the initial acid volume, "water" is the initial water volume, and "lost" is the fractional volume of water added. The amount of acid remaining in the solution after this first dip is, therefore

$$\text{acid\_left} = \frac{\text{acid}}{(1 + \text{lost})}$$

This means that, when the second part is dipped into the acid–water bath, the concentration is

$$\text{con} = \frac{\text{acid\_left}}{(\text{acid} + \text{water}) + \text{water added}}$$

$$= \frac{\text{acid\_left}}{(1 + \text{lost})(\text{acid} + \text{water})}$$

$$= \frac{\text{initial\_con}}{(1 + \text{lost})^2}$$

Following this process, after n dips, the concentration of the acid–water bath is

$$\text{con} = \frac{\text{initial\_con}}{(1 + \text{lost})^n}$$

If min_con is the minimum acceptable concentration, the maximum number of dips is the integer less than or equal to

$$n = \frac{\log(\text{initial\_con}/\text{min\_con})}{\log(1 + \text{lost})}$$

In MATLAB, the solution is

```
EDU» initial_con=90
initial_con =
    90
EDU» min_con=50
min_con =
    50
EDU» lost=0.01;
EDU» n=floor(log(initial_con/min_con)/log(1+lost))
n =
    59
```

Fifty-nine dips can be completed before the concentration drops below 50%. Note that the `floor` function was used to round n down to the nearest integer. Also note that while the natural logarithm was used, `log10` or `log2` could have also been used.

Example: Interest Calculations

Problem: You've agreed to buy a new car for $18,500. The car dealer is offering two financing options: (1) 2.9% interest over 4 years, or (2) 8.9% interest over 4 years, with a factory rebate of $1500. Which one is the better deal?

Solution: The monthly payment P on a loan of A dollars, having a monthly interest rate of R, paid off in M months, is

$$P = A\left[\frac{R(1 + R)^M}{(1 + R)^M - 1}\right]$$

giving a total amount paid of $T = P \cdot M$.

In MATLAB, the solution is

```
EDU» format bank % use bank display format
EDU» A=18500;  % amount of loan
EDU» M=12*4;   % number of months
EDU» FR=1500;  % factory rebate
EDU» % first financing offer
EDU» R=(2.9/100)/12; % monthly interest rate

EDU» P=A*( R*(1+R)^M/( (1+R)^M −1)) % payment
P =
        408.67

EDU» T1=P*M % total car cost
T1 =
          19616.06

EDU» % second financing offer
EDU» R=(8.9/100)/12; % monthly interest rate

EDU» P=(A−FR)*( R*(1+R)^M/( (1+R)^M −1)) % payment
P =
        422.24

EDU» T2=P*M % total car cost
T2 =
          20267.47

EDU» Diff=T2−T1
Diff =
        651.41
```

Based on these results, the first financing offer is the better of the two.

Command Window
Features

3.1 Managing the MATLAB Workspace

3.2 Saving and Retrieving Data

3.3 Number Display Formats

The MATLAB *Command* window has numerous features, some of which were introduced in prior chapters.

3.1 Managing the MATLAB Workspace

The data and variables created in the *Command* window reside in what is called the **MATLAB workspace.** To see what variable names are in the MATLAB workspace, issue the command who:

```
EDH» who

Your variables are:

initial_con   min_con
lost          n
```

These are the variables used in the acid–water bath example. For more detailed information, use the command whos:

```
EDU» whos
  Name          Size          Bytes Class

  initial_con   1x1           8 double array
  lost          1x1           8 double array
  min_con       1x1           8 double array
  n             1x1           8 double array

Grand total is 4 elements using 32 bytes
```

Each variable is listed along with its size, the number of bytes used, and its class. In this particular example, our variables are all scalars having double precision representation. The command whos will be more useful later, after the introduction to arrays and other data types.

In addition to these functions, the **Show Workspace** item in the **File** menu creates a GUI window, called the **Workspace Browser,** that contains the same information as the whos command. Moreover, it gives you the ability to delete or clear selected variables. This window is also created by pressing the **Workspace Browser** button on the *Command* window toolbar.

As shown earlier, the command clear deletes variables from the MATLAB workspace. For example:

```
EDU» clear lost n
EDU» who

Your variables are:

initial_con   min_con
```

deletes the variables `lost` and `n`. Other options for the `clear` function can be found by asking for help:

```
EDU» help clear

 CLEAR Clear variables and functions from memory.
    CLEAR removes all variables from the workspace.
    CLEAR VARIABLES does the same thing.
    CLEAR GLOBAL removes all global variables.
    CLEAR FUNCTIONS removes all compiled M-functions.
    CLEAR MEX removes all links to MEX-files.
    CLEAR ALL removes all variables, globals, functions, and MEX
    links.

    CLEAR VAR1 VAR2...clears the variables specified. The
    wildcard character '*' can be used to clear variables that
    match a pattern. For instance, CLEAR X* clears all the
    variables in the current workspace that start with X.

    If X is global, CLEAR X removes X from the current
    workspace, but leaves it accessible to any functions
    declaring it global. CLEAR GLOBAL X completely removes the
    global variable X.

    CLEAR ALL also has the side effect of removing all debugging
    breakpoints since the breakpoints for a file are cleared
    whenever the m-file changes or is cleared.

    Use the functional form of CLEAR, such as CLEAR('name'),
    when the variable name is stored in a string.
    See also WHO, WHOS.
```

Clearly, the `clear` function deletes more than just variables. These other features will demonstrated later.

Finally, when working in the MATLAB workspace, it is often convenient to save or print a copy of your work. The `diary` command saves user input and *Command* window output to an ASCII text file named `diary` in the current directory or folder. `EDU» diary fname` saves the diary to file `fname`. `EDU» diary off` terminates the `diary` command and closes the file. When the *Command* window is active, selecting **Print...** from the **File** menu prints a copy of the entire *Command* window. Alternatively, if you highlight a portion of the *Command* window using the mouse, selecting **Print Selection...** from the **File** menu prints the selected text.

3.2   Saving and Retrieving Data

In addition to remembering variables, MATLAB can save and load data from files on your computer. The **Save Workspace as...** menu item in the **File** menu opens a standard file dialog box for saving all current variables. Similarly, the **Load Workspace...** menu item in the **File** menu opens a dialog box for loading variables from a previously saved workspace. Saving variables does not delete them from the MATLAB workspace. Loading variables of the same name as those found in the MATLAB workspace changes the variable values to those loaded from the file.

If the **File** menu approach is not available or does not meet your needs, MATLAB provides two commands—save and load—that offer more flexibility. In particular, the save command allows you to save one or more variables in the file format of your choice. For example:

```
EDU» save
```

stores all variables in MATLAB binary format in the file matlab.mat.

```
EDU» save data
```

saves all variables in MATLAB binary format in the file data.mat.

```
EDU» save data erasers pads tape
```

saves the variables erasers, pads, and tape in binary format in the file data.mat.

```
EDU» save data erasers pads tape —ascii
```

saves the variables erasers, pads, and tape in 8-digit ASCII format in the file data. ASCII-formatted files may be edited using any common text editor. Note that ASCII files do not get the extension .mat.

```
EDU» save data erasers pads tape —ascii —double
```

saves the variables erasers, pads, and tape in 16-digit ASCII format in the file data.

The load command uses the same syntax, with the obvious difference of loading variables into the MATLAB workspace.

3.3   Number Display Formats

When MATLAB displays numerical results, it follows several rules. By default, if a result is an integer, MATLAB displays it as an integer. Likewise, when a result is a real number, MATLAB displays it with approximately four digits to the right of the decimal point. If the significant digits in the result are outside this range, MATLAB displays the result in scientific notation, similar to scien-

Scrip

tific calculators. You can override this default behavior by specifying a different numerical format within the **Preferences** menu item in the **File** menu, if available, or by typing the appropriate MATLAB command at the prompt. Using the variable `average_cost` from an earlier example, these numerical formats are:

MATLAB Command	average_cost	Comments
`format short`	50.833	5 digits
`format long`	50.83333333333334	16 digits
`format short e`	5.0833e+01	5 digits plus exponent
`format long e`	5.083333333333334e+01	16 digits plus exponent
`format short g`	50.833	better of `format short` or `format short e`
`format long g`	50.83333333333333	better of `format long` or `format long e`
`format hex`	40496aaaaaaaaaab	hexadecimal
`format bank`	50.83	2 decimal digits
`format +`	+	positive, negative, or zero
`format rat`	305/6	rational approximation

It is important to note that MATLAB does not change the internal representation of a number when different display formats are chosen; only the display changes.

When a MATLAB command is not terminated by a semicolon, the results of the command are displayed in the *Command* window with the variable name identified. For a prettier display, it is sometimes convenient to suppress the variable name. In MATLAB, this is accomplished with the command `disp`:

```
EDU» initial_con  % traditional way to display result
initial_con =
    90

EDU» disp(initial_con)  % display result without variable name
      90
```

To save you from repeatedly editing a script file when computations for a variety of cases are desired, the `input` command allows you to prompt for input as a script file is executed. For example, reconsider the `example1.m` script file with modifications:

```
% Example1.m script file for acid-water bath problem

initial_con=90
min_con=50
lost=input('Enter Percentage Lost With Each Dip > ')/100
n=floor(log2(initial_con/min_con)/log2(1+lost))
```

Running this script file produces:

```
Enter Percentage Lost With Each Dip > 5
lost =
      0.05
n =
   12
```

In response to the prompt, the number 5 was entered and the **Return** or **Enter** key was pressed. The remaining commands were evaluated with `lost=5/100`. Note that the `input` function can be mixed with other operations, just like other common functions. Here the number input is divided by 100 to convert the entered percentage to the desired value for `lost`. The function `input` accepts any valid MATLAB expression. For example, running the script file again and providing different values gives:

```
EDU» example1

Enter Percentage Lost With Each Dip > round(sqrt(13))+3
lost =
        0.07
n =
     8
```

File Manag

In this case, the `lost` was set equal to the result of evaluating the expression `round(sqrt(13))+3`, then dividing by 100.

To see the effect of the `echo` command, add it to the script file and execute:

```
echo on

% Example1.m script file for acid-water bath problem

initial_con=90
min_con=50
lost=input('Enter Percentage Lost With Each Dip > ')/100
n=floor(log2(initial_con/min_con)/log2(1+lost))

echo off
```

```
EDU» example1

% Example1.m script file for acid-water bath problem

initial_con=90
initial_con =
    90
min_con=50
min_con =
    50

lost=input('Enter Percentage Lost With Each Dip > ')/100
Enter Percentage Lost With Each Dip > 20
lost =
        0.2

n=floor(log2(initial_con/min_con)/log2(1+lost))
n =
    3

echo off
```

As you can see in this case, the `echo` command made the result much harder to read. On the other hand, the `echo` command can be very helpful when debugging more complicated script files.

MATLAB's search path `matlabpath` is a listing of all the directories where MATLAB stores its files. Moreover, if you create a directory of M-files, its path must be added to `matlabpath`, or MATLAB will be unable to access your files unless this directory happens to be your current directory. To understand how MATLAB uses the `matlabpath`, consider the scenario illustrated in the following table:

MATLAB Search Path

In general, when you enter » `cow`, MATLAB does the following:

(1) It checks to see if `cow` is a **variable** in the MATLAB workspace; if not. . . .

(2) It checks to see if `cow` is a **built-in function**; if not. . . .

(3) It checks to see if an M-file named `cow.m` exists in the **current directory**; if not. . . .

(4) It checks to see if `cow.m` exists anywhere on the **MATLAB search path,** by searching the path in the order in which it is specified.

Whenever a match is found, MATLAB accepts it and acts accordingly. For example, if `cow` exists as a variable in the MATLAB workspace, MATLAB cannot use a function or command called `cow`. As a result, you should avoid creating variables having the same name as functions, e.g., » `sqrt=1.2;sqrt(2);` produces an error because `sqrt` is not the square root function here, but rather is a variable having a value of 1.2. The preceding path-searching procedure is also followed when the `load` command is issued. First MATLAB looks in the current directory, then it begins searching the MATLAB search path for the desired data file.

The actual MATLAB search procedure is more complicated than shown above, because MATLAB uses more than just files ending in `.m`. Function M-files can contain more than one function, directories on the `matlabpath` can have subdirectories named `private`, and MATLAB supports object-oriented programming with operator-overloading M-files residing in subdirectories beginning with the character @. If all of these features were added to the previous table, the table would be more complete, but also much harder to understand. If you wish to explore these more advanced features, see the documentation provided on the CD.

If you have M-files or MAT-files stored in a directory not on the MATLAB search path and not in the current directory, MATLAB cannot find them. There are two solutions to this problem: (1) Make the desired directory the current directory using the cd or pwd command from the previous table, or (2) add the desired directory to the MATLAB search path.

This last approach is easily accomplished using the path browser or the *Command* window commands, path and addpath. To access the path browser, select **Set Path** from the **File** menu or click on the **Path Browser Button** on the *Command* window toolbar. Doing so brings up the window, similar to that shown in Fig. 5.1 for the Macintosh.

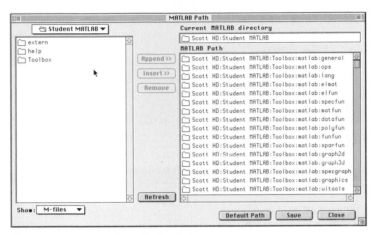

Figure 5.1   Macintosh Path Browser

As with all well-designed GUIs, this one is relatively straightforward to use. The present matlabpath is shown on the right, a directory selection window appears on the left, and path alteration buttons appear in the middle. To save the modified matlabpath for future MATLAB sessions, press the **Save** button before closing the GUI.

The window layout is different for the path browser on the PC, but the functionality is the same (Fig. 5.2).

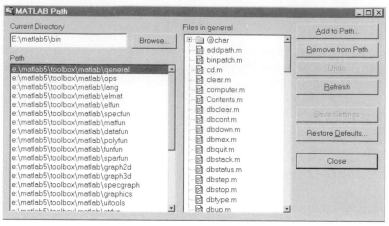

Figure 5.2   PC Path Browser

Here, the current directory is listed in the upper left with a standard **Browse** button. The present `matlabpath` is shown below. The files in the currently selected path directory are shown in the middle box. Path alteration buttons appear on the right. Again, to save the modified `matlabpath` for future MATLAB sessions, press the **Save** button before closing the GUI.

5.1   MATLAB at Startup

When MATLAB starts up, it executes two script M-files, `matlabrc.m` and `startup.m`. Of these, `matlabrc.m` comes with MATLAB and generally should not be modified. The commands in this M-file set the default *Figure* window size and placement, as well as a number of other default features. On Windows95 and NT systems, the default MATLAB search path is set by calling the script file `pathdef.m` from `matlabrc.m`. On all platforms, commands in `matlabrc.m` check for the existence of the script M-file `startup.m` on the MATLAB search path. If it exists, the commands in it are executed.

The optional M-file `startup.m` typically contains commands that add personal default features to MATLAB. For example, it is very common to put one or more `addpath` or `path` commands in `startup.m` to append additional directories to the MATLAB search path. Similarly, the default number display format can be changed, e.g., `format compact`. If you have a grayscale monitor, the command `graymon` is useful for setting default grayscale graphics features. Further still, if you want plots to have different default characteristics, a call to `colordef` could appear in `startup.m`. Since `startup.m` is a standard script M-file, there are no restrictions as to what commands can be placed in it. However, it's probably unwise to place the `quit` command in `startup.m`.

Array Operations

These are the first through fifth elements in x. 1:5 says "start with 1 and count up to 5."

```
EDU» x(7:end)
ans =
        1.885    2.1991    2.5133    2.8274    3.1416
```

starts with the seventh element and continues to the last element. Here, the word end signifies the last element in the array x.

```
EDU» y(3:-1:1)
ans =
    0.5878    0.3090         0
```

These are the third, second, and first elements in reverse order. 3:-1:1 says "start with 3, count down by 1, and stop at 1."

```
EDU» x(2:2:7)
ans =
    0.3142    0.9425    1.5708
```

These are the second, fourth, and sixth elements in x. 2:2:7 says "start with 2, count up by 2, and stop when you get to 7." In this case, adding 2 to 6 gives 8, which is greater than 7, so the eighth element is not included.

```
EDU» y([8 2 9 1])
ans =
    0.8090    0.3090    0.5878         0
```

Here we used another array [8 2 9 1] to extract the elements of the array y in the order we wanted them! The first element taken is the eighth, the second is the second, the third is the ninth, and the fourth is the first. In fact, [8 2 9 1] is an array that addresses the desired elements of y.

6.3   Array Construction

Earlier we entered the values of x by typing each individual element in x. While this is fine when there are only 11 values in x, what if there are 111 values? Using the colon notation, two other ways of entering x are:

```
EDU» x=(0:0.1:1)*pi
x =
  Columns 1 through 7
        0    0.3142    0.6283    0.9425    1.2566    1.5708    1.8850
  Columns 8 through 11
    2.1991    2.5133    2.8274    3.1416
```

```
EDU» x=linspace(0,pi,11)
x =
  Columns 1 through 7
        0     0.3142    0.6283    0.9425    1.2566    1.5708    1.8850
  Columns 8 through 11
    2.1991    2.5133    2.8274    3.1416
```

In the first case, the colon notation $(0:0.1:1)$ creates an array that starts at 0, increments by 0.1, and ends at 1. Each element in this array is then multiplied by π to create the desired values in x. In the second case, the MATLAB function linspace is used to create x. This function's arguments are described by:

```
linspace(first_value,last_value,number_of_values)
```

Both of these array creation forms are common in MATLAB. The colon notation form allows you to directly specify the increment between data points, but not the number of data points. linspace, on the other hand, allows you to directly specify the number of data points, but not the increment between the data points.

Both of the preceding array creation forms create arrays where the individual elements are linearly spaced with respect to each other. For the special case where a logarithmically spaced array is desired, MATLAB provides the logspace function:

```
EDU» logspace(0,2,11)
ans =
  Columns 1 through 7
    1.0000    1.5849    2.5119    3.9811    6.3096   10.0000   15.8489
  Columns 8 through 11
   25.1189   39.8107   63.0957  100.0000
```

Here, we created an array starting at 10^0, ending at 10^2, containing **11** values. The function arguments are described by:

```
logspace(first_exponent,last_exponent,number_of_values)
```

Though it is common to begin and end at integer powers of ten, logspace works equally well with nonintegers.

Sometimes an array is required that is not conveniently described by a linearly or logarithmically spaced element relationship. There is no uniform way to create these arrays. However, array addressing and the ability to combine expressions can help eliminate the need to enter individual elements one at a time:

```
EDU» a=1:5,b=1:2:9
a =
      1     2     3     4     5
b =
      1     3     5     7     9
```

creates two arrays. Remember that multiple statements can appear on a single line if they are separated by commas or semicolons.

```
EDU» c=[b a]
c =
   1    3    5    7    9    1    2    3    4    5
```

creates an array c composed of the elements of b followed by those of a.

```
EDU» d=[a(1:2:5) 1 0 1]
d =
      1     3     5     1     0     1
```

creates an array d composed of the first, third, and fifth elements of a followed by three additional elements.

The basic array construction features of MATLAB are summarized in the following table.

Basic Array Construction	
`x=[2 2*pi sqrt(2) 2-3j]`	Create row vector x containing elements specified
`x=first:last`	Create row vector x starting with `first`, counting by one, ending at or before `last`
`x=first:increment:last`	Create row vector x starting with `first`, counting by `increment`, ending at or before `last`
`x=linspace(first,last,n)`	Create row vector x starting with `first`, ending at `last`, having n elements
`x=logspace(first,last,n)`	Create logarithmically spaced row vector x starting with 10^{first}, ending at 10^{last}, having n elements

6.4 Array Orientation

In the preceding examples, arrays contained one row and multiple columns. As a result of this row orientation, they are commonly called ***row vectors***. It is also possible for an array to be a ***column vector***, having one column and multiple rows. In this case, all of the above array manipulation and mathematics apply without change. The only difference is that results are displayed as columns, rather than as rows.

Since the array creation functions illustrated previously all create row vectors, there must be some way to create column vectors. One straightforward way to create a column vector is to specify it element by element, separating values with semicolons:

```
EDU» c=[1;2;3;4;5]
c =
     1
     2
     3
     4
     5
```

Based on this example, **separating elements by spaces or commas specifies elements in different columns, whereas separating elements by semicolons specifies elements in different rows**.

Another way is to construct a row vector (using colon rotation, linspace, logspace, or other means), then transpose it into a column vector using the MATLAB transpose operator ('):

```
EDU» a=1:5
a =
     1   2   3   4   5
```

creates a row vector using the colon notation format.

```
EDU» b=a'
b =
     1
     2
     3
     4
     5
```

uses the transpose operator to change the row vector a into the column vector b.

```
EDU» c=b'
c =
     1    2    3    4    5
```

applies the transpose again and changes the column back to a row.

In addition to the simple transpose just noted, MATLAB also offers a transpose operator with a preceding dot. This **dot-transpose operator** is interpreted as the non-complex conjugate transpose. When an array is complex, the transpose (') gives the complex-conjugate transpose, i.e., the sign on the imaginary part is changed as part of the transpose operation. On the other hand, the dot-transpose (.') transposes the array, but does not conjugate it.

```
EDU» c=a.'
c =
     1
     2
     3
     4
     5
```

shows that .' and ' are identical for real data.

```
EDU» d=a+i*a
d =
  Columns 1 through 4
   1.0000 + 1.0000i   2.0000 + 2.0000i   3.0000 + 3.0000i   4.0000 + 4.0000i
  Column 5
   5.0000 + 5.0000i
```

creates a simple complex row vector from the array a using the default value i=sqrt(−1).

```
EDU» e=d'
e =
   1.0000 − 1.0000i
   2.0000 − 2.0000i
   3.0000 − 3.0000i
   4.0000 − 4.0000i
   5.0000 − 5.0000i
```

creates a column vector e that is the *complex conjugate* transpose of d.

```
EDU» f=d.'
f =
   1.0000 + 1.0000i
   2.0000 + 2.0000i
   3.0000 + 3.0000i
```

```
       4.0000 + 4.0000i
       5.0000 + 5.0000i
```

creates a column vector f that is the transpose of d.

If an array can be a row vector or a column vector, it makes sense that arrays could just as well have both multiple rows and multiple columns. **That is, arrays can also be in the form of *matrices*.** Creation of matrices follows that of row and column vectors. Commas or spaces are used to separate elements in a specific row, and semicolons are used to separate individual rows:

```
EDU» g=[1 2 3 4;5 6 7 8]
g =
       1       2       3       4
       5       6       7       8
```

Here, g is an array, or matrix having 2 rows and 4 columns, i.e., it is a *2-by-4 matrix*, or it is a *matrix of dimension 2 by 4.* The semicolon tells MATLAB to start a new row between the 4 and 5.

```
EDU» g=[1 2 3 4
5 6 7 8
9 10 11 12]
g =
       1       2       3       4
       5       6       7       8
       9      10      11      12
```

In addition to semicolons, pressing the **Return** or **Enter** key while entering a matrix also tells MATLAB to start a new row.

```
EDU» h=[1 2 3;4 5 6 7]
???  All rows in the bracketed expression must have the same
number of columns.
```

MATLAB strictly enforces the fact that all rows must contain the same number of columns. A new MATLAB 5 structure, the cell array, may be used if your rows don't have the same number of columns. We'll discuss this later.

Scalar–Array Mathematics

In the first array example previously given, the array x is multiplied by the scalar π. Other simple mathematical operations between scalars and arrays follow the same natural interpretation. Addition, subtraction, multiplication, and division by a scalar simply apply the operation to all elements of the array:

```
EDU» g—2
ans =
    —1     0     1     2
     3     4     5     6
     7     8     9    10
```

subtracts 2 from each element in g.

```
EDU» 2*g—1
ans =
     1     3     5     7
     9    11    13    15
    17    19    21    23
```

multiplies each element in g by two, and subtracts one from each element of the result. Note that scalar–array mathematics uses the same order of precedence used in scalar expressions to determine the order of evaluation.

Array–Array Mathematics

Mathematical operations between arrays are not quite as simple as those between scalars and arrays. Clearly, array operations between arrays of different sizes or dimensions are difficult to define, and moreover of dubious value. **However, when two arrays have the same dimensions, addition, subtraction, multiplication, and division apply on an element-by-element basis in MATLAB.** For example:

```
EDU» g % recall previous array
g =
     1     2     3     4
     5     6     7     8
     9    10    11    12
EDU» h=[1 1 1 1;2 2 2 2;3 3 3 3] % create new array
h =
     1     1     1     1
     2     2     2     2
     3     3     3     3
EDU» g+h % add h to g on an element-by-element basis
ans =
     2     3     4     5
     7     8     9    10
    12    13    14    15
EDU» ans—h % subtract h from the previous answer to get g back
ans =
     1     2     3     4
     5     6     7     8
     9    10    11    12
```

```
EDU» 2*g−h % multiplies g by 2 and subtracts h from the result
ans =
     1     3     5     7
     8    10    12    14
    15    17    19    21
```

Note that array–array mathematics also uses the same order of precedence used in scalar expressions to determine the order of evaluation.

Element-by-element multiplication and division work similarly, but use slightly unconventional notation:

```
EDU» g.*h
ans =
     1     2     3     4
    10    12    14    16
    27    30    33    36
```

Here we multiplied the arrays g and h element-by-element using the **_dot multiplication_** symbol .*. The dot preceding the standard asterisk multiplication symbol tells MATLAB to perform element-by-element array multiplication. Multiplication without the dot signifies **_matrix multiplication_**, which will be discussed later. For this particular example, matrix multiplication is not defined:

```
EDU» g*h
??? Error using ==> *
Inner matrix dimensions must agree.
```

Array division, or dot division, also requires use of the dot symbol:

```
EDU» g./h
ans =
    1.0000    2.0000    3.0000    4.0000
    2.5000    3.0000    3.5000    4.0000
    3.0000    3.3333    3.6667    4.0000

EDU» h.\g
ans =
    1.0000    2.0000    3.0000    4.0000
    2.5000    3.0000    3.5000    4.0000
    3.0000    3.3333    3.6667    4.0000
```

As with scalars, division is defined using both the forward and backward slashes. In both cases, the array *below* the slash is divided into the array above the slash.

Division without the dot is the matrix **_division_** operation, which is an entirely different operation:

```
EDU» g/h

Warning: Rank deficient, rank = 1 tol =  5.3291e−15.
```

```
ans =
            0         0     0.8333
            0         0     2.1667
            0         0     3.5000
```

EDU» h/g

Warning: Rank deficient, rank = 2 tol = 1.8757e−14.

```
ans =
      −0.1250          0     0.1250
      −0.2500          0     0.2500
      −0.3750          0     0.3750
```

Matrix division gives results that are not necessarily the same size as g and h. Matrix operations are discussed later.

Array powers are defined in several ways. As with multiplication and division, ^ is reserved for matrix powers, and .^ is used to denote element-by-element powers:

```
EDU» g,h
g =
      1      2      3      4
      5      6      7      8
      9     10     11     12
h =
      1      1      1      1
      2      2      2      2
      3      3      3      3
```

recalls the arrays used earlier.

```
EDU» g.^2
ans =
      1      4      9     16
     25     36     49     64
     81    100    121    144
```

squares the individual elements of g.

```
EDU» g.^−1
ans =
            1         0.5     0.33333         0.25
          0.2     0.16667     0.14286        0.125
      0.11111         0.1    0.090909     0.083333
```

finds the reciprocal of each element in g.

```
EDU» 2.^g
ans =
           2          4          8         16
          32         64        128        256
         512       1024       2048       4096
```

raises 2 to the power of each element in the array g.

```
EDU» g.^h
ans =
           1          2          3          4
          25         36         49         64
         729       1000       1331       1728
```

raises the elements of g to the corresponding elements in h. In this case, the first row is unchanged, the second row is squared, and the third row is cubed.

```
EDU» g.^(h−1)
ans =
           1          1          1          1
           5          6          7          8
          81        100        121        144
```

shows that scalar and array operations can be combined.

The following table summarizes basic array operations.

Element-by-Element Array Mathematics	
Illustrative data: $a = [a_1\ a_2\ \ldots\ a_n]$, $b = [b_1\ b_2\ \ldots\ b_n]$, $c = $ `<a scalar>`	
Scalar addition	$a + c = [a_1 + c\ \ a_2 + c\ \ \ldots\ \ a_n + c]$
Scalar multiplication	$a * c = [a_1 * c\ \ a_2 * c\ \ \ldots\ \ a_n * c]$
Array addition	$a + b = [a_1 + b_1\ \ a_2 + b_2\ \ \ldots\ \ a_n + b_n]$
Array multiplication	$a .* b = [a_1 * b_1\ \ a_2 * b_2\ \ \ldots\ \ a_n * b_n]$
Array right division	$a ./ b = [a_1 / b_1\ \ a_2 / b_2\ \ \ldots\ \ a_n / b_n]$
Array left division	$a .\backslash b = [a_1 \backslash b_1\ \ a_2 \backslash b_2\ \ \ldots\ \ a_n \backslash b_n]$
Array powers	$a .^\wedge c = [a_1{}^\wedge c\ \ a_2{}^\wedge c\ \ \ldots\ \ a_n{}^\wedge c]$
	$c .^\wedge a = [c^\wedge a_1\ \ c^\wedge a_2\ \ \ldots\ \ c^\wedge a_n]$
	$a .^\wedge b = [a_1{}^\wedge b_1\ \ a_3{}^\wedge b_2\ \ \ldots\ \ a_n{}^\wedge b_n]$

6.5 Arrays of Ones or Zeros

Because of their general utility, MATLAB provides functions for creating arrays containing either all ones or all zeros:

```
EDU» ones(3)
ans =
        1       1       1
        1       1       1
        1       1       1

EDU» zeros(2,5)
ans =
        0       0       0       0       0
        0       0       0       0       0

EDU» size(g)
ans =
        3       4

EDU» ones(size(g))
ans =
        1       1       1       1
        1       1       1       1
        1       1       1       1
```

When called with a single input argument, `ones(n)` or `zeros(n)`, MATLAB creates an n-by-n array containing ones or zeros, respectively. When called with two input arguments, `ones(r,c)` or `zeros(r,c)`, MATLAB creates an array having r rows and c columns. To create an array of ones or zeros the same size as another array, use the `size` function (discussed later in this chapter) in the argument to `ones` or `zeros`.

6.6 Array Manipulation

Since arrays and matrices are fundamental to MATLAB, there are many ways to manipulate them in MATLAB. Once matrices are formed, MATLAB provides powerful ways to insert, extract, and rearrange subsets of them by identifying subscripts of interest. Knowledge of these features is key to using MATLAB efficiently. To illustrate the matrix and array manipulation features of MATLAB, consider the following examples:

```
EDU» A=[1 2 3;4 5 6;7 8 9]
A =
        1       2       3
        4       5       6
        7       8       9
```

```
EDU» A(3,3)=0   % set element in 3rd row, 3rd column to zero
A =
      1      2      3
      4      5      6
      7      8      0
```

changes the element in the third row and third column to zero.

```
EDU» A(2,6)=1   % set element in 2nd row, 6th column to one
A =
      1      2      3      0      0      0

      4      5      6      0      0      1

      7      8      0      0      0      0
```

places one in the second row, sixth column. Since A does not have six columns, the size of A is increased as necessary and filled with zeros so that the matrix remains rectangular.

```
EDU» A(:,4)=4
A =
      1      2      3      4      0      0
      4      5      6      4      0      1
      7      8      0      4      0      0
```

sets the fourth column of A equal to 4. Since 4 is a scalar, it is *expanded* to fill all the elements specified.

```
EDU» A=[1 2 3;4 5 6;7 8 9];   % restore original data

EDU» B=A(3:-1:1,1:3)
B =
      7      8      9
      4      5      6
      1      2      3
```

creates a matrix B by taking the rows of A in reverse order.

```
EDU» B=A(3:-1:1,:)
B =
      7      8      9
      4      5      6
      1      2      3
```

does the same as the preceding example. Here, the final **single colon means take all columns**. That is, : is short for $1:end$, or $1:3$, in this example, because A has three columns.

```
EDU» C=[A B(:,[1 3])]
C =
     1     2     3     7     9
     4     5     6     4     6
     7     8     9     1     3
```

creates C by appending all rows in the first and third columns of B to the right of A.

```
EDU» B=A(1:2,2:3)
B =
     2     3
     5     6
```

creates B by extracting the first two rows and last two columns of A.

```
EDU» C=[1 3]
C =
     1     3

EDU» B=A(C,C)
B =
     1     3
     7     9
```

uses the array C to index the matrix A rather than specifying them directly using the colon notation start:increment:end or start:end. In this example, B is formed from the first and third rows and the first and third columns of A.

```
EDU» B=A(:)
B =
     1
     4
     7
     2
     5
     8
     3
     6
     9
```

builds B by stretching A into a column vector, taking its columns one at a time in order.

```
EDU» B=B.'
B =
     1     4     7     2     5     8     3     6     9
```

illustrates the dot-transpose operation introduced earlier.

```
EDU» B=A
B =
        1       2       3
        4       5       6
        7       8       9

EDU» B(:,2)=[ ]
B =
        1       3
        4       6
        7       9
```

redefines B by throwing away all rows in the second column of original B. **When you set something equal to the empty matrix [ ], it gets deleted, causing the matrix to collapse to what remains.** Note that you must delete whole rows or columns so that the result remains rectangular.

```
EDU» B=B.'
B =
        1       4       7
        3       6       9
```

illustrates the transpose of a matrix. In general, the ith row becomes the ith column of the result, so the original 3-by-2 matrix becomes a 2-by-3 matrix.

```
EDU» B(2,:)=[ ]
B =
        1       4       7
```

throws out the second row of B.

```
EDU» A(2,:)=B
A =
        1       2       3
        1       4       7
        7       8       9
```

replaces the second row of A with B.

```
EDU» B=A(:,[2 2 2 2])
B =
        2               2
        4       4       4       4
        8       8       8       8
```

creates B by duplicating all rows in the second column of A four times.

```
EDU» A   % show A again
A =
      1     2     3
      1     4     7
      7     8     9
EDU» A(2,2)=[ ]
???   Indexed empty matrix assignment is not allowed.
```

shows that you can throw out only entire rows or columns. MATLAB does not know how to collapse a matrix when partial rows or columns are thrown out.

```
EDU» B=A(4,:)
???   Index exceeds matrix dimensions.
```

since A does not have a fourth row, MATLAB doesn't know what to do, and it says so.

```
EDU» B(1:2,:)=A
???   In an assignment A(matrix,:) = B, the number of columns in
A and B must be the same.
```

shows that you can't squeeze one matrix into another one having a different size.

```
EDU» B(3:4,:)=A(2:3,:)
B =
      1     4     7
      0     0     0
      1     4     7
      7     8     9
```

But you can place the second and third columns of A into a same-size area of B. Since the second through fourth rows of B did not exist, they are created as necessary. Moreover, the second row of B is unspecified, so it is filled with zeros.

```
EDU» G(1:6)=A(:,2:3)
G =
      2     4     8     3     7     9
```

creates a row vector G by extracting all rows in the second and third columns of A. Note that the shape of the matrices is different on either side of the equals sign.

When the right-hand side of an assignment is a scalar and the left-hand side is an array, *scalar expansion* is used. For example:

```
EDU» A(2,:)=0
A =
      1     2     3
      0     0     0
      7     8     9
```

replaces the second row of A with zeros. The single zero on the right-hand side is expanded to fill all indices specified on the left. This example is equivalent to

```
EDU» A(2,:)=[0 0 0]
A =
     1     2     3
     0     0     0
     7     8     9
```

Sometimes it is more convenient to address matrix elements with a *single index*. When a single index is used in MATLAB, the index counts elements down the columns, starting with the first. For example:

```
EDU» D=[1 2 3 4;5 6 7 8; 9 10 11 12] % new data
D =
     1     2     3     4
     5     6     7     8
     9    10    11    12

EDU» D(2)   % second element
ans =
     5

EDU» D(5)   % fifth element (3 in first column plus 2 in second
column)
ans =
     6

EDU» D(end)   % last element in matrix
ans =
    12

EDU» D(4:7)   % fourth through seventh elements
ans =
     2     6    10     3
```

In addition to addressing matrices based on their subscripts, we can also address them with **logical arrays** that result from logical operations (to be discussed more thoroughly later) **if the size of the array is equal to that of the array it is addressing.** In this case, True (1) elements are retained and False (0) elements are discarded.

```
EDU» x=−3:3   % Create data
x =
    −3    −2    −1     0     1     2     3
EDU» abs(x)>1
ans =
     1     1     0     0     0     1     1
```

returns a logical array with ones where the absolute value of x is greater than 1.

```
EDU» y=x(abs(x)>1)
y =
     -3    -2     2     3
```

creates y by taking those values of x where its absolute value is greater than 1. Note, however, that

```
EDU» y=x([1 1 0 0 0 1 1])
??? Index into matrix is negative or zero. See release notes on
changes to logical indices.
```

gives an error even though the abs(x)>1 and [1 1 0 0 0 1 1] appear to be the same vector. In this second case, [1 1 0 0 0 1 1] is a numeric array, as opposed to a logical array. As a result, MATLAB tries to address the element numbers specified in [1 1 0 0 0 1 1], and generates an error because there is no element 0. Naturally, MATLAB provides the function logical for converting numerical arrays to logical arrays:

```
EDU» y=x(logical([1 1 0 0 0 1 1]))
y =
     -3    -2     2     3
```

Now we once again have the desired result. **Logical arrays are a special kind of double-precision array in MATLAB.** Up to now, we've considered only numerical arrays. Specifying array subscripts with numerical arrays extracts the elements having the given numerical indices. On the other hand, specifying array subscripts with logical arrays, which are returned by logical expressions and the function logical, extract elements which are logical True ($\neq 0$).

Logical arrays work on matrices, as well as vectors, also:

```
EDU» B=[5 -3;2 -4]
B =
      5    -3
      2    -4
EDU» x=abs(B)>2
x =
      1     1
      0     1
```

Likewise, 0–1 logical array extraction works for matrices as well.

```
EDU» y=b(x)
y =
      5
     -3
      4
```

However, the results are converted to a column vector, since there is no way to define a matrix having only three elements.

The above array-addressing techniques are summarized in the following table.

Array Addressing	
A(r,c)	Address a subarray within A defined by the index vector of desired rows in r and index vector of desired columns in c
A(r,:)	Address a subarray within A defined by the index vector of desired rows in r and all columns
A(:,r)	Address a subarray within A defined by all rows and the index vector of desired columns in r
A(:)	Address all elements of A as a column vector taken column by column
A(i)	Address a subarray within A defined by the single index vector of desired elements in i, as if A was the column vector, a(:)
A(x)	Address a subarray within A defined by the logical array x. x must be the same size as A

6.7   Subarray Searching

Many times, it is desirable to know the indices or subscripts of those elements of an array that satisfy some relational expression. In MATLAB, this task is performed by the function find, which returns the subscripts where a relational expression is True:

```
EDU» x=-3:3
x =
    -3   -2   -1    0    1    2    3
EDU» k=find(abs(x)>1)
k =
     1    2    6    7
```

finds those subscripts where abs(x)>1.

```
EDU» y=x(k)
y =
    -3   -2    2    3
```

creates y using the indexes in k.

The find function also works for matrices:

```
EDU» A=[1 2 3;4 5 6;7 8 9]
```

Executing the script produces the following data and stem plot:

```
EDU» example6_2
lost =
        1     2     3     4     5     6     7     8     9    10
n =
       59    29    19    14    12    10     8     7     6     6
```

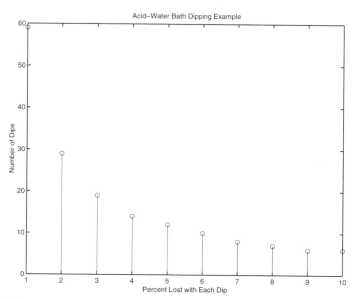

Figure 6.2

Note that dot-division is required in the expression for n because log(1+lost/100) is a vector.

Example: Searching for a Solution using Vectors

Problem: The "Problem of the Week" in middle school is to find all numbers less than 1000 that are divisible by 7, but have remainder 1 when divided by 2, 3, 4, 5, and 6.

Solution: There is no analytic solution to this problem, so it must be found by searching. If you start with all multiples of 7 less than 1000, all the numbers that don't satisfy the remainder conditions can be thrown out, leaving the desired solution. In MATLAB, the solution is given by the script file:

```
% pow.m script file to solve the problem of the week

n=7:7:1000;  % all multiples of 7 less than 1000
number=length(n)    % number of potential solutions

n(rem(n,2)~=1)=[];  % throw out nonsolutions by
number=length(n)
n(rem(n,3)~=1)=[];  % setting them equal to an empty array,
number=length(n)
n(rem(n,4)~=1)=[];  % the function rem computes remainders.
number=length(n)
n(rem(n,5)~=1)=[];
number=length(n)
n(rem(n,6)~=1)=[]
```

Running this script file produces two solutions

```
EDU» pow
number =
    142
number =
    71
number =
    24
number =
    12
number =
    2
n =
   301    721
```

Clearly, it doesn't take long to eliminate most of the potential solutions.

In addition to "traditional" mathematical operations, MATLAB supports relational and logical operations. You may be familiar with these if you've had some experience with other programming languages. The purpose of these operators and functions is to provide answers to True-False questions. One important use of this capability is to control the flow or order of execution of a series of MATLAB commands (usually in an M-file) based on the results of True/False questions.

As inputs to all relational and logical expressions, MATLAB considers any nonzero number to be True, and zero to be False. The output of all relational and logical expressions produces *one for True* and *zero for False*, and the array is flagged as *logical*. That is, the result contains numerical values 1 and 0 that can be used in mathematical statements, but also allow logical array-addressing as described in Chapter 6.

8.1   Relational Operators

MATLAB relational operators include all common comparisons:

Relational Operator	Description
<	less than
<=	less than or equal to
>	greater than
>=	greater than or equal to
=	equal to
~=	not equal to

MATLAB relational operators can be used to compare two arrays of the same size or to compare an array to a scalar. In the second case, the scalar is compared with all elements of the array, and the result has the same size as the array. Some examples include:

```
EDU» A=1:9,B=9-A
A =
     1     2     3     4     5     6     7     8     9
B =
     8     7     6     5     4     3     2     1     0
EDU» tf=A>4
tf =
     0     0     0     0     1     1     1     1     1
```

finds elements of A that are greater than 4. Zeros appear in the result where
A≤4, and ones appear where A>4.

```
EDU» tf=(A==B)
tf =
     0    0    0    0    0    0    0    0    0
```

finds elements of A that are equal to those in B. Note that = and == mean two
different things: == compares two variables and returns ones where they are
equal and zeros where they are not; =, on the other hand, is used to assign the
output of an operation to a variable.

```
EDU» tf=B-(A>2)
tf =
     8    7    5    4    3    2    1    0   -1
```

finds where A>2 and subtracts the resulting vector from B. This example shows
that since the output of logical operations are numerical arrays of ones and
zeros, they can be used in mathematical operations, too.

```
EDU» B=B+(B==0)*eps
B =
  Columns 1 through 7
    8.0000    7.0000    6.0000    5.0000    4.0000    3.0000    2.0000
  Columns 8 through 9
    1.0000    0.0000
```

is a demonstration of how to replace zeros in an array with the special MATLAB
number eps, which is approximately $2.2e{-}16$. This particular expression is
sometimes useful to avoid dividing by zero, as in:

```
EDU» x=(-3:3)/3
x =
   -1.0000   -0.6667   -0.3333        0    0.3333    0.6667    1.0000
EDU» sin(x)./x
Warning: Divide by zero
ans =
    0.8415    0.9276    0.9816      NaN    0.9816    0.9276    0.8415
```

Computing the function $\sin(x)/x$ gives a warning because the fifth data point
is zero. Since $\sin(0)/0$ is undefined, MATLAB returns NaN (meaning Not-
a-Number) at that location in the result. Try again, after replacing the zero
with eps:

```
EDU» x=x+(x==0)*eps;
EDU» sin(x)./x
ans =
    0.8415    0.9276    0.9816    1.0000    0.9816    0.9276    0.8415
```

Now $\sin(x)/x$ for $x = 0$ gives the correct limiting answer.

8.2 Logical Operators

Logical operators provide a way to combine or negate relational expressions. MATLAB logical operators include:

Logical Operator	Description
&	AND
|	OR
~	NOT

Some examples of the use of logical operators are:

```
EDU» A=1:9;B=9-A;

EDU» tf=A>4
tf =
    0    0    0    0    1    1    1    1    1
```

finds where A is greater than 4.

```
EDU» tf=~(A>4)
tf =
    1    1    1    1    0    0    0    0    0
```

negates this result, i.e., swaps where the ones and zeros appear.

```
EDU» tf=(A>2)&(A<6)
tf =
    0    0    1    1    1    0    0    0    0
```

returns ones where A is greater than 2 AND less than 6.

8.3 Relational and Logical Functions

In addition to the previously mentioned basic relational and logical operators, MATLAB provides other relational and logical functions, including the following:

Other Relational and Logical Functions	
xor(x,y)	Exclusive OR operation. Return ones where either x or y is nonzero (True). Return zeros where both x and y are zero (False) or both are nonzero (True).
any(x)	Return one if *any* element in a vector x is nonzero. Return one for each column in a matrix x that has nonzero elements.
all(x)	Return one if *all* elements in a vector x are nonzero. Return one for each column in a matrix x that has all nonzero elements.

MATLAB also provides numerous functions that test for the existence of specific values or conditions and return logical results:

Test Functions	
`isa(X,'name')`	True if X has object class `'name'`
`iscell(X)`	True if argument is a cell array
`iscellstr(S)`	True if argument is a cell array of strings
`ischar(S)`	True if argument is a character string
`isempty(X)`	True if argument is empty
`isequal(A,B)`	True if A and B are identical
`isfield(S,'name')`	True if `'name'` is a field of structure S
`isfinite(X)`	True where elements are finite
`isglobal(X)`	True if argument is a global variable
`ishandle(h)`	True if argument is a valid object handle
`ishold`	True if current plot hold state is ON
`isieee`	True if computer performs IEEE arithmetic
`isinf(X)`	True where elements are infinite
`isletter(S)`	True where elements are letters of the alphabet
`islogical(X)`	True if argument is a logical array
`ismember(A,B)`	True where elements of A are also in B
`isnan(X)`	True where elements are NaNs
`isnumeric(X)`	True if argument is a numeric array
`isppc`	True for Macintosh with PowerPC processor
`isprime(X)`	True where elements are prime
`isreal(X)`	True if argument has no imaginary part
`isspace(S)`	True where elements are white-space characters
`issparse(A)`	True if argument is a sparse matrix
`isstruct(S)`	True if argument is a structure
`isstudent`	True if Student Edition of MATLAB
`isunix`	True if computer is UNIX
`isvms`	True if computer is VMS

9

Text

MATLAB's true power is its ability to crunch numbers. However, there are times when it is desirable to manipulate text, such as when putting labels and titles on plots. In MATLAB, text variables are referred to as **character strings,** or simply **strings.**

9.1 Character Strings

Character strings in MATLAB are arrays of ASCII values that are displayed as their character string representation. For example:

```
EDU» t='How about this character string?'
t =
How about this character string?

EDU» size(t)
ans =
     1    32

EDU» whos
  Name         Size           Bytes  Class

    t          1x32             64   char array

Grand total is 32 elements using 64 bytes
```

A character string is simply text surrounded by single quotes. Each character in a string is one element in the array, with each element occupying 2 bytes.

To see the underlying ASCII representation of a character string, you need only perform some arithmetic operation on the string, or convert it using the function double. For example:

```
EDU» double(t)
ans =
  Columns 1 through 12
     72   111   119    32    97    98   111   117   116    32   116   104
  Columns 13 through 24
    105   115    32    99   104    97   114    97    99   116   101   114
  Columns 25 through 32
     32   115   116   114   105   110   103    63

EDU» abs(t)
ans =
  Columns 1 through 12
     72   111   119    32    97    98   111   117   116    32   116   104
```

```
Columns 13 through 24
 105    115     32     99    104     97    114     97     99    116    101    114
Columns 25 through 32
  32    115    116    114    105    110    103     63
```

The function char provides the reverse transformation:

```
EDU» char(t)
ans =
How about this character string?
```

Since strings are numerical arrays with special attributes, they can be manipulated with all the array-manipulation tools available in MATLAB. For example:

```
EDU» u=t(16:24)
u =
character
```

Strings are addressed just like arrays. Here, elements 16 through 24 contain the word *character*.

```
EDU» u=t(24:-1:16)
u =
retcarahc
```

This is the word "character" spelled backward.

```
EDU» u=t(16:24)'
u =
c
h
a
r
a
c
t
e
r
```

Using the transpose operator changes the word "character" to a column.

```
EDU» v='I can'' t find the manual!'
v =
I can't find the manual!
```

Single quotes within a character string are symbolized by two consecutive quotes.

String catenation follows directly from array catenation:

```
EDU» u='If a woodchuck could chuck wood,';
EDU» v=' how much wood would a woodchuck chuck?';
EDU» w=[u v]
w =
If a woodchuck could chuck wood, how much wood would a woodchuck chuck
```

The function disp allows you to display a string without printing its variable name. For example:

```
EDU» disp(u)
If a woodchuck could chuck wood,
```

Note that the u = statement is suppressed. This is useful for displaying helpful text within a script file.

As with matrices, character strings can have multiple rows, **but each row must have an equal number of columns**. Again, print forward to cell arrays. Therefore, blanks are explicitly required to make all rows the same length. For example:

```
EDU» v=['Character strings having more than'
        'one row must have the same number '
        'of columns just like matrices!    '] % note added blanks
v =
Character strings having more than
one row must have the same number
of columns just like matrices!

EDU» w=['This';'does not';'work!']  % second row is too long
???  All rows in the bracketed expression must have the same
number of columns.

EDU» w=char('However, this','does work!')  % char function again
w =
However, this
does work!

EDU» size(w)
ans =
     2    13
```

The function char also creates string arrays from individual strings, and pads them with blanks properly to make a valid array.

9.2 String Conversions

In addition to the conversion, discussed previously, between the string and its ASCII representation, MATLAB offers a number of other useful string conversion functions. They include the following:

String Conversions	
base2dec	Base x string to decimal integer
bin2dec	Binary string to decimal integer
char	String to ASCII
dec2base	Decimal integer to base x string
dec2bin	Decimal number to binary string
dec2hex	Decimal number to hexadecimal string
double	ASCII to string
fprintf	Write formatted text to file or screen
hex2dec	Hexadecimal string to decimal integer
hex2num	Hexadecimal string to IEEE floating point number
int2str	Integer to string
mat2str	Numerical matrix to eval'able string
num2str	Number to string
double	ASCII to string
sprintf	Number to string with format control
sscanf	Convert string to number under format control
str2num	String to number

In many situations, it is desirable to embed a numerical result within a string. Several string conversions perform this task.

```
EDU» rad=2.5;area=pi*rad^2;
EDU» t=['A circle of radius ' num2str(rad) ...
  ' has an area of ' num2str(area) '.'];
EDU» disp(t)
A circle of radius 2.5 has an area of 19.63.
```

Here, the function num2str has been used to convert numbers to strings, and string concatenation was used to embed the converted numbers in a character-string sentence. In a similar manner, int2str converts integers to strings. Both num2str and int2str call the function sprintf, which uses C-like syntax for converting numbers to strings.

9.3 String Functions

MATLAB offers a number of string functions, including those listed in the following table.

String Functions	
blanks(n)	Return a string of n blanks or spaces
deblank(s)	Remove trailing blanks from a string
eval(string)	Evaluate string as a MATLAB command
eval(try,catch)	Evaluate string and catch errors
feval(f,x,y,...)	Evaluate function given by string
findstr(s1,s2)	Find one string within another
ischar(s)	True if input is a string
isletter(s)	True where alphabet characters exist
isspace(s)	True where white-space characters exist
lasterr	String of last MATLAB error issued
lower(s)	String to lowercase
strcat(s1,s2,...)	Horizontal string concatenation
strcmp(s1,s2)	True if strings are identical
strjust(s)	Right-justify string array
strmatch(s1,s2)	Find possible matches for string
strncmp(s1,s2,n)	True if first n characters are identical
strrep(s1,s2)	Replace one string with another
strtok(s)	Find first token in a string
strvcat(s1,s2,...)	Vertical string concatenation
upper(s)	String to uppercase

A number of the string functions listed in the table provide basic string-parsing capabilities. For example, findstr returns the starting indices of one string within another:

```
EDU» b='Peter Piper picked a peck of pickled peppers';
EDU» findstr(b,' ')  % find spaces
ans =
      6    12    19    21    26    29    37
EDU» findstr(b,'p')  % find the letter p
ans =
      9    13    22    30    38    40    41
EDU» find(b=='p')  % find command works for single characters
ans =
      9    13    22    30    38    40    41
EDU» findstr(b,'cow')  % find the word cow
ans =
      [ ]
EDU» findstr(b,'pick')  % find the string pick
ans =
     13    30
```

Note that this function is case sensitive and returns the empty matrix when no match is found. findstr does not work on string matrices.

```
EDU» strrep(b,'p','P')  % capitalize all p's
ans =
Peter PiPer Picked a Peck of Pickled PePPers
EDU» strrep(b,'Peter','Pamela') % change Peter to Pamela
ans =
Pamela Piper picked a peck of pickled peppers
```

As shown above, strrep performs simple string replacement. strrep does not work on string matrices, so you would need to reshape the matrix into a vector first.

9.4   Cell Arrays of Strings

The fact that all rows in arrays must have the same number of columns is sometimes cumbersome, especially when the nonblank portions vary significantly from row to row. This cumbersome issue is eliminated by using cell arrays. All data forms can be placed in cell arrays, but their most frequent use is with character strings. **A cell array is a data type that allows you to name and manipulate a group of data of various sizes and types simply.** For example:

```
EDU» C={'How';'about';'this for a';'cell array of strings?'}
C =
    'How'
    'about'
    'this for a'
    'cell array of strings?'
EDU» size(C)
ans =
     4     1
```

Note that curly brackets are used to create cell arrays, and that the quotes around each string is displayed. In this example, the cell array C has 4 rows and 1 column. However, each element of the cell array contains a character string of different lengths. **Cell arrays are containers that hold other MATLAB data.**

Cell arrays are addressed just like arrays:

```
EDU» C(2:3)
ans =
    'about'
    'this for a'
EDU» C([4 3 2 1])
ans =
    'cell array of strings?'
    'this for a'
    'about'
    'How'
EDU» C(1)
ans =
    'How'
```

Here, the results are still cell arrays. To retrieve the **contents** of a particular cell, use curly brackets:

```
EDU» s=C{4}
s =
cell array of strings?
EDU» size(s)
ans =
     1     22
```

To extract more than one cell, use the function deal:

```
EDU» [a,b,c,d]=deal(C{:})
a =
How
b =
about
c =
this for a
d =
cell array of strings?
```

Here, C{:} denotes all the cells as a list. That is, it's the same as

```
EDU» [a,b,c,d]=deal(C{1},C{2},C{3},C{4})
a =
How
b =
about
c =
this for a
d =
cell array of strings?
```

The char function converts the contents of a cell array to a conventional string array:

```
EDU» s=char(C)
s =
How
about
this for a
cell array of strings?

EDU» size(s)  % result is a standard STRING array with blanks
ans =
      4    22

EDU» ss=char(C(1:2))  % naturally you can extract pieces
ss =
How
about

EDU»size(ss)  % result is a standard STRING array with blanks
ans =
      2     5
```

The inverse conversion is performed by the function `cellstr`:

```
EDU» cellstr(s)
ans =
    'How'
    'about'
    'this for a'
    'cell array of strings?'
```

Most of the string functions in MATLAB work with either string arrays or cell arrays of strings.

Cell arrays are discussed in more detail in Chapter 19.

10

Time

MATLAB offers a number of functions to manipulate time. You can do arithmetic with dates and times, print calendars, and find specific days. MATLAB does this by storing the date and time as a double-precision number representing the number of days since the beginning of year zero. For example, January 1, 1997 at midnight is represented as 729391, and the same day at noon is 729391.5. This format may make calculations easier for the computer, but it can be difficult to interpret. That's why MATLAB supplies a number of functions to help convert between numbers and character strings and to manipulate dates and times.

10.1   Current Time and Date

The clock function returns the current date and time in an array. For example,

```
EDU» T=clock
T =
    1997    1    21    16    33    39.934708
```

The now function returns the current date and time as a double-precision date number or, simply, a date number.

```
EDU» t=now
t =
    729411.690045541
```

Both results represent the same information.

The date function returns the current date as a string in the dd-mmm-yyyy format.

```
EDU» date
ans =
    21-Jan-1997
```

10.2   Format Conversions

You can convert the date number to a string using the datestr function. The format is datestr(date_number,format_spec). Here is the help text for datestr:

```
EDU» help datestr

 DATESTR String representation of date.
    DATESTR(D,DATEFORM) converts a serial date number D (as
    returned by DATENUM) into a date string. The string is
    formatted according to the format number or string DATEFORM
    (see table below). By default, DATEFORM is 1, 16, or 0
    depending on whether D contains dates, times, or both.
```

```
DATEFORM number    DATEFORM string         Example
      0            'dd-mmm-yyyy HH:MM:SS'   01-Mar-1995
                                           15:45:17
      1            'dd-mmm-yyyy'            01-Mar-1995
      2            'mm/dd/yy'               03/01/95
      3            'mmm'                    Mar
      4            'm'                      M
      5            'mm'                     3
      6            'mm/dd'                  03/01
      7            'dd'                     1
      8            'ddd'                    Wed
      9            'd'                      W
     10            'yyyy'                   1995
     11            'yy'                     95
     12            'mmmyy'                  Mar95
     13            'HH:MM:SS'               15:45:17
     14            'HH:MM:SS PM'             3:45:17 PM
     15            'HH:MM'                  15:45
     16            'HH:MM PM'                3:45 PM
     17            'QQ-YY'                  Q1-96
     18            'QQ'                     Q1
```

See also DATE, DATENUM, DATEVEC

and some examples:

```
EDU» datestr(t)
ans =
    21-Jan-1997 16:33:40

EDU» datestr(t,14)
ans =
    4:33:40 PM
```

The function datenum is the inverse of datestr. That is, datenum converts a date string using the form datenum(str), or from individual numbers or vectors to date number format using the forms datenum(year,month,day) or datenum(year,month,day,hour,minute,second).

```
EDU» datenum('21-Jan-1997 16:33:40')
ans =
       729411.690045541

EDU» datenum(1997,01,21)
ans =
       729411
```

```
EDU» datenum(1997,01,21,16,33,40)
ans =
        729411.690045541

EDU» datenum(T(1),T(2),T(3),T(4),T(5),T(6))
ans =
        729411.690045541
```

The datevec function converts from a date string (using datestr formats 0, 1, 2, 6, 13, 14, 15, or 16) or date number into a vector.

```
EDU» c=datevec('12/24/1984')
c =
    1984    12    24     0     0     0

EDU» [yr,mo,day,hr,min,sec]=datevec('24-Dec-1984 08:22')
yr =
    1984
mo =
    12
day =
    24
hr =
    8
min =
    22
sec =
    0
```

10.3 Date Functions

The day of the week may be found from a date string or a date number using weekday. MATLAB uses the convention that Sunday = 1 and Saturday = 7.

```
EDU» [d w]=weekday(728647)
d =
    2
w =
    Mon

EDU» [d w]=weekday('21-Dec-1994')
d =
    4
w =
    Wed
```

The last day of any month may be found using eomday. The year and month must be supplied.

```
EDU» eomday(1996,2)   % 1996 was a leap year
ans =
    29
```

MATLAB can generate a calendar for any month you request, and display it in the *Command* window or place it in a 6-by-7 matrix.

```
EDU» calendar('7/17/95')
                    Jul 1995
     S      M     Tu      W     Th      F      S
     0      0      0      0      0      0      1
     2      3      4      5      6      7      8
     9     10     11     12     13     14     15
    16     17     18     19     20     21     22
    23     24     25     26     27     28     29
    30     31      0      0      0      0      0

EDU» S=calendar(1994,12)
S =
     0      0      0      0      1      2      3
     4      5      6      7      8      9     10
    11     12     13     14     15     16     17
    18     19     20     21     22     23     24
    25     26     27     28     29     30     31
     0      0      0      0      0      0      0
```

10.4   Timing Functions

The tic and toc commands may be used to time an operation.

```
EDU» tic; plot(rand(5)); toc
elapsed_time =
    1.009768

EDU» tic; plot(rand(5)); toc
elapsed_time =
    0.04925
```

Notice the difference between the elapsed time for the identical plot commands. The second plot was faster because MATLAB had already created the *Figure* window and compiled the functions it needed into memory.

The cputime function returns the amount of Central Processing Unit (cpu) time, in seconds, that MATLAB has used since the current session was started. The etime function calculates the elapsed time between two time vectors. The vectors must be 6-element row vectors such as those returned by clock and datevec. At the present time, etime does not work across month and year boundaries. Both of these functions can be used to compute the time it takes for an operation to complete:

```
EDU» t0=cputime; myoperation; cputime-t0
ans =
    0.149999999999991
EDU» t1=clock; myoperation; etime(clock,t1)
ans =
    11.284853
```

See the on-line help or the MATLAB CD for more information.

10.5   Plot Labels

Sometimes it is useful to plot data and use dates or time strings for one or more of the axis labels. The datetick function automates this task. If the plot was drawn using date numbers for one or more axes, datetick generates date labels for the tick marks. Here, in Fig. 10.1, is a simple example:

```
EDU» t=(1900:10:1990)';
EDU» p=[ 75.995;  91.972; 105.711; 123.203; 131.669;
         150.697; 179.323; 203.212; 226.505; 249.633];
EDU» plot(datenum(t,1,1),p)
EDU» datetick('x','yyyy')  % use 4-digit year on the x-axis
EDU» title('Population by Year')
```

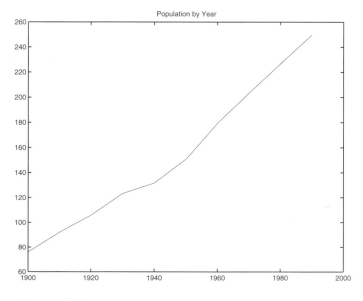

Figure 10.1

Here, in Fig. 10.2, we create a bar chart of company sales from November 1994 to December 1995:

```
EDU» y=[1994 1994 1995*ones(1,12)]';
EDU» m=[11 12 (1:12)]';
EDU» s=[1.1 1.3 1.2 1.4 1.6 1.5 1.7 1.6 1.8 1.3 1.9 1.7 1.6 1.95]';

EDU» bar(datenum(y,m,1),s)
EDU» datetick('x','mmmyy')
EDU» ylabel('$ Million')
EDU» title('Monthly Sales')
```

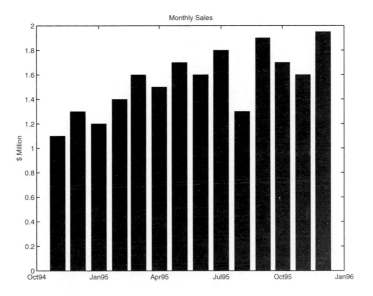

Figure 10.2

Examples: Finding Friday the 13th

Now that we have been introduced to the time and date commands, let's use them in some useful functions. If you are a cautious person, you might like to know in advance when Friday the 13th will occur. Here is a function M-file that will give you that information.

```
function m=friday(start)
%FRIDAY Date of the next Friday the 13th
% FRIDAY display the next occurrence of Friday the 13th.
% FRIDAY(START) start the search at the date specified by START.
% M=FRIDAY return the date number of the next Friday the 13th.
%

if nargin == 0, start=now; end   % use the current date if none
                                 % was supplied

[yr,mo,da]=datevec(start);
da=da+6-weekday(start);          % start with the Friday in
                                 % this week
start=datenum(yr,mo,da,0,0,0);
while 1
    [yr,mo,da]=datevec(start);
    if (weekday(start) == 6) & (da == 13)
       break;
    end
    start=datenum(start+7);      % skip to the next Friday
end

if nargout == 0
  disp(['Friday, ' datestr(start,1)]) % display the result
else
  m=start;                       % or return the resulting date
                                 % number
end
```

If you want to be forewarned for a whole year, consider the function fridays:

```
function F=fridays(ynum)
%FRIDAYS List the Friday the 13ths in the year ynum.
%   M=FRIDAYS return the date numbers found.
%
if nargin == 0                        % use the current year
   [ynum dummy]=datevec(now);
end
M=[];
trynum=datenum(ynum,1,13,0,0,0);     % check January 13 first
trynum=friday(trynum);               % find the first one
[tyr dummy]=datevec(trynum);
while tyr==ynum;                     % maybe there are more
                                     % this year

  MM=[MM; trynum];
  trynum=friday(trynum+7);           % skip to the next week
  [tyr dummy]=datevec(trynum);
end

if nargout == 0
   disp(' Fridays');                 % display the results
   disp(datestr(M,1))
else
  F=M;                               % or return a vector of
                                     % date numbers

end
```

11

Control Flow

Computer programming languages and programmable calculators offer features that allow you to control the flow of command execution based on decision-making structures. If you have used these features before, this section will be familiar to you. On the other hand, if control flow is new to you, this material may seem complicated at first; if this is so, take it slow.

Control flow is extremely powerful, since it lets past computations influence future operations. MATLAB offers four decision-making or control-flow structures. They are: `for` loops, `while` loops, `if-else-end` constructions, and `switch-case` constructions. Because these constructions often encompass numerous MATLAB commands, they often appear in M-files, rather than being typed directly at the MATLAB prompt.

11.1 for **Loops**

`for` loops allow a group of commands to be repeated a fixed, predetermined number of times. The general form of a `for` loop is

```
for x = array
    commands...
end
```

The `commands...` **between the** `for` **and** `end` **statements are executed once for every column in** `array`. At each iteration, x is assigned to the next column of `array`, i.e., during the nth time through the loop, $x=array(:,n)$. For example:

```
EDU» for n=1:10
        x(n)=sin(n*pi/10);
    end

EDU» x
x =
  Columns 1 through 7
    0.3090    0.5878    0.8090    0.9511    1.0000    0.9511    0.8090
  Columns 8 through 10
    0.5878    0.3090  0.0000
```

In words, the first statement says: *For* n *equals one to ten, evaluate all statements until the next* end *statement.* The first time through the `for` loop $n = 1$, the second time $n = 2$, and so on until the $n = 10$ case. After the $n = 10$ case, the `for` loop ends and any commands after the `end` statement are evaluated, which, in this case, is to display the computed elements of x.

A `for` loop cannot be terminated by reassigning the loop variable n within the `for` loop:

```
EDU» for n=1:10
       x(n)=sin(n*pi/10);
       n=10;
     end

EDU» x
x =
  Columns 1 through 7
    0.3090     0.5878     0.8090     0.9511     1.0000     0.9511     0.8090
  Columns 8 through 10
    0.5878     0.3090     0.0000
```

The statement $1:10$ is a standard MATLAB array creation statement. Any valid MATLAB array is acceptable in the for loop:

```
EDU» data=[3 9 45 6; 7 16 −1 5]
data =
      3      9     45      6
      7     16     −1      5

EDU» for n=data
       x=n(1)−n(2)
     end
x =
    −4
x =
    −7
x =
    46
x =
     1
```

Naturally, for loops can be nested as desired:

```
EDU» for n=1:5
       for m=5:−1:1
           A(n,m)=n^2+m^2;
       end
       disp(n)
     end
     1
     2
     3
     4
     5
```

```
EDU» A
A =
      2      5     10     17     26
      5      8     13     20     29
     10     13     18     25     34
     17     20     25     32     41
     26     29     34     41     50
```

for loops should be avoided whenever there is an equivalent array approach to solving a given problem. For example, the first example just considered may be rewritten as:

```
EDU» n=1:10;
```

```
EDU» x=sin(n*pi/10)
x =
  Columns 1 through 7
    0.3090    0.5878    0.8090    0.9511    1.0000    0.9511    0.8090
  Columns 8 through 10
    0.5878    0.3090   0.0000
```

While both approaches lead to identical results, the second approach executes faster, is more intuitive, and requires less typing.

To maximize speed, arrays should be preallocated before a for loop (or while loop) is executed. For example, in the first case considered previously, every time the commands within the for loop are executed, the size of the variable x is increased by one. This forces MATLAB to take the time to allocate more memory for x every time through the loop. To eliminate this step, the for loop example should be rewritten as:

```
EDU» x=zeros(1,10); % preallocated memory for x

EDU» for n=1:10
        x(n)=sin(n*pi/10);
      end
```

Now, only the values of x(n) need to be changed.

11.2   while **Loops**

While for loop evaluates a group of commands a fixed number of times, a while loop evaluates a group of statements an indefinite number of times.

The general form of a while loop is

```
while expression
    commands...
  end
```

The commands... **between the** while **and** end **statements are executed as long as ALL elements in** expression **are True.** Usually evaluation of expression gives a scalar result, but array results are also valid. In the array case, all elements of the resulting array must be True. Consider the following example:

```
EDU» num=0;EPS=1;
EDU» while (1+EPS)>1
        EPS=EPS/2;
        num=num+1;
    end
EDU» num
num =
    53
EDU» EPS=2*EPS
EPS =
    2.2204e-16
```

This example shows one way of computing the special MATLAB value eps, which is the smallest number that can be added to 1 such that the result is greater than 1 using finite precision. Here, we used uppercase EPS so that the MATLAB value eps is not overwritten. In this example, EPS starts at 1. As long as (1+FPS)>1 is True (nonzero), the commands inside the while loop are evaluated. Since EPS is continually divided in two, EPS eventually gets so small that adding EPS to 1 is no longer greater than 1. (Recall that this happens because a computer uses a fixed number of digits to represent numbers. MATLAB uses 16 digits, so you would expect EPS to be near 10^{-16}.) At this point, (1 + EPS) > 1 is False (zero) and the while loop terminates. Finally, EPS is multiplied by 2 because the last division by 2 made it too small by a factor of two.

11.3   if-else-end **Constructions**

Many times, sequences of commands must be conditionally evaluated based on a relational test. In programming languages, this logic is provided by some variation of an if-else-end construction. The simplest if-else-end construction is

```
if expression
    commands...
end
```

The commands... **between the** if **and** end **statements are evaluated if all elements in** expression **are True (nonzero).** In those cases where expression involves several logical subexpressions, all subexpressions are evaluated even if a prior one determines the final logical state of `expression`. For example:

```
EDU» apples=10;             % number of apples
EDU» cost=apples*25         % cost of apples
cost =
    250
EDU» if apples>5            % give 20% discount for larger
        cost=(1-20/100)*cost;  % purchases
      end
EDU» cost
cost =
    200
```

In cases where there are two alternatives, the `if-else-end` construction is

```
if expression
    commands evaluated if True
else
    commands evaluated if False
end
```

Here, the first set of commands is evaluated if `expression` is True; the second set is evaluated if `expression` is False.

When there are three or more alternatives, the `if-else-end` construction takes the form

```
if expression1
    commands evaluated if expression1 is True
elseif expression2
    commands evaluated if expression2 is True
elseif expression3
    commands evaluated if expression3 is True
elseif expression4
    commands evaluated if expression4 is True
elseif ...
      .
      .
      .
else
    commands evaluated if no other expression is True
end
```

In this last form, only the commands associated with the *first* True expression encountered are evaluated; ensuing relational expressions are not tested, and

the rest of the `if-else-end` construction is skipped. Furthermore, the final `else` command may or may not appear.

Now that we know how to make decisions with `if-else-end` structures, it is possible to show a legal way for jumping or breaking out of `for` loops and `while` loops:

```
EDU» EPS=1;

EDU» for num=1:1000
        EPS=EPS/2;
        if (1+EPS)<=1
          EPS=EPS*2
          break
        end
      end
EPS =
    2.2204e-16

EDU» num
num =
    53
```

This example demonstrates another way of estimating `eps`. In this case, the `for` loop is instructed to run some sufficiently large number of times. The `if-else-end` structure tests to see if `EPS` has gotten small enough. If it has, `EPS` is multiplied by two, and the `break` command forces the `for` loop to end prematurely, i.e., at `num=53`, in this case.

In this example, when the `break` statement is executed, MATLAB jumps to the next statement outside the loop in which it appears. In this case, it returns to the MATLAB prompt and displays `EPS`. If a `break` statement appears in a nested `for` loop or `while` loop structure, MATLAB jumps out of only the loop in which it appears; it does not jump all the way out of the entire nested structure.

11.4 switch-case **Constructions**

When sequences of commands must be conditionally evaluated based on repeated use of an equality test with one common argument, a `switch-case` construction is often easier. `switch-case` constructions have the form

```
switch expression
    case test_expression1
        commands1...
    case {test_expression2,test_expression3,test_expression4}
        commands2...
    otherwise
        commands3...
end
```

Here, expression must be either a scalar or a character string. If expression is a scalar, expression ==test_expression is tested by the case statement. If expression is a character string, strcmp(expression, test_expression) is tested. In the preceding example, expression is compared with test_expression1 at the first case statement. If they are equal, commands1... are evaluated, and the rest of the statements before the end statement are skipped. If the first comparison is not true, the second is considered. In the preceding example, expression is compared with test_expression2, test_expression3, and test_expression4, which are held or contained in a cell array. If any of these is equal to expression, commands2... are evaluated, and the rest of the statements before the end are skipped. If all case comparisons are false, commands3... following the optional otherwise statement are executed. Note that this implementation of the switch-case construction allows one, at most, of the command groups to be executed.

A simple example demonstrating the switch-case construction is

```
x=2.7;
units='m';
switch units  % convert x to centimeters
      case {'inch','in'}
            y=x*2.54;
      case {'feet','ft'}
            y=x*2.54*12;
      case {'meter','m'}
            y=x/100;
      case {'millimeter','mm'}
            y=x*10;
      case {'centimeter','cm'}
            y=x;
      otherwise
            disp(['Unknown Units: ' units])
            y=nan;
end
```

Executing this example gives a final value of y=0.027.

Example: An Amortization Example

Problem: To purchase a car, you borrow $10,000 at 8.9% interest for 3 years. How much interest and principal are paid with each payment? In addition, what is the remaining balance after each payment is made?

Solution: From Chapter 2, the monthly payment P on a loan of A dollars, having a monthly interest rate of R, paid off in M months, is

$$P = A\left[\frac{R(1 + R)^M}{(1 + R)^M - 1}\right]$$

At the first payment, the interest paid is $Ip_1 = R \cdot A$. Given a payment P, the principal paid is $Pr_1 = P - Ip_1$, and the remaining loan balance is $B_1 = A - Pr_1$. At all remaining payments, the interest paid is $Ip_m = R \cdot B_{m-1}$, and the balance remaining is $B_m = B_{m-1} - Pr_m$. Using this information, the MATLAB solution is

```
% amort.m script file

A=10000; % amount of loan
M=3*12;    % number of months
R=8.9;   % annual interest rate %

r=(R/100)/12; % monthly interest rate

P=A*( r*(1+r)^M/( (1+r)^M −1)); % payment required

B=zeros(M,1);   % storage for balance remaining per month
Ip=B;           % storage for interest paid per month
Pr=B;           % storage for principal paid per month

for m=1:M

    if m==1  % compute interest when balance is original amount
        Ip(m)=r*A;
    else     % balance is B(m−1)
        Ip(m)=r*B(m−1);
    end

    Pr(m)=P−Ip(m);  % principal paid this month

    if m==1  % compute balance remaining after payment
        B(m)=A−Pr(m);
    else
        B(m)=B(m−1)−Pr(m);
    end
end

format bank
disp(['Amount = ' num2str(A)])
disp(['Interest Rate = ' num2str(R)])
disp(['Number of Months = ' int2str(M)])
disp(['Payment = ' num2str(P)])
disp(' ')
disp('                      Amortization Schedule')
disp('      Payment      Balance         Interest       Principal')
disp([(1:M)' B Ip Pr])
format short g
```

Running this script M-file produces

```
Amount = 10000
Interest Rate = 8.9
Number of Months = 36
Payment = 317.5321
```

```
                  Amortization Schedule
      Payment        Balance      Interest       Principal
        1.00        9756.63         74.17          243.37
        2.00        9511.46         72.36          245.17
        3.00        9264.48         70.54          246.99
        4.00        9015.65         68.71          248.82
        5.00        8764.99         66.87          250.67
        6.00        8512.46         65.01          252.53
        7.00        8258.07         63.13          254.40
          .
          .
          .
       30.00        1856.70         16.01          301.53
       31.00        1552.94         13.77          303.76
       32.00        1246.92         11.52          306.01
       33.00         938.64          9.25          308.28
       34.00         628.07          6.96          310.57
       35.00         315.19          4.66          312.87
       36.00          -0.00          2.34          315.19
```

This example demonstrates `for` loops and `if-else-end` constructions. It also shows the utility of script M-files. To compute any desired loan, you just have to change the input data at the beginning of the script and rerun it.

Example: The up/down Sequence

Problem: Let x_0 be any integer. Suppose that the following rule is used to define a sequence of numbers based on x_0.

$$x_{k+1} = \begin{cases} x_k/2 & \text{if } x_k \text{ is even} \\ 3x_k + 1 & \text{if } x_k \text{ is odd} \end{cases}$$

What properties does this sequence have? If you stop generating values when $x_k = 1$, does the sequence diverge to infinity or converge to 1?

Solution: What is needed is a `while` loop that stops when $x_k = 1$, and an `if-else-end` construction to implement the foregoing rule. In MATLAB, the solution is

```
% up_down.m script file for up/down sequence problem

x=zeros(500,1);  % preallocate storage for x(k)

x(1)=round(abs(input('Enter a number > ')));
k=1;

    while (x(k)>1) & (k<500)
        if rem(x(k),2)==0  % x(k) is even
        x(k+1)=x(k)/2;
    else                % x(k) is odd
        x(k+1)=3*x(k)+1;
    end
    k=k+1;  % increment sequence counter
end

x=x(x>0) % keep values generated only and display them
```

This M-file produces interesting results. For example, $x = 2^m$ where m is an integer produces the shortest sequences. (Why?) Moreover, whenever a sequence value reaches any power of two, the sequence quickly terminates. Some relatively small numbers produce interesting sequences, e.g., $x(1) = 27$. Almost all initial values produce sequences that have interesting plots, as shown for $x(1) = 837799$ in the following example. Can you find a sequence that diverges?

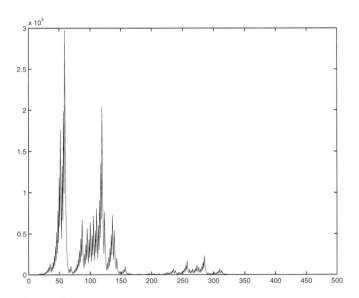

Figure 11.1

Function M-files

12.1 Rules and Properties

When you use MATLAB functions such as `inv`, `abs`, `angle`, and `sqrt`, MATLAB takes the variables you pass it, computes the required results using your input, and then passes those results back to you. The commands evaluated by the function (as well as any intermediate variables created by those commands) are hidden. All you see is what goes in and what comes out—i.e., a function is a black box.

These properties make functions very powerful tools for evaluating commands that encapsulate useful mathematical functions or sequences of commands that appear often when solving some larger problem. Because of this power, MATLAB provides a structure for creating functions of your own in the form of text M-files stored on your computer. The MATLAB function `flipud` is a good example of an M-file function:

```
function y = flipud(x)
%FLIPUD Flip matrix in up/down direction.
%   FLIPUD(X) returns X with columns preserved and rows flipped
%   in the up/down direction.  For example,
%
%   X = 1 4        becomes  3 6
%       2 5                 2 5
%       3 6                 1 4
%
%   See also FLIPLR, ROT90, FLIPDIM.

%   Copyright (c) 1984-96 by The MathWorks, Inc.
%   $Revision: 5.3 $ $Date: 1996/10/24 18:41:14 $

if ndims(x)~=2, error('X must be a 2-D matrix.'); end
[m,n] = size(x);
y = x(m:-1:1,:);
```

A function M-file is similar to a script file in that it is a text file having a `.m` extension. As with script M-files, function M-files are not entered in the *Command* window, but rather are external text files created with a text editor. A function M-file is different than a script file in that a function communicates with the MATLAB workspace only through the variables passed to it and through the output variables it creates. Intermediate variables within the function do not appear in, or interact with, the MATLAB workspace. As you can see in the preceding example, the first line of a function M-file defines the M-file as a function and specifies its name (its file name without the `.m` extension). It also defines its input and output variables. The next continuous sequence of comment lines is the text displayed in response to the `help` command: » `help flipud` or » `helpwin flipud`. The first help line, called the H1 line, is the line searched by the `lookfor` command. Finally, the remainder of the M-file contains MATLAB commands that create the output variables.

12.1 Rules and Properties

Function M-files must follow specific rules. In addition, they have a number of important properties. They include the following:

- The function name and file name are identical. For example, the function `flipud` is stored in a file named `flipud.m`.

- The first time MATLAB executes a function M-file, it opens the corresponding text file and *compiles* the commands into an internal representation in memory that speeds their execution for all ensuing function calls. If the function contains references to other function M-files, they too are compiled into memory.

- Comment lines up to the first noncomment line in a function M-file are the help text returned when you request help, e.g., » `help flipud` returns the first nine comment lines above. The very first help line, known as the H1 line, is the line searched by the `lookfor` command.

- Each function has its own workspace separate from the MATLAB workspace. The only connections between the variables within a function and the MATLAB workspace are the function's input and output variables. If a function changes values in any input variable, the changes appear within the function only, and do not affect the variable in the MATLAB workspace. Variables created within a function reside only in the function's workspace; furthermore, they exist only temporarily during function execution and disappear afterwards. Thus, it is not possible to store information in function workspace variables from one call to the next.

- The number of input and output arguments used when a function is called are available within that function. The function workspace variable `nargin` contains the number of input arguments. The function workspace variable `nargout` contains the number of output arguments. In practice, these variables are commonly used to set default input variables and determine what output variables the user desires. For example, consider the MATLAB function `linspace`:

```
function y = linspace(d1, d2, n)
%LINSPACE Linearly spaced vector.
%    LINSPACE(x1, x2) generates a row vector of 100 linearly
%    equally spaced points between x1 and x2.
%
%    LINSPACE(x1, x2, N) generates N points between x1 and x2.
%
%    See also LOGSPACE, :.

%    Copyright (c) 1984-96 by The MathWorks, Inc.
%    $Revision: 5.2 $  $Date: 1996/03/29 20:24:44 $

if nargin == 2
    n = 100;
end
y = [d1+(0:n-2)*(d2-d1)/(n-1) d2];
```

Here, if the user calls linspace with only two input arguments, e.g., linspace(0,10), linspace makes the number of points equal to 100. On the other hand, if the number of input arguments is three, e.g., linspace(0,10,50), the third argument determines the number of data points.

- Functions can share variables with other functions, the MATLAB workspace and recursive calls to themselves if the variables are declared **global.** To gain access to a global variable within a function or the MATLAB workspace, the variable must be declared global within each desired workspace. An example of the use of global variables can be found in the MATLAB functions tic and toc, which together act as a stopwatch:

```
function tic
%TIC Start a stopwatch timer.
%    The sequence of commands
%        TIC, operation, TOC
%    prints the time required for the operation.
%
%    See also TOC, CLOCK, ETIME, CPUTIME.

%    Copyright (c) 1984-96 by The MathWorks, Inc.
%    $Revision: 5.2 $  $Date: 1996/03/29 20:29:26 $

% TIC simply stores CLOCK in a global variable.
global TICTOC
TICTOC = clock;
```

```
function t = toc
%TOC Read the stopwatch timer.
%    TOC, by itself, prints the elapsed time since TIC was used.
%    t = TOC; saves the elapsed time in t, instead of printing it out.
%
%    See also TIC, ETIME, CLOCK, CPUTIME.

%    Copyright (c) 1984-96 by The MathWorks, Inc.
%    $Revision: 5.2 $  $Date: 1996/03/29 20:30:02 $

% TOC uses ETIME and the value of CLOCK saved by TIC.
global TICTOC
if nargout < 1
    elapsed_time = etime(clock,TICTOC)
else
    t = etime(clock,TICTOC);
end
```

In the function tic, the variable TICTOC is declared global, then its value is set by calling the function clock. Later in the function toc, the variable TICTOC is also declared global, giving toc access to the value stored in TICTOC. Using this value, toc computes the elapsed time since the function tic was executed. It is important to note that the variable TICTOC exists in the workspaces of tic and toc, but not in the **MATLAB** workspace.

- Function M-files terminate execution and return when they reach the end of the M-file, or, alternatively, when the command return is encountered. The return command provides a simple way to terminate a function without reaching the end of the file.

- The MATLAB function error displays a character string in the *Command* window, aborts function execution, and returns control to the keyboard. This function is useful for flagging improper function usage, as in the file fragment:

```
if length(val)>1
    error('VAL must be a scalar.')
end
```

Here, if the variable val is not a scalar, error displays the informative character string and returns control to the *Command* window and keyboard.

- Function M-files may contain more than one function. The first or primary function appearing in the M-file shares the file name as previously discussed. Other functions beginning with a function statement are simply appended below the first function. These *sub*functions can be called from the primary function only; that is, subfunctions cannot be called from other functions or from the *Command* window. This feature provides a convenient way to encapsulate parts of the primary function that are used repeatedly, or to improve the readability of the primary function.

In summary, function M-files provide a simple way to extend the capabilities of MATLAB. In fact, many of the standard functions in MATLAB are function M-files.

Example: Amortization Schedule Function

Problem: Consider a loan of A dollars at R percent annual interest, to be paid off in M months. Write a function M-file that displays an amortization schedule if no output arguments are given, the monthly payment P if one output argument is provided, or the monthly payment P and a numerical matrix containing the amortization schedule if two output arguments are provided.

Solution: From Chapter 11, the monthly payment P on a loan of A dollars, having a monthly interest rate of R, paid off in M months, is:

$$P = A\left[\frac{R(1 + R)^M}{(1 + R)^M - 1}\right]$$

At the first payment, the interest paid is $Ip_1 = R \cdot A$. Given a payment P, the principal paid is $Pr_1 = P - Ip_1$, and the remaining loan balance is $B_1 = A - Pr_1$. At all remaining payments, the interest paid is $Ip_m = R \cdot B_{m-1}$, and the balance remaining is $B_m = B_{m-1} - Pr_m$. Using this information, the function M-file solution is

```
function [P,S]=loan(a,r,m)
%LOAN Loan Payment and Amortization Table. (H1 help line)
% P=LOAN(A,R,M) computes the monthly payment on a loan
% amount of A, having an annual interest rate of R, to be
% paid off in equal amounts over M months.
%
% [P,S]=LOAN(A,R,M) also returns an amortization table S,
% which is an M-by-4 matrix where S(:,1) = Payment Number,
% S(:,2) = Remaining Balance, S(:,3) = Interest Paid, and
% S(:,4) = Principal Paid.
%
% If no output arguments are provided the table is displayed.

% start with some error checking
if nargin<3,  error('Three Input Arguments are Required.'),  end
if fix(m)~=m, error('Number of Months Must Be An Integer.'), end

% now calculate
rm=(r/100)/12;  % monthly interest rate
p=a*( rm*(1+rm)^m/( (1+rm)^m −1)); % payment required

if nargout==1 % done if only payment is required.
     P=p; % copy output into output variable
     return
end

B=zeros(m,1);  % storage for balance remaining per month
Ip=B;          % storage for interest paid per month
Pr=B;          % storage for principal paid per month

for i=1:m  % create table data

    if i==1  % compute interest when balance is original amount
        Ip(i)=rm*a;
    else     % balance is B(i−1)
        Ip(i)=rm*B(i−1);
    end

    Pr(i)=p−Ip(i);  % principal paid this month

    if i==1  % compute balance remaining after payment
        B(i)=a−Pr(i);
    else
        B(i)=B(i−1)−Pr(i);
    end

end

end
```

```
B(abs(B)<0.001)=0;  % set near zero balances to zero
s=[(1:m)' B Ip Pr];
if nargout==0  % display table
    disp(['Amount = ' num2str(a)])
    disp(['Interest Rate = ' num2str(r)])
    disp(['Number of Months = ' int2str(m)])
    disp(['Payment = ' num2str(p)])
    disp(' ')
    disp('                    Amortization Schedule')
    disp('Payment        Balance        Interest     Principal')
    fprintf('  %5.0f  %12.2f  %12.2f  %12.2f\n',s') % better formatting
else  % two output arguments requested
    P=p;
    S=s;
end
```

Example: Decoding Resistor Color Bands

Problem: The values of resistors used in electrical circuits are determined by color-coded rings around the resistors. On resistors having 5% tolerance, there are three bands, denoted A, B, and C, that determine the resistance. The numerical value assigned to each color is:

Color	Value
Black	0
Brown	1
Red	2
Orange	3
Yellow	4
Green	5
Blue	6
Violet	7
Gray	8
White	9

If A, B, and C denote the values associated with these color bands, the resistance of a resistor is:

$$R = (10 \cdot A + B) \cdot 10^C$$

Using this information, create a function M-file that returns the resistance value associated with any standard resistor.

Solution: This problem requires string manipulation and comparison to perform the conversion described in the preceding table. A MATLAB solution is:

```
function r=resistor(a,b,c)
%RESISTOR(A,B,C) Resistor Value from Color Code.
% RESISTOR(A,B,C) returns the resistance value of a resistor
% given its three color bands, A, B, and C.
% A, B, and C must be one of the following character strings:
%
% 'black', 'brown', 'red', 'orange', 'yellow',
% 'green', 'blue', 'violet', 'gray', 'white'

% first some error checking
if nargin~=3
    error('Three Input Arguments Required.')
end
if ~ischar(a) | ~ischar(b) | ~ischar(c)
    error('Inputs Must be Character Strings.')
end

% now solve problem
vals=zeros(1,3);  % storage for the three code values

abc={a,b,c};  % string cell array of the three inputs

for i=1:3  % do each color band in turn

    band=lower(abc{i});  % get (i)th input and make lowercase

    if strncmp(band,'bla',3)        % black (compare min # of
        vals(i)=0;                  % chars for unique match)
    elseif strncmp(band,'br',2)     % brown
        vals(i)=1;
    elseif strncmp(band,'r',1)      % red
        vals(i)=2;
    elseif strncmp(band,'o',1)      % orange
        vals(i)=3;
```

```
        elseif strncmp(band,'y',1)     % yellow
            vals(i)=4;
        elseif strncmp(band,'gre',3)  % green
            vals(i)=5;
        elseif strncmp(band,'blu',3)  % blue
            vals(i)=6;
        elseif strncmp(band,'v',1)     % violet
            vals(i)=7;
        elseif strncmp(band,'gra',3)  % gray
            vals(i)=8;
        elseif strncmp(band,'w',1)     % white
            vals(i)=9;
        else
            error(['Unknown Color Band: ' band ])
        end
end
if vals(1)==0
    error('First Color Band Cannot Be Black.')
end
r=(10*vals(1)+vals(2)) * 10^vals(3);
```

Using the function for several examples produces

```
EDU » resistor('brown','black','red')  % 1 kiloohm
ans =
        1000

EDU » resistor('br','bla','r')
ans =
        1000

EDU » resistor('r','g')
??? Error using ==> resistor
Three Input Arguments Required.

EDU » resistor('yellow','violet','ORAN')  % 47 kiloohm
ans =
       47000

EDU » resistor('red','g','blue')
??? Error using ==> resistor
Unknown Color Band: g
```

Data Analysis

13.1 Data Analysis Functions

Because of its matrix orientation, MATLAB readily performs statistical analyses on data sets. While MATLAB, by default, considers data sets stored in column-oriented arrays, data analysis can be conducted along any specified dimension. That is, unless specified otherwise, the columns of a data array represent a different measured variable, and each row represents individual samples or observations. For example, let's assume that the daily high temperature (in Celsius) of three cities over a 31-day month was recorded and assigned to the variable temps in a script M-file. Running the M-file puts the variable temps in the MATLAB workspace. Doing this work, the variable temps contains:

```
EDU» temps
temps =
     12       8      18
     15       9      22
     12       5      19
     14       8      23
     12       6      22
     11       9      19
     15       9      15
      8      10      20
     19       7      18
     12       7      18
     14      10      19
     11       8      17
      9       7      23
      8       8      19
     15       8      18
      8       9      20
     10       7      17
     12       7      22
      9       8      19
     12       8      21
     12       8      20
     10       9      17
     13      12      18
      9      10      20
     10       6      22
     14       7      21
     12       5      22
     13       7      18
     15      10      23
     13      11      24
     12      12      22
```

Each row contains the high temperatures for a given day. Each column contains the high temperatures for a different city. To visualize the data, plot it:

```
EDU» d=1:31;    % number the days of the month

EDU» plot(d,temps)

EDU» xlabel('Day of Month'),ylabel('Celsius')

EDU» title('Daily High Temperatures in Three Cities')
```

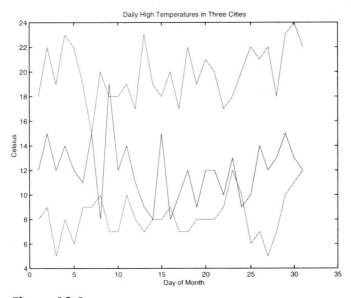

Figure 13.1

The `plot` command just given illustrates yet another form of `plot` command usage. The variable d is a vector of length 31, whereas `temps` is a 31-by-3 matrix. Given these data, the `plot` command plots each column of `temps` versus d.

To illustrate some of the data analysis capabilities of MATLAB, consider the following commands based on the foregoing temperature data:

```
EDU» avg_temp=mean(temps)
avg_temp =
    11.9677    8.2258    19.8710
```

shows that the third city has the highest average temperature. Here, MATLAB found the average of each column individually. Taking the average again gives:

```
EDU» avg_avg=mean(avg_temp)
avg_avg =
    13.3548
```

finds the overall average temperature of the three cities. When the input to a data analysis function is a row or column vector, MATLAB simply performs the operation on the vector, returning a scalar result.

Alternatively, you can specify the dimension to work on:

```
EDU» avg_temp=mean(temps,1)   % same as above, work down each
                              % column
avg_temp =
        11.968        8.2258        19.871

EDU» avg_tempr=mean(temps,2)  % compute means across each row
avg_tempr =
        12.667
        15.333
            12
            15
        13.333
            13
            13
        12.667
        14.667
        12.333
        14.333
            12
            13
        11.667
        13.667
        12.333
        11.333
        13.667
            12
        13.667
        13.333
            12
        14.333
            13
        12.667
            14
            13
```

```
    12.667
       16
       16
    15.333
```

This is the average city temperature on each day.

Consider the problem of finding the daily deviation from the mean of each city. That is, avg_temp(i) must be subtracted from column i of temps. You cannot simply issue the statement

```
EDU» temps—avg_temp
??? Error using ==> —
Matrix dimensions must agree.
```

because the operation is not a defined array operation (temps is 31-by-3 and avg_temp is 1-by-3). Perhaps the most straightforward approach is to use a for loop:

```
EDU» for i=1:3
        tdev(:,i)=temps(:,i)—avg_temp(i);
  end

EDU» tdev
tdev =
      0.0323   —0.2258   —1.8710
      3.0323    0.7742    2.1290
      0.0323    3.2258   —0.8710
      2.0323   —0.2258    3.1290
      0.0323   —2.2258    2.1290
     —0.9677    0.7742   —0.8710
      3.0323    0.7742   —4.8710
     —3.9677    1.7742    0.1290
      7.0323   —1.2258   —1.8710
      0.0323   —1.2258   —1.8710
      2.0323    1.7742   —0.8710
     —0.9677   —0.2258   —2.8710
     —2.9677   —1.2258    3.1290
     —3.9677   —0.2258   —0.8710
      3.0323   —0.2258   —1.8710
     —3.9677    0.7742    0.1290
     —1.9677   —1.2258   —2.8710
      0.0323   —1.2258    2.1290
     —2.9677   —0.2258   —0.8710
      0.0323   —0.2258    1.1290
      0.0323   —0.2258    0.1290
     —1.9677    0.7742   —2.8710
```

```
    1.0323    3.7742   -1.8710
   -2.9677    1.7742    0.1290
   -1.9677   -2.2258    2.1290
    2.0323   -1.2258    1.1290
    0.0323   -3.2258    2.1290
    1.0323   -1.2258   -1.8710
    3.0323    1.7742    3.1290
    1.0323    2.7742    4.1290
    0.0323    3.7742    2.1290
```

While this approach works, it is slower than using the array manipulation features of MATLAB. It is much faster to duplicate avg_temp to make it the size of temps, and then do the subtraction:

```
EDU» tdev=temps-avg_temp(ones(31,1),:)
tdev =
    0.0323   -0.2258   -1.8710
    3.0323    0.7742    2.1290
    0.0323   -3.2258   -0.8710
    2.0323   -0.2258    3.1290
    0.0323   -2.2258    2.1290
   -0.9677    0.7742   -0.8710
    3.0323    0.7742   -4.8710
   -3.9677    1.7742    0.1290
    7.0323   -1.2258   -1.8710
    0.0323   -1.2258   -1.8710
    2.0323    1.7742   -0.8710
   -0.9677   -0.2258   -2.8710
   -2.9677   -1.2258    3.1290
   -3.9677   -0.2258   -0.8710
    3.0323   -0.2258   -1.8710
   -3.9677    0.7742    0.1290
   -1.9677   -1.2258   -2.8710
    0.0323   -1.2258    2.1290
   -2.9677   -0.2258   -0.8710
    0.0323   -0.2258    1.1290
    0.0323   -0.2258    0.1290
   -1.9677    0.7742   -2.8710
    1.0323    3.7742   -1.8710
   -2.9677    1.7742    0.1290
   -1.9677   -2.2258    2.1290
    2.0323   -1.2258    1.1290
    0.0323   -3.2258    2.1290
```

```
        1.0323    -1.2258    -1.8710
        3.0323     1.7742     3.1290
        1.0323     2.7742     4.1290
        0.0323     3.7742     2.1290
```

Here, `avg_temp(ones(31,1),:)` duplicates the first (and only) row of `avg_temp` 31 times, creating a 31-by-3 matrix whose ith column is `avg_temp(i)`.

```
EDU» max_temp=max(temps)
max_temp =
    19    12    24
```

finds the maximum high temperature of each city over the month.

```
EDU» [max_temp,x]=max(temps)
max_temp =
    19    12    24
x =
     9    23    30
```

finds the maximum high temperature of each city and the row index x where the maximum appears. For this example, x identifies the day of the month when the highest temperature occurred.

```
EDU» min_temp=min(temps)
min_temp =
     8     5    15
```

finds the minimum high temperature of each city.

```
EDU» [min_temp,n]=min(temps)
min_temp =
     8     5    15
n =
     8     3     7
```

finds the minimum high temperature of each city and the row index n where the minimum appears. For this example, n identifies the day of the month when the lowest high temperature occurred.

```
EDU» s_dev=std(temps)
s_dev =
    2.5098    1.7646    2.2322
```

finds the standard deviation in `temps`.

```
EDU» daily_change=diff(temps)
daily_change =
     3     1     4
    -3    -4    -3
     2     3     4
    -2    -2    -1
    -1     3    -3
     4     0    -4
    -7     1     5
    11    -3    -2
    -7     0     0
     2     3     1
    -3    -2    -2
    -2    -1     6
    -1     1    -4
     7     0    -1
    -7     1     2
     2    -2    -3
     2     0     5
    -3     1    -3
     3     0     2
     0     0    -1
    -2     1    -3
     3     3     1
    -4    -2     2
     1    -4     2
     4     1    -1
    -2    -2     1
     1     2    -4
     2     3     5
    -2     1     1
    -1     1    -2
```

computes the difference between successive daily high temperatures, which describes how much the daily high temperature varied from day to day. For example, the first row of daily_change is the amount the daily high changed between the first and second days of the month.

13.1 Data Analysis Functions

Data analysis in MATLAB is performed on column-oriented matrices. Different variables are stored in individual columns, and each row represents a different observation of each variable. MATLAB statistical functions include:

Data Analysis Functions	
`corrcoef(x)`	Correlation coefficients
`cov(x)`	Covariance matrix
`cplxpair(x)`	Sort vector into complex conjugate pairs
`cross(x,y)`	Vector cross product
`cumprod(x)`	Cumulative product of columns
`cumprod(x,n)`	Cumulative product along dimension n
`cumsum(x)`	Cumulative sum of columns
`cumsum(x,n)`	Cumulative sum along dimension n
`cumtrapz(x,y)`	Cumulative trapezoidal integration
`cumtrapz(x,y,n)`	Cumulative trapezoidal integration along dimension n
`del2(A)`	Five-point discrete Laplacian
`diff(x)`	Compute differences between elements
`diff(x,m)`	m^{th} order difference between elements
`diff(x,m,n)`	m^{th} order difference along dimension n
`dot(x,y)`	Vector dot product
`gradient(Z,dx,dy)`	Approximate gradient
`histogram(x)`	Histogram or bar chart
`max(x), max(x,y)`	Maximum component
`max(x,n)`	Maximum along dimension n
`mean(x)`	Mean or average value of columns
`mean(x,n)`	Mean along dimension n
`median(x)`	Median value of columns
`median(x,n)`	Median along dimension n
`min(x), min(x,y)`	Minimum component
`min(x,n)`	Minimum along dimension n
`prod(x)`	Product of elements in columns
`prod(x,n)`	Product along dimension n
`rand(x)`	Uniformly distributed random numbers

	Data Analysis Functions (Continued)
`randn(x)`	Normally distributed random numbers
`sort(x)`	Sort columns in ascending order
`sort(x,n)`	Sort along dimension `n`
`sortrows(A)`	Sort rows in ascending order
`std(x)`, `std(0)`	Standard deviation of columns normalized by $N-1$
`std(x,1)`	Standard deviation normalized by N
`std(x,flag,n)`	Standard deviation along dimension `n`
`subspace(A,B)`	Angle between two subspaces
`sum(x)`	Sum of elements in each column
`sum(x,n)`	Sum along dimension `n`
`trapz(x,y)`	Trapezoidal integration of `y=f(x)`
`trapz(x,y,n)`	Trapezoidal integration along dimension `n`

14

Polynomials

14.1 Roots

Finding the roots of a polynomial, i.e., the values for which the polynomial is zero, is a problem that arises in many disciplines. MATLAB solves this problem and provides other polynomial manipulation tools as well. **In MATLAB, a polynomial is represented by a *row* vector of its coefficients in *descending* order**. For example, the polynomial $x^4 - 12x^3 + 0x^2 + 25x + 116$ is entered as:

```
EDU» p=[1 −12 0 25 116]
p =
        1    −12      0     25    116
```

Note that terms with zero coefficients must be included. MATLAB has no way of knowing which terms are zero unless you specifically identify them. Given this form, the roots of a polynomial are found by using the function roots:

```
EDU» r=roots(p)
r =
   11.7473
    2.7028
   −1.2251 + 1.4672i
   −1.2251 − 1.4672i
```

Since both a polynomial and its roots are vectors in MATLAB, **MATLAB adopts the convention that polynomials are *row* vectors and roots are *column* vectors**. Given the roots of a polynomial, it is also possible to construct the associated polynomial. In MATLAB, the command poly performs this task:

```
EDU» pp=poly(r)
pp =
              1           −12  −1.7764e−14              25             116
EDU» pp(abs(pp)<1e−12)=0   % change small element to zero!
pp =
              1           −12            0              25             116
```

Because of truncation errors, it is not uncommon for the results of poly to have near-zero components, or to have components with small imaginary parts. As just shown, near-zero components can be corrected by array manipulation. Similarly, eliminating spurious imaginary parts is simply a matter of using the function real to extract the real part of the result.

14.2 Multiplication

Polynomial multiplication is supported by the function conv (which performs the *convolution* of two arrays). Consider the product of the two polynomials $a(x) = x^3 + 2x^2 + 3x + 4$ and $b(x) = x^3 + 4x^2 + 9x + 16$:

```
EDU» a=[1  2  3  4];  b=[1  4  9  16];

EDU» c=conv(a,b)
c =
        1      6     20     50     75     84     64
```

This result is $c(x) = x^6 + 6x^5 + 20x^4 + 50x^3 + 75x^2 + 84x + 64$. Multiplication of more than two polynomials requires repeated use of conv.

14.3 Addition

MATLAB does not provide a direct function for adding polynomials. Standard array addition works if both polynomial vectors are the same size. Add the polynomials $a(x)$ and $b(x)$ given above:

```
EDU» d=a+b
d =
        2      6     12     20
```

which is $d(x) = 2x^3 + 6x^2 + 12x + 20$. When two polynomials are of different orders, the one having lower order must be padded with leading zeros to make it have the same effective order as the higher-order polynomial. Consider the addition of polynomials c and d above:

```
EDU» e=c+[0  0  0  d]
e =
        1      6     20     52     81     96     84
```

which is $e(x) = x^6 + 6x^5 + 20x^4 + 52x^3 + 81x^2 + 96x + 84$. Leading zeros are required rather than trailing zeros, because coefficients associated with like powers of x must line up.

If desired, you can create a function M-file using the editor to perform general polynomial addition:

```
function p=polyadd(a,b)
%POLYADD Polynomial addition.
% POLYADD(A,B) adds the polynomials A and B

if nargin<2, error('Not enough input arguments'),end  % error checking
a=a(:).';  % make sure inputs are row vectors
b=b(:).';
na=length(a);  % find lengths of a and b
nb=length(b);
p=[zeros(1,nb-na) a]+[zeros(1,na-nb) b];  % pad with zeros as necessary
```

Now, to illustrate the use of `polyadd`, reconsider the preceding example:

```
EDU» f=polyadd(c,d)
f =
     1     6    20    52    81    96    84
```

which is the same as `e` above. Of course, `polyadd` may also be used for subtraction:

```
EDU» g=polyadd(c,-d)
g =
     1     6    20    48    69    72    44
```

which is $g(x) = x^6 + 6x^5 + 20x^4 + 48x^3 + 69x^2 + 72x + 44$.

14.4   Division

In some special cases, it is necessary to divide one polynomial into another. In MATLAB, this is accomplished with the function `deconv`. Using the polynomials `b` and `c` from the foregoing:

```
EDU» [q,r]=deconv(c,b)
q =
     1     2     3     4
r =
     0     0     0     0     0     0     0
```

This result says that `b` divided into `c` gives the quotient polynomial `q` and the remainder `r`, which is zero in this case since the product of `b` and `q` is exactly `c` (`c` was formed as the product of `b` and `q=a` earlier).

14.5   Derivatives

Because differentiation of a polynomial is simple to express, MATLAB offers the function `polyder` for polynomial differentiation:

```
EDU» g
g =
     1     6    20    48    69    72    44
EDU» h=polyder(g)
h =
     6    30    80   144   138    72
```

14.6   Evaluation

Given that you can add, subtract, multiply, divide, and differentiate polynomials based on row vectors of their coefficients, you should be able to evaluate them also. In MATLAB, this is accomplished with the function `polyval`:

```
EDU» x=linspace(-1,3);
```

chooses 100 data points between -1 and 3.

```
EDU» p=[1  4  -7  -10];
```

uses the polynomial $p(x) = x^3 + 4x^2 - 7x - 10$.

```
EDU» v=polyval(p,x);
```

evaluates $p(x)$ at the values in x and stores the result in v. The result is then plotted using

```
EDU» plot(x,v), title('x^3 + 4x^2 - 7x -10'), xlabel('x')
```

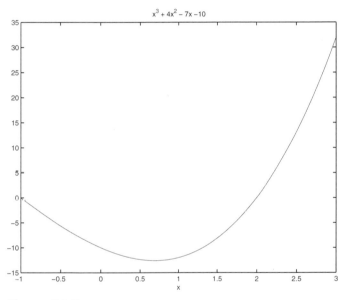

Figure 14.1

14.7   Rational Polynomials

Sometimes you may encounter ratios of polynomials, e.g., transfer functions and Pade approximations to functions, having the form:

$$\frac{n(x)}{d(x)} = \frac{N_1 x^m + N_2 x^{m-1} + \cdots + N_{m+1}}{D_1 x^n + D_2 x^{n-1} + \cdots + D_{n+1}}$$

In MATLAB, these are manipulated by considering the two polynomials separately. For example,

```
EDU» n=[1  -10  100]  % a numerator
n =
      1    -10    100
```

```
EDU» d=[1 10 100 0]  % a denominator
d =
     1    10    100     0
EDU» z=roots(n)  % the zeros of n(x)/d(x)
z =
          5 + 8.6603i
          5 - 8.6603i
EDU» p=roots(d)  % the poles of n(x)/d(x)
p =
          0
         -5 + 8.6603i
         -5 - 8.6603i
```

The derivative of this rational polynomial with respect to x is found using polyder:

```
EDU» [nd,dd]=polyder(n,d)
nd =
         -1         20        -100       -2000      -10000
dd =
  Columns 1 through 6
          1         20         300        2000       10000        0
  Column 7
          0
```

Here, nd and dd are the numerator and denominator of the derivative.

Another common operation is to find the partial fraction expansion of a rational polynomial.

```
EDU» [r,p,k]=residue(n,d)
r =
  9.7954e-17 + 1.1547i
  9.7954e-17 - 1.1547i
          1
p =
         -5 + 8.6603i
         -5 - 8.6603i
          0
k =
     []
```

In this case, the residue function returns the residues or partial fraction expansion coefficients r, their associated poles p, and direct term polynomial k. Since the order of the numerator is less than that of the denominator, there are no direct terms. For this example, the partial fraction expansion of the rational polynomial given previously is

$$\frac{n(x)}{d(x)} = \frac{1.1547i}{x + 5 - 8.6603i} + \frac{-1.1547i}{x - 5 + 8.6603i} + \frac{1}{x}$$

Given this information, the original rational polynomial is found by using residue yet again:

```
EDU» [nn,dd]=residue(r,p,k)
nn =
         1          -10          100
dd =
         1           10          100           0
```

So, in this case, the function residue performs two operations that are inverses of one another, based on how many input and output arguments are used.

15

Curve Fitting and Interpolation

In numerous application areas, the task arises to describe data, often measured, with an analytic function. There are two approaches to this problem. In *interpolation*, the data are assumed to be correct, and what is desired is some way to describe what happens between the data points. In the other method, *curve fitting* or *regression*, you are seeking to find some smooth curve that "best fits" the data, but does not necessarily pass through any data points. Fig. 15.1 illustrates these two approaches. The 'o' marks are the data points; the solid lines connecting them depict linear interpolation, and the dashed curve is a "best fit" to the data.

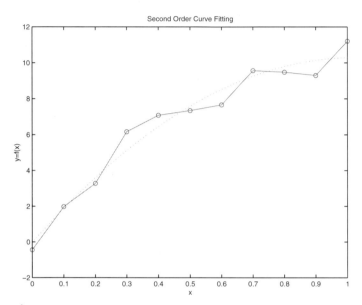

Figure 15.1

Let's look more closely at curve fitting. We'll explore interpolation later.

15.1 Curve Fitting

Curve fitting involves answering two fundamental questions: What is meant by "best fit," and what kind of a curve should be used? "Best fit" can be defined in many different ways, and there is an infinite number of curves. So where do we go from here? As it turns out, when "best fit" is interpreted as minimizing the sum of the squared error at the data points and the curve used is restricted to polynomials, curve fitting is fairly straightforward. Mathematically, this is called **least squares curve fitting** to a polynomial. If this description is confusing, study Fig. 15.1 again. The vertical distance between the dashed curve and a marked data point is the error at that point. Squaring this distance at each data point and adding together the squared distances is the "sum of the squared error." The dashed curve is the curve that makes this sum of squared error as small as it can be, i.e., it is a "best fit." The term "least squares" is an abbreviated way of saying "minimizing the sum of the squared error."

In MATLAB, the function polyfit solves the least squares curve fitting problem. To illustrate the use of this function, let's start with the data in the preceding plot:

```
EDU» x=[0 .1 .2 .3 .4 .5 .6 .7 .8 .9 1];
EDU» y=[−.447 1.978 3.28 6.16 7.08 7.34 7.66 9.56 9.48 9.30 11.2];
```

To use polyfit, we must give it the preceding data and the order or degree of the polynomial we wish to best fit to the data. If we choose n=1 as the order, the best straight line approximation will be found. This is often called **linear regression**. On the other hand, if we choose n=2 as the order, a quadratic polynomial will be found. For now, let's choose a quadratic polynomial:

```
EDU» n=2;
EDU» p=polyfit(x,y,n)
p =
   −9.8108    20.1293    −0.031/
```

The output of polyfit is a row vector of the polynomial coefficients. Here, the solution is $y = -9.8108x^2 + 20.1293x - 0.0317$. To compare the curve fit solution to the data points, let's plot both:

```
EDU» xi=linspace(0,1,100);
```

creates x-axis data for plotting the polynomial.

```
EDU» z=polyval(p,xi);
```

calls the MATLAB function polyval to evaluate the polynomial p at the data points in xi.

```
EDU» plot(x,y,'−o',xi,z,':')
```

plots the original data x and y, marking the data points with 'o' and connecting them with straight lines. In addition, it plots the polynomial data xi and z using a dotted line ':'.

```
EDU» xlabel('x'),ylabel('y=f(x)'),title('Second Order Curve Fitting')
```

labels the plot. The result of these steps is shown in the plot given at the beginning of this section.

The choice of polynomial order is somewhat arbitrary. It takes two points to define a straight line, or first-order polynomial. It takes three points to define a quadratic, or second-order polynomial. Following this progression, it takes $n+1$ data points to uniquely specify an nth-order polynomial. Thus, in the previous case where there are 11 data points, we could choose up to a tenth-order polynomial. However, given the poor numerical properties of higher-order polynomials, you should not choose a polynomial order any higher than necessary. In addition, as the polynomial order increases, the approximation becomes less smooth, since higher-order polynomials can be differentiated more times before they become zero. For example, choosing a tenth-order polynomial:

```
EDU» pp=polyfit(x,y,10)

EDU» format short e  % change display format

EDU» pp.'  % display polynomial coefficients as a column
ans =
  -4.6436e+05
   2.2965e+06
  -4.8773e+06
   5.8233e+06
  -4.2948e+06
   2.0211e+06
  -6.0322e+05
   1.0896e+05
  -1.0626e+04
   4.3599e+02
  -4.4700e-01
```

Note the size of the polynomial coefficients in this case compared to those of the earlier quadratic fit. Note also the seven orders of magnitude difference between the smallest $(-4.4700e-01)$ and largest $(5.8233e+06)$ coefficients. Try plotting this solution and comparing it to the original data and quadratic curve fit.

```
EDU» zz=polyval(pp,xi);  % evaluate 10th order polynomial

EDU» plot(x,y,'o',xi,z,':',xi,zz) % plot data

EDU» xlabel('x'),ylabel('y=f(x)')

EDU» title('2nd and 10th Order Curve Fitting')
```

In Fig. 15.2, the original data is marked with 'o', the quadratic curve fit is dotted, and the tenth-order fit is solid. Note the wave-like ripples that appear between the data points at the left and right extremes in the tenth-order fit. Based on this plot, it is clear that the "more is better" philosophy does not necessarily apply here.

Curve Fitting and Interpolation   Chapter 15

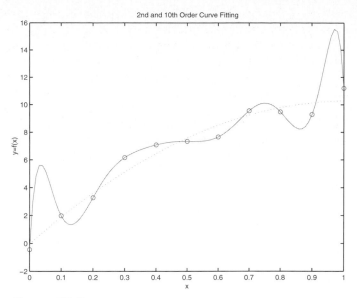

Figure 15.2

15.2 One-Dimensional Interpolation

As described in the introduction to this section, interpolation is defined as a way of estimating values of a function between those given by some set of data points. Interpolation is a valuable tool when one cannot quickly evaluate the function at the desired intermediate points. For example, this is true when the data points are the result of some experimental measurements or lengthy computational procedure.

Perhaps the simplest example of interpolation is MATLAB plots. By default, MATLAB draws straight lines connecting the data points used to make a plot. **This *linear* interpolation guesses that intermediate values fall on a straight line between the entered points.** Certainly, as the number of data points increases and the distance between them decreases, linear interpolation becomes more accurate. For example:

```
EDU» x1=linspace(0,2*pi,60);

EDU» x2=linspace(0,2*pi,6);

EDU» plot(x1,sin(x1),x2,sin(x2),'—')

EDU» xlabel('x'),ylabel('sin(x)'),title('Linear Interpolation')
```

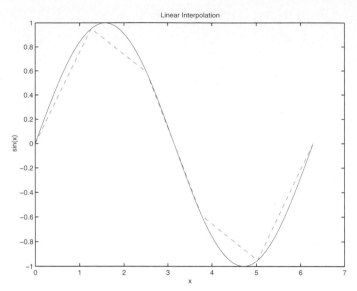

Figure 15.3

Of the two plots of the sine function, the one using 60 points is much smoother and more accurate between the data points than the one using only 6 points.

As with curve fitting, there are decisions to be made. There are multiple approaches to interpolation depending on the assumptions made. Moreover, it is possible to interpolate in more than one dimension. That is, if you have data reflecting a function of two variables, $z = f(x, y)$, you can interpolate between values of both x and y to find intermediate values of z. MATLAB provides a number of interpolation functions. `interp1` interpolates one-dimensional data; `interp2` interpolates two-dimensional data; `interp3` interpolates three-dimensional data; `interpn` interpolates higher-dimensional data. One-dimensional and two-dimensional data will be discussed later.

To illustrate one-dimensional interpolation, consider the following example: The threshold of audibility, i.e., the lowest perceptible sound level, of the human ear varies with frequency. Typical measurement data are:

```
EDU» Hz=[20:10:100 200:100:1000 1500 2000:1000:10000];
EDU»     % frequencies in Hertz
EDU» spl=[76 66 59 54    49  46   43 40 38 22 ...
     14   9   6 3.5 2.5 1.4 0.7   0 −1 −3 ...
     −8 −7 −2    2    7    9   11 12];
EDU»     % sound pressure level in dB
```

The sound-pressure levels are normalized so that 0 dB appears at 1000 Hz. Since the frequencies span such a large range, plot the data using a logarithmic *x*-axis:

```
EDU» semilogx(Hz,spl,'-o')
EDU» xlabel('Frequency, Hz')
EDU» ylabel('Relative Sound Pressure Level, dB')
EDU» title('Threshold of Human Hearing')
EDU» grid on
```

Based on Fig. 15.4, the human ear is most sensitive to tones around 3 kHz. Given these data, let's estimate the sound-pressure level in several different ways at a frequency of 2.5 kHz.

```
EDU» s=interp1(Hz,spl,2.5e3)   % linear interpolation
s =
          -5.5

EDU» s=interp1(Hz,spl,2.5e3,'linear')   % linear interpolation again
```

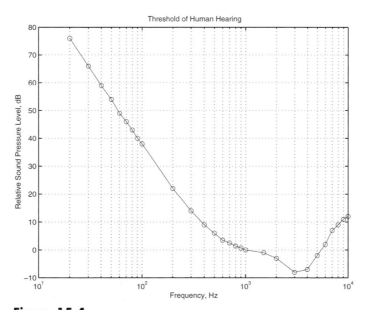

Figure 15.4

```
s =
        −5.5
EDU» s=interp1(Hz,spl,2.5e3,'cubic')  % cubic interpolation
s =
        −5.6875
EDU» s=interp1(Hz,spl,2.5e3,'spline')  % spline interpolation
s =
        −5.6641
EDU» s=interp1(Hz,spl,2.5e3,'nearest')  % nearest-neighbor
s =
      −8
```

Note the differences in these results. The first two results return exactly what is shown in the figure at 2.5 kHz, since MATLAB linearly interpolates between data points on plots. Cubic and spline interpolation fit cubic, i.e., third-order, polynomials to each data interval using different constraints. As a result, these results are close to each, but different than the linear interpolation solution. The poorest interpolation in this case is nearest-neighbor, which returns the input data point nearest to the given value.

So, how do you choose an interpolation method for a given problem? In many cases, linear interpolation is sufficient. In fact, that's why it is the default method. While nearest-neighbor produced poor results here, it is often used when speed is important or the data set is large. The most time-consuming method is spline, but it often produces the most desirable results.

While the abovementioned case considered only a single interpolation point, interp1 can handle any arbitrary number. In fact, one of the most common uses of cubic or spline interpolation is to smooth data. That is, given a set of data, use interpolation to evaluate the data at a finer interval. For example:

```
EDU» Hzi=linspace(2e3,5e3);  % look closely near minimum
EDU» spli=interp1(Hz,spl,Hzi,'cubic');  % interpolate near minimum
EDU» i=find(Hz>=2e3 & Hz<=5e3);
EDU» % find original data indices near minimum
EDU» semilogx(Hz(i),spl(i),'−o',Hzi,spli)  % plot old and new data
EDU» xlabel('Frequency, Hz')
EDU» ylabel('Relative Sound Pressure Level, dB')
EDU» title('Threshold of Human Hearing')
EDU» grid on
```

In Fig. 15.5, the dashed line is linear interpolation, the solid line is the cubic interpolation, and the original data are marked with 'o'. By asking for a finer

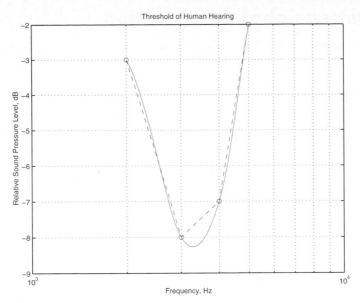

Figure 15.5

resolution on the frequency axis and using cubic interpolation, we have a smoother estimate of the sound-pressure level. In particular, note how the slope of the cubic solution does not change abruptly at the data points.

With these data, we can make a better estimate of the frequency of greatest sensitivity:

```
EDU» [spl_min,i]=min(spli)  % minimum and index of minimum
spl_min =
      -8.2682
i =
     43
EDU» Hz_min=Hzi(i)  % frequency at minimum
Hz_min =
       3272.7
```

The human ear is most sensitive to tones near 3.3 kHz.

Before discussing two-dimensional interpolation, it is important to recognize the two major restrictions enforced by interp1. First, asking for results outside the range of the independent variable, e.g., interp1(Hz,spl,1e5), produces NaN results. Second, the independent variable must be **monotonic**. That is, the independent variable must always increase or must always decrease. In our example, Hz is monotonic.

15.3 Two-Dimensional Interpolation

Two-dimensional interpolation is based on the same underlying ideas as one-dimensional interpolation. However, as the name implies, two-dimensional interpolation interpolates functions of two variables, $z = f(x,y)$. To understand this added dimension, consider the following example: An exploration company is using sonar to map the ocean floor. At points every 0.5 km on a rectangular grid, the ocean depth in meters is recorded for later analysis. A portion of the data collected is entered into MATLAB in the script M-file ocean.m:

```
% ocean depth data
x=0:.5:4;  % x-axis (varies across the rows of z)

y=0:.5:6;  % y-axis (varies down the columns of z)

z=[100    99   100    99   100    99    99    99   100
   100    99    99    99   100    99   100    99    99
    99    99    98    98   100    99   100   100   100
   100    98    97    97    99   100   100   100    99
   101   100    98    98   100   102   103   100   100
   102   103   101   100   102   106   104   101   100
    99   102   100   100   103   108   106   101    99
    97    99   100   100   102   105   103   101   100
   100   102   103   101   102   103   102   100    99
   100   102   103   102   101   101   100    99    99
   100   100   101   101   100   100   100    99    99
   100   100   100   100   100    99    99    99    99
   100   100   100    99    99   100    99   100    99];
```

A plot of these data can be displayed by

```
mesh(x,y,z)
xlabel('X-axis, km')
ylabel('Y-axis, km')
zlabel('Ocean Depth, m')
title('Ocean Depth Measurements')
```

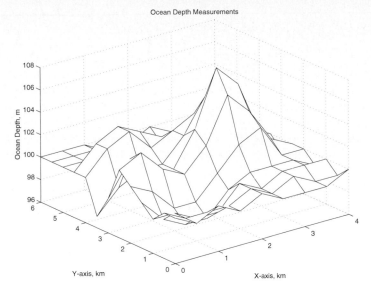

Figure 15.6

Using these data, the depth at arbitrary points within the rectangle can be found by using the function `interp2`. For example:

```
EDU» zi=interp2(x,y,z,2.2,3.3)
zi =
      103.92

EDU» zi=interp2(x,y,z,2.2,3.3,'linear')
zi =
      103.92

EDU» zi=interp2(x,y,z,2.2,3.3,'cubic')
zi =
      104.19

EDU» zi=interp2(x,y,z,2.2,3.3,'nearest')
zi =
      102
```

As was the case with one-dimensional interpolation, several interpolation methods are available, with the default method being linear. Once again, we can interpolate on a finer scale or mesh to smooth the plot:

15.3 Two-Dimensional Interpolation

```
xi=linspace(0,4,30);  % finer x-axis
yi=linspace(0,6,40);  % finer y-axis
[xxi,yyi]=meshgrid(xi,yi);  % grid of all combinations of xi and yi
zzi=interp2(x,y,z,xxi,yyi,'cubic');  % interpolate

mesh(xxi,yyi,zzi)  % plot smoothed data
hold on
[xx,yy]=meshgrid(x,y);    % grid original data
plot3(xx,yy,z+0.1,'ok')  % plot original data up a bit to show nodes
hold off
```

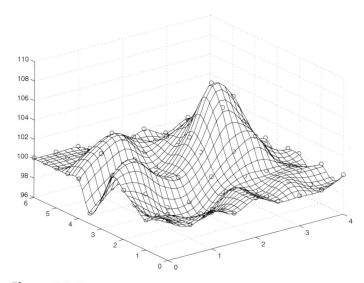

Figure 15.7

Here, the function meshgrid was used to create interpolation arrays covering all combinations of the x and y points requested. As shown in Fig. 15.7, meshgrid performs this operation by generating two-dimensional arrays from the vectors xi and yi. Using these data, we can now estimate the peak and its location.

```
EDU» zmax=max(max(zzi))
zmax =
       108.05
```

```
EDU» [i,j]=find(zmax==zzi);
EDU» xmax=xi(j)
xmax =
        2.6207

EDU» ymax=yi(i)
ymax =
        2.9231
```

16

Numerical Analysis

Whenever it is difficult to integrate, differentiate, or determine some specific value of a function analytically, a computer may be called upon to numerically approximate the desired solution. This area of computer science and mathematics is known as numerical analysis. As you may have guessed by now, MATLAB provides tools to solve these problems. In this chapter, the use of these tools will be examined.

16.1   Plotting

Up to this point, plots of a function have been generated by simply evaluating the function over some range and plotting the resulting vectors. In many cases, this is sufficient; however, sometimes a function is flat and unexciting over some range and then acts wildly over another. Using the traditional plotting approach in this case may lead to a plot that misrepresents the true nature of a function. As a result, MATLAB provides a smart plotting function called `fplot`. This function carefully evaluates the function to be plotted, and makes sure that all its oddities are represented in the output plot. As its input, this function needs to know the name of the function as a character string and the plotting range as a two-element array. For example:

```
» fplot('humps',[0 2])
» title('FPLOT of humps')
```

evaluates the function `humps` between 0 and 2 and displays the plot in Fig. 16.1.

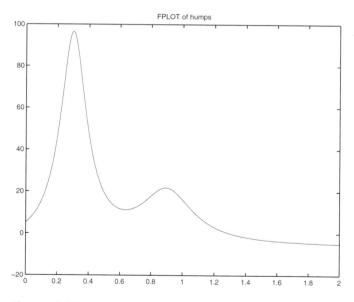

Figure 16.1

In this example, 'humps' is a function M-file that ships with MATLAB:

```
function [out1,out2] = humps(x)
%HUMPS   A function used by QUADDEMO, ZERODEMO and FPLOTDEMO.
%    Y = HUMPS(X) is a function with strong maxima near x = .3
%    and x = .9.
%
%    [X,Y] = HUMPS(X) also returns X.  With no input arguments,
%    HUMPS uses X = 0:.05:1.
%
%    Example:
%       plot(humps)
%
%    See QUADDEMO, ZERODEMO and FPLOTDEMO.

%    Copyright (c) 1984-96 by The MathWorks, Inc.
%    $Revision: 5.2 $  $Date: 1996/01/01 22:05:14 $

if nargin==0, x = 0:.05:1; end

y = 1 ./ ((x-.3).^2 + .01) + 1 ./ ((x-.9).^2 + .04) - 6;

if nargout==2,
  out1 = x; out2 = y;
else
  out1 = y;
end
```

fplot works for any function M-file with one equally-sized vector input and one vector output. That is, as in humps above, the output variable y returns an array the same size as the input x, with y and x associated in the array-to-array sense. The most common mistake made in using fplot (as well as other numerical analysis functions) is forgetting to put the name of the function in quotes. That is, fplot needs to know the name of the function as a character string. If fplot(humps,[0 2]) is typed, MATLAB thinks humps is a variable in the workspace rather than the name of a function.

For simple functions that can be expressed as a single character string, such as $y = 2e^{-x}\sin(x)$, fplot can plot the function without creating an M-file by simply writing the function to be plotted as a complete character string using x as the independent variable:

```
» f='2*exp(-x).*sin(x)';
```

Here, the function $f(x) = 2e^{-x}\sin x$ is defined using array multiplication.

```
» fplot(f,[0 8])
» title(f),xlabel('x')
```

plots the function over the range $0 \leq x \leq 8$, producing the plot in Fig. 16.2.

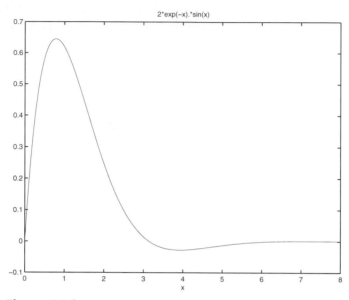

Figure 16.2

Beyond these basic features, the function `fplot` has many more powerful capabilities. See on-line help and the MATLAB on-line reference for more information.

16.2 Minimization

In addition to the visual information provided by plotting, it is often necessary to determine other more specific attributes of a function. Of particular interest in many applications are function extremes, i.e., their *maxima* (peaks) and their *minima* (valleys). Mathematically, these extremes are found analytically by determining where the derivative (slope) of a function is zero. This fact can be readily understood by inspecting the slope of the `humps` plot at its peaks and valleys. Clearly, when a function is simply defined, this process often works. However, even for many simple functions that can be differentiated readily, it often is not possible to find where the derivative is zero. In these cases, and in cases where it is difficult or impossible to find the derivative analytically, it is necessary to search for function extremes numerically. MATLAB provides two functions that perform this task, fmin and fmins. These two functions find minima of one-dimensional and n-dimensional functions, respectively. Only fmin will be discussed here. Further information regarding fmins can be found in on-line help. Since a maximum of $f(x)$ is equal to a minimum of $-f(x)$, fmin and fmins can be used to find both minima and maxima. If you are unclear about this, visualize the preceding plot flipped upside-down. In the upside-down state, the peaks become valleys and the valleys become peaks.

To illustrate one-dimensional minimization and maximization, consider the preceding example once again. From Fig. 16.2, there is a maximum near $x_{max} = 0.7$ and a minimum near $x_{min} = 4$. Analytically, these points can be shown to be $x_{max} = \pi/4 \approx 0.785$ and $x_{min} = 5\pi/4 \approx 3.93$. Writing a script M-file using the editor for convenience and using fmin to find them numerically gives:

```
% ex_fmin.m

fn='2*exp(-x)*sin(x)';     % define function for min
xmin=fmin(fn,2,5)          % search over range 2<x<5

emin=5*pi/4-xmin           % find error

x=xmin;                    % eval needs x since fn has x as its variable
ymin=eval(fn)              % evaluate at xmin

fx='-2*exp(-x)*sin(x)';    % define function for max: note minus sign
xmax=fmin(fx,0,3)          % search over range 0<x<3

emax=pi/4-xmax             % find error

x=xmax;                    % eval needs x since fn has x as its variable
ymax=eval(fn)              % evaluate at xmax
```

Running this M-file results in the following:

```
» ex_fmin
xmin =
    3.9270
emin =
    1.4523e-06
ymin =
   -0.0279
```

```
xmax =
    0.7854
emax =
   -1.3781e-05
ymax =
    0.6448
```

These results agree well with the preceding plot. Note that `fmin` works a lot like `fplot`. The function to be evaluated can be expressed in a function M-file, or can be given just as a character string with `x` being the independent variable. The latter was done here. This example also introduces the function `eval`, which takes a character string and interprets it as if the string were typed at the MATLAB prompt. Since the function to be evaluated was given as a character string with an independent variable `x`, setting `x` equal to `xmin` and `xmax` allows `eval` to evaluate the function to find `ymin` and `ymax`.

Finally, it is important to note that numerical minimization involves searching for a minimum; `fmin` evaluates the function over and over looking for a minimum. This searching can take a significant amount of time if evaluating the function requires a lot of computations, or if the function has more than one minimum within the search range. In some cases, the searching process does not find a solution at all! When `fmin` cannot find a minimum, it stops and provides an explanation.

16.3   Zero Finding

Just as you may be interested in finding function extremes, it is sometimes important to find out where a function crosses zero or some other constant value. Trying to find this point analytically often is difficult, and many times is impossible. In the preceding `humps` function plot, repeated here as Fig. 16.3, the function crosses zero near $x = 1.2$.

Once again, MATLAB provides a numerical solution to this problem. The function `fzero` searches for the zero of a one-dimensional function. To illustrate the use of this function, let's use the `humps` example again:

```
» xzero=fzero('humps',1.2)  % look for a zero near 1.2
xzero =
    1.2995
» yzero=humps(xzero)  % evaluate at xzero

yzero =

    3.5527e-15
```

So, the zero actually occurs close to 1.3. As before, the zero-searching process may not find a solution. If `fzero` does not find one, it will stop and provide an explanation.

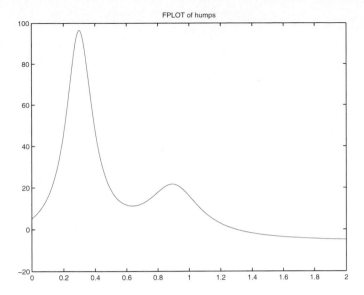

Figure 16.3

The function `fzero` must be given the name of a function when it is called. For some reason, it was never given the capability to accept a function described by a character string using x as the independent variable. Thus, even though this feature is available in both `fplot` and `fmin`, `fzero` does not support this syntax.

While `fzero` finds where a function is zero, it can also be used to find where a function is equal to any constant. All that is required is a simple redefinition. For example, to find where the function $f(x)$ equals the constant c, define the function $g(x)$ as $g(x) = f(x) - c$. Then, using $g(x)$ in `fzero` will find the value of x where $g(x)$ is zero, which occurs when $f(x) = c$!

16.4   Integration

The integral, or the area under a function, is yet another useful attribute. MATLAB provides three functions for numerically computing the area under a function over a finite range: `trapz`, `quad`, and `quad8`. The function `trapz` approximates the integral under a function by summing the area of trapezoids formed from the data points, as shown in Fig. 16.4 using the function `humps`.

As is apparent from Fig. 16.4, the area of individual trapezoids underestimates the true area in some segments, and overestimates it in others. As with linear interpolation, this approximation gets better as the number of trapezoids increases. For example, if we roughly double the number of trapezoids used in Fig. 16.4, we get a much better approximation, as shown in Fig. 16.5.

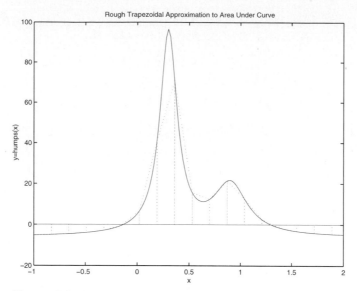

Figure 16.4

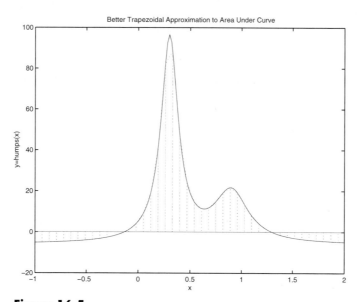

Figure 16.5

Numerical Analysis   Chapter 16

To compute the area under y=humps(x) over the range $-1 < x < 2$ using trapz for each of the two plots shown above:

```
» x=−1:.17:2;        % rough approximation

» y=humps(x);

» area=trapz(x,y)    % call trapz just like the plot command
area =
    25.9174

» x=−1:.07:2;        % better approximation

» y=humps(x);

» area=trapz(x,y)
area =
    26.6243
```

Naturally, the solutions are different. Based on inspection of the plots, the rough approximation probably underestimates the area. Nothing certain can be said about the better approximation, except that it is likely to be much more accurate. Clearly, if you were to somehow change individual trapezoid widths to match the characteristics of the function, i.e., make them narrower where the function changes more rapidly, much greater accuracy would be achieved.

The MATLAB functions quad and quad8, which are based on the mathematical concept of quadrature, take this approach. Both of these integration functions operate in the same way. Both evaluate the function to be integrated at whatever intervals are necessary to achieve accurate results. Moreover, both functions make higher-order approximations than a simple trapezoid, with quad8 being more rigorous than quad. These functions are called in the same way that fzero is:

```
» area=quad('humps',−1,2)  % find area between −1 and 2
area =
    26.3450

» area=quad8('humps',−1,2)
area =
    26.3450
```

Note that both of these functions return essentially the same estimate of the area, and that the estimate is between the two trapz estimates.

For more information on MATLAB's integration functions, see on-line help or MATLAB on-line reference.

16.5 Differentiation

Compared to integration, numerical differentiation is much more difficult. Integration describes an overall or macroscopic property of a function, whereas differentiation describes the slope of a function at a point, which is a microscopic property of a function. As a result, integration is not sensitive to minor changes in the shape of a function, whereas differentiation is. Any small change in a function can easily create large changes in its slope in the neighborhood of the change.

Because of this inherent difficulty with differentiation, numerical differentiation is avoided whenever possible, especially if the data to be differentiated are obtained experimentally. In this case, it is best to perform a least squares curve fit to the data, and then differentiate the resulting polynomial. For example, reconsider the curve fitting example from Chapter 15:

```
» x=[0 .1 .2 .3 .4 .5 .6 .7 .8 .9 1];
» y=[−.447 1.978 3.28 6.16 7.08 7.34 ...
      7.66 9.56 9.48 9.30 11.2]; % data
» n=2; % order of fit
» p=polyfit(x,y,n)  % find polynomial coefficients
p =
    −9.8108    20.1293    −0.0317
» xi=linspace(0,1,100);
» z=polyval(p,xi); % evaluate polynomial
» plot(x,y,'o',x,y,xi,z,':')
» xlabel('x'),ylabel('y=f(x)'),
EDU» title('Second Order Curve Fitting')
```

The derivative, in this case, is found by using the polynomial derivative function `polyder`:

```
» pd=polyder(p)
pd =
  −19.6217    20.1293
```

The derivative of $y = -9.8108x^2 + 20.1293x - 0.0317$ is $dy/dx = -19.6217x + 20.1293$. Since the derivative of a polynomial is yet another polynomial of the next lowest order, the derivative can also be evaluated and plotted:

```
» z=polyval(pd,xi);  % evaluate derivative
» plot(xi,z)
» xlabel('x'),ylabel('dy/dx')
EDU» title('Derivative of a Curve Fit Polynomial')
```

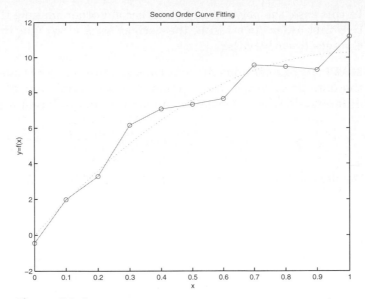

Figure 16.6

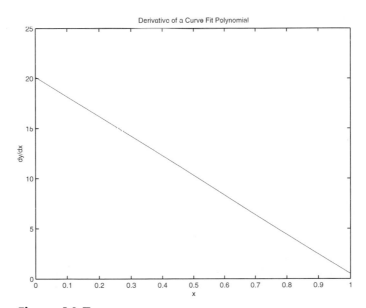

Figure 16.7

16.5 Differentiation

In this case, the polynomial fit was second-order, making the resulting derivative first-order. As a result, the derivative is a straight line, meaning that it changes linearly with x.

MATLAB provides one function for computing a very rough derivative, given the data describing some function. This function, named `diff`, computes the difference between elements in an array. Since differentiation is defined as

$$\frac{dy}{dx} = \lim_{h \to 0} \frac{f(x + h) - f(x)}{(x + h) - (x)}$$

the derivative of $y = f(x)$ can be approximated by

$$\frac{dy}{dx} = \frac{f(x + h) - f(x)}{(x + h) - (x)} \quad \text{where } h > 0$$

which is the **finite difference of y divided by the finite difference of x**. Since `diff` computes differences between array elements, differentiation can be approximated in MATLAB. Continuing with the prior example:

```
» dy=diff(y)./diff(x);  % compute differences and use array division
» xd=x(1:length(x)-1);  % create new x axis array since dy is
                        % shorter than y
```

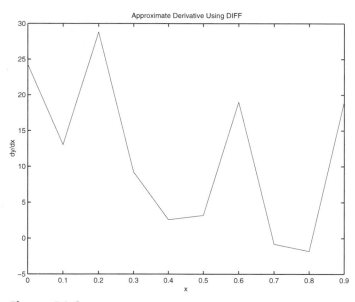

Figure 16.8

```
» plot(xd,dy)

» title('Approximate Derivative Using DIFF')

» ylabel('dy/dx'),xlabel('x')
```

Since `diff` computes the difference between elements of an array, the resulting output contains one fewer element than the original array. Thus, to plot the derivative, one element of the x array must be thrown out. Comparing the last two plots, it is overwhelmingly apparent that approximating the derivative by finite differences can lead to poor results.

16.6 Differential Equations

You may already be familiar with the fact that the actions of many physical systems can be modeled by ordinary differential equations. If you are, then this section may be of interest to you.

Ordinary differential equations describe how the rate of change of variables within a system are influenced by variables within the system and by external stimuli, i.e., inputs. When ordinary differential equations can be solved analytically, features in the *Symbolic Math Toolbox* can be used to find exact solutions.

In those cases where the equations cannot be readily solved analytically, it is convenient to solve them numerically. For illustrative purposes, consider the classical Van der Pol differential equation, which describes an oscillator:

$$\frac{d^2x}{dt^2} - \mu(1 - x^2)\frac{dx}{dt} + x = 0$$

As with all numerical approaches to solving differential equations, higher-order differential equations must be rewritten in terms of an equivalent set of first-order differential equations. For the above differential equation, this is accomplished by defining two new variables:

$$\text{let} \quad y_1 = x, \quad \text{and} \quad y_2 = \frac{dx}{dt}$$

$$\text{then} \quad \frac{dy_1}{dt} = y_2$$

$$\frac{dy_2}{dt} = \mu(1 - y_1^2) - y_1$$

For sets of equations like these, MATLAB provides a whole suite of ODE functions for numerically approximating their solution. Their individual capabilities and internal workings are beyond the scope of this tutorial. To explore the various ODE functions applied to a variety of test problems, type » `odedemo` at the MATLAB prompt. Following the advice provided in the suite, the ODE function to try first on a new problem is `ode45`. Doing so requires that we write a function M-file that returns the above derivatives given the current time and the current values of y_1 and y_2. In MATLAB, the derivatives are given by a column vector, called `yprime` in this case. Similarly, y_1 and y_2 are written as a column vector `y`. The resulting function M-file is:

```
function yprime=vdpol(t,y);
%VDPOL(t,y) returns the state derivatives of the Van der Pol equation:
%
%      x'' - mu*(1-x^2)*x' + x = 0     (' = d/dx, '' = d^2/dx^2)
%
%      let y(1) = x    and y(2) = x'
%
%      then  y(1)' = y(2)
%            y(2)' = mu*(1-y(1)^2)*y(2) -y(1)

mu=2; % choose 0< mu < 10

yprime=[y(2)
        mu*(1-y(1)^2)*y(2)-y(1)];  % output must be a column
```

Next, let the desired time span be 0 to 30 seconds, i.e., `tspan=[0 30]`, and let the initial conditions be `yo=[1;0]`. Then, given `vdpol`, the solution is computed as:

```
» tspan=[0 30];
» yo=[1;0];
» ode45('vdpol',tspan,yo);
```

When used with no output arguments, ODE functions generate a time plot of the solution dynamically. To gain access to the data, simply provide output arguments:

```
» [t,y]=ode45('vdpol',tspan,yo);
```

Here, `t` is a column vector containing the time points where the solution was computed, and `y` is a matrix having two columns and `length(t)` rows. The first column of `y` is the variable $y(1)$, and the second is the variable $y(2)$.

Given these results, we can make a phase plane plot, which in this case is a plot of $y(2)$ versus $y(1)$.

```
» plot(y(:,1),y(:,2))
```

Numerical Analysis   Chapter 16

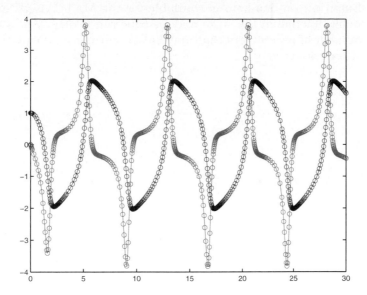

Figure 16.9

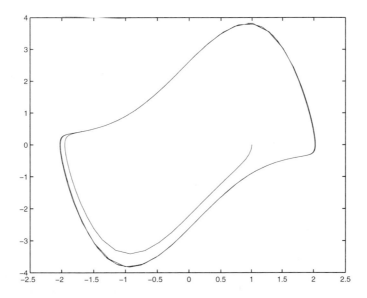

Figure 16.10

16.6   Differential Equations

Extensive on-line help is available for the MATLAB ODE suite of functions. Each function in the suite may be called in a variety of ways, and each has a number of parameters that may be set. For more information, see on-line help or on-line reference.

17

Two-Dimensional Graphics

MATLAB® 5

PLATE 3 ▶

Surface plots of sin(R)/R illustrating the use of color to add a fourth dimension.

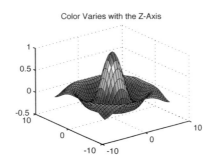

Color Varies with the Z-Axis

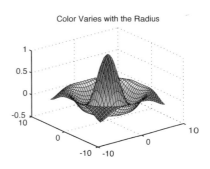

Color Varies with the Radius

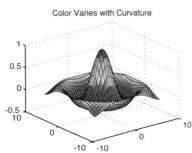

Color Varies with Curvature

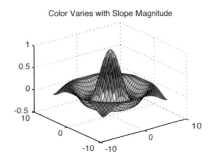

Color Varies with Slope Magnitude

PLATE 4 ▶

Pseudocolor plots illustrating the use of the `caxis` *command to affect the color range.*

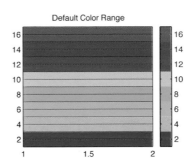

Default Color Range

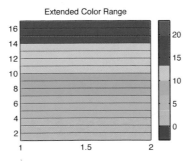

Extended Color Range

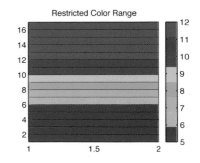

Restricted Color Range

MATLAB® 5

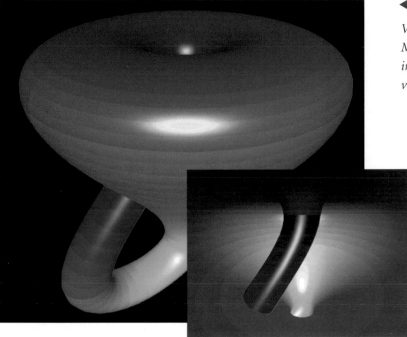

◄ PLATE 5

*Viewpoint control in
MATLAB 3-D graphics result
in these outside and inside
views of a Klein bottle.*

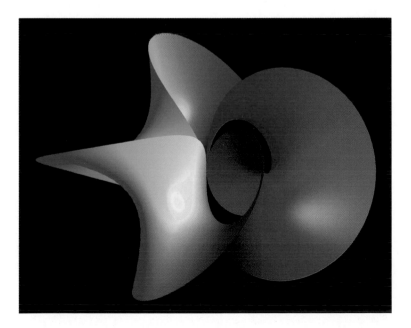

◄ PLATE 6

*3-D model of the familiar
Möbius strip, with four
half-twists instead of the
usual one.*

MATLAB 5

MATLAB®

PLATE 7 ▶

*Lit and Gouraud shaded
rendering of a penny, based
on its height data.*

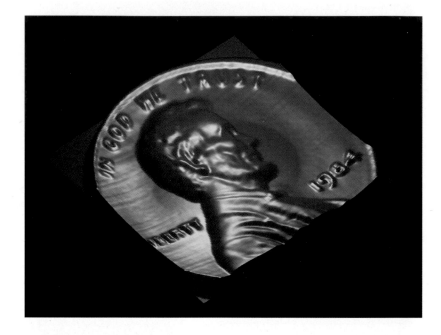

PLATE 8 ▶

*Four steps in gridding
and visualizing
irregularly sampled
elevations of an
undersea mountain.*

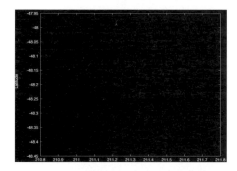

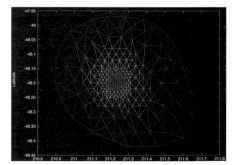

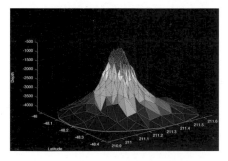

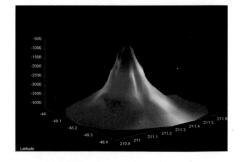

Let's plot a sine and cosine on the same plot:

```
EDU» z=cos(x);
EDU» plot(x,y,x,z)
```

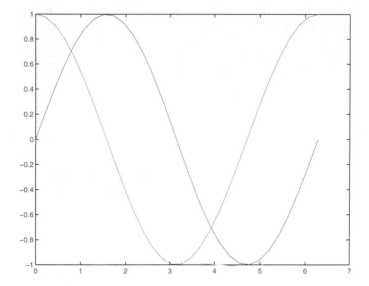

Figure 17.2

This example shows that you can plot more than one set of data at the same time, just by giving plot another pair of arguments. This time, sin(x) versus x and cos(x) versus x were plotted on the same plot. plot automatically drew the second curve in a different color on the screen. Many curves may be plotted at one time if you supply additional pairs of arguments to plot.

If one of the arguments is a matrix and the other is a vector, the plot command plots each column of the matrix versus the vector:

```
EDU» W=[y;z]; % create a matrix of the sine and cosine

EDU» plot(x,W) % plot the columns of W vs. x
```

If you change the order of the arguments, the plot rotates 90 degrees:

```
EDU» plot(W,x) % plot x vs. the columns of W
```

When the plot command is called with only one argument, e.g., plot(Y), the plot function acts differently, depending on the data contained in Y. If Y is a *complex*-valued vector, plot(Y) is interpreted as plot(real(Y),imag(Y)). In all other cases, the imaginary components of the input vectors are ignored.

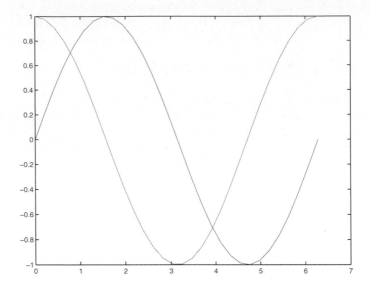

Figure 17.3

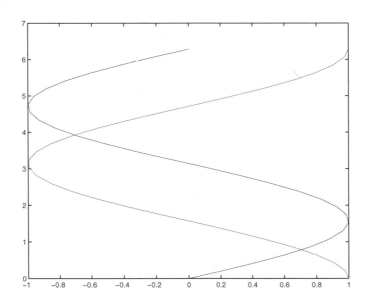

Figure 17.4

Two-Dimensional Graphics   Chapter 17

On the other hand, if Y is *real*-valued, then `plot(Y)` is interpreted as `plot(1:length(Y),Y)`, i.e., Y is plotted versus an index of its values. When Y is a matrix, these interpretations are applied to each column of Y.

17.2 Line Styles, Markers, and Colors

In the previous examples, MATLAB chose the **solid** line style, and the colors **blue** and **green** for the plots. You can specify your own colors, markers, and line styles by giving `plot` a third argument after each pair of data arrays. This optional additional argument is a character string consisting of one or more characters from the following table:

Symbol	Color	Symbol	Marker	Symbol	Line style
b	blue	.	point	—	solid line
g	green	o	circle	:	dotted line
r	red	x	x-mark	−.	dash-dot line
c	cyan	+	plus	−−	dashed line
m	magenta	*	star		
y	yellow	s	square		
k	black	d	diamond		
w	white	∨	triangle (down)		
		∧	triangle (up)		
		<	triangle (left)		
		>	triangle (right)		
		p	pentagram		
		h	hexagram		

If you do not specify a color and you are using the default color scheme, MATLAB starts with **blue** and cycles through the first seven colors in the table for each additional line. The default line style is the solid line, unless you specify a different line stylc. There is no default marker; if no marker is selected, no markers are drawn. The use of any marker places the chosen symbol at each data point, but does not connect the data points with a straight line unless a line style is selected as well.

If a color, marker, and line style are all included in the string, the color applies to both the marker and the line. To specify a different color for the markers, plot the same data with a different specification string. Here is an example using different line styles, colors, and point markers:

```
EDU» plot(x,y,'b:p',x,z,'c-',x,z,'m+')
```

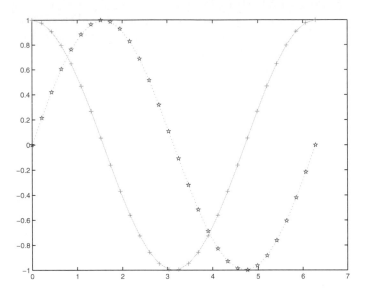

Figure 17.5a

As with many of the plots in this section, your computer displays color, but the figures printed here do not. If you are following along in MATLAB, just enter the commands listed in the examples to really see the effects of color.

17.3   Plotting Styles

The colordef command lets you select an overall style for your plots. The default style is colordef white. This style uses a white axis background, a light gray figure background, and black axis labels, and it uses blue, dark green, and red as the first three plot colors. If you like a black background, use colordef black. This style uses a black axis background, a dark gray figure background, and white axis labels, and it uses yellow, magenta, and cyan as the first three plot colors. If you use colordef none, MATLAB will default to the same style that was used in previous versions of MATLAB. This style uses a black axis and figure background color, uses white axis labels, and uses yellow, magenta, and cyan as the first three plot colors.

17.4 Plot Grids, Axes Box, Labels, and Legends

The `grid on` command adds grid lines to the current plot at the tick marks. The `grid off` command removes the grid. `grid` with no arguments alternately turns them on and off, i.e., **toggles** them. MATLAB starts up with `grid off` by default for two-dimensional plots. Normally, two-dimensional axes are enclosed by solid lines, called an *axes box*. This box can be turned off with `box off`; `box on` restores the axes box. The `box` command toggles the state of the axes box. Horizontal and vertical axes can be labeled with the `xlabel` and `ylabel` commands, respectively. The `title` command adds a line of text at the top of the plot. Let's use the sine and cosine plot again as an example.

```
EDU» x=linspace(0,2*pi,30);
EDU» y=sin(x);
EDU» z=cos(x);
EDU» plot(x,y,x,z)
```

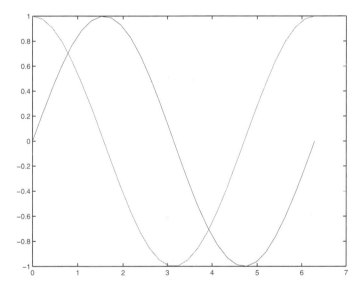

Figure 17.5b

Now remove the axes box, and add a plot title and axis labels:

```
EDU» box off        % turn off the axes box
EDU» xlabel('Independent Variable X')        % label horizontal axis
```

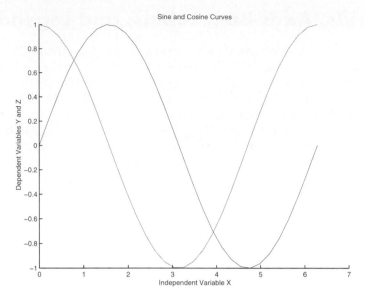

Figure 17.6

```
EDU» ylabel('Dependent Variables Y and Z') % label vertical axis

EDU» title('Sine and Cosine Curves')        % title the plot
```

You can add a label or any other text string to any specific location on your plot with the `text` command. The format is `text(x,y,'string')`, where `(x,y)` represents the coordinates of the center left edge of the text string in units taken from the plot axes. To add a label identifying the sine curve at the location `(2.5,0.7)`:

```
EDU» grid on, box on % turn axes box and grid lines on

EDU» text(2.5,0.7,'sin(x)')
```

If you want to add a label but don't want to stop to figure out the coordinates to use, you can place a text string with the mouse. The `gtext` command switches to the current *Figure* window, puts up a cross-hair that follows the mouse, and waits for a mouse click or keypress. When either one occurs, the text is placed with the lower left corner of the first character at that location. Try labeling the second curve in the plot:

```
EDU» gtext('cos(x)')
```

Rather than using individual text strings to identify the data sets on your plot, you may use a legend. The `legend` command creates a legend box in the upper right corner of the plot, keying any text you supply to each line in your plot. If you wish to move the legend, simply click and hold the left mouse button near

Two-Dimensional Graphics   Chapter 17

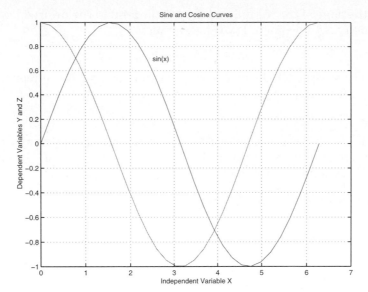

Figure 17.7

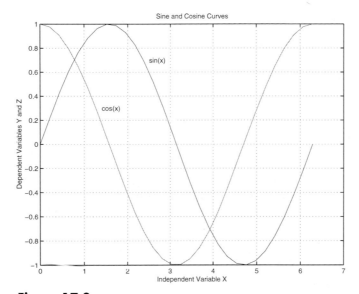

Figure 17.8

17.4   Plot Grids, Axes Box, Labels, and Legends

the edge of the legend and drag the legend to the desired location. `legend off` deletes the legend. Try this example:

```
EDU» legend('sin(x)','cos(x)')
```

Try moving the legend around on your plot with the mouse. Then remove the legend with:

```
EDU» legend off
```

The `legend` function works with other types of plots and has an optional argument specifying an initial location for the legend. Consult on-line help for more details or reference.

17.5 Customizing Plot Axes

MATLAB gives you complete control over the scaling and appearance of both the horizontal and vertical axes of your plot with the `axis` command. Because this command has so many features, only the most useful ones will be described here. For a more complete description of `axis`, see on-line help or reference. The primary features of the `axis` command are given in the following table.

Commands	Description
`axis([xmin xmax ymin ymax])`	Set the minimum and maximum values of the axes using values given in the row vector.
`V=axis`	V is a row vector containing the scaling for the current plot: `[xmin xmax ymin ymax]`
`axis auto` `axis('auto')`	Return the axis scaling to its automatic defaults: `xmin=min(x)`, `xmax=max(x)`, `etc.`
`axis manual`	Freeze scaling at the current limits, so that if hold is turned on, subsequent plots use the same axis limits.
`axis xy`	Use the (default) Cartesian coordinate form, where the *system origin* (the smallest coordinate pair) is at the lower left corner. The horizontal axis increases left to right, and the vertical axis increases bottom to top.
`axis ij`	Use the *matrix* coordinate form, where the system origin is at the top left corner. The horizontal axis increases left to right, but the vertical axis increases top to bottom.
`axis square`	Set the current plot to be a square rather than the default rectangle.
`axis equal`	Set the scaling factors for both axes to be equal.
`axis tightequal` `axis tight`	Same as `axis equal`, but the plot box fits tightly to the data as well.
`axis vis3d`	Keeps MATLAB from altering the proportions of axes if the view is changed.
`axis normal`	Turn off `axis square`, `equal`, `tight`, and `vis3d`
`axis off`	Turn off axis background, labeling, grid, box, and tick marks. Leave the title and any labels placed by the `text` and `gtext` commands.
`axis on`	Turn on axis background, labeling, tick marks, and, if they are enabled, box and grid.

Try out some of the `axis` commands on your plots. Using the preceding example plot produces the following results:

```
EDU» axis off                 % turn off the axes
```

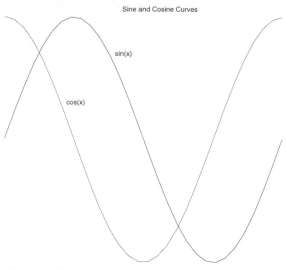

Figure 17.9

```
EDU» axis on, grid off  % turn the axes back on, turn the grid off
```

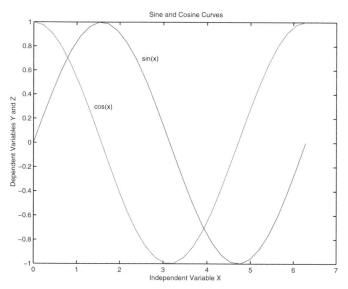

Figure 17.10

EDU» axis ij   % turn the plot upside-down

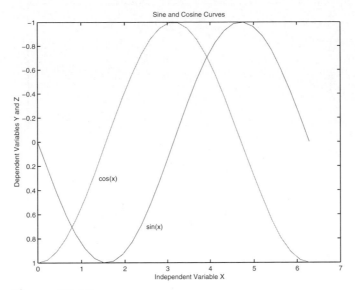

Figure 17.11

```
EDU» axis square equal   % give axis two commands at once
```

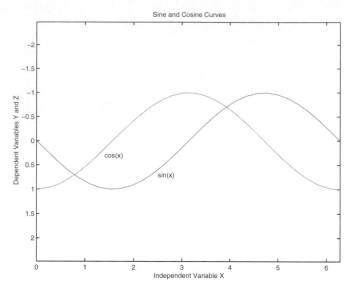

Figure 17.12

```
EDU» axis xy normal      % return to the defaults
```

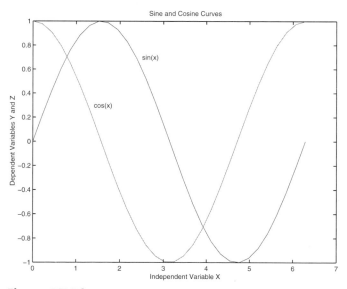

Figure 17.13

Two-Dimensional Graphics   Chapter 17

17.6   Printing Figures

What good is a plot if you can't print it? The printing of plots can be accomplished by using a command from the menu bar or MATLAB commands.

To print a plot using commands from the menu bar, make the *Figure* window the active window by clicking it with the mouse. Then use the **Print** menu item from the **File** menu (on the *Figure* window menu bar on the Windows version). Using the parameters set in the **Print Setup** or **Page Setup** menu item, the current plot is sent to the printer.

MATLAB has its own printing commands that can be used from the *Command* window. To print a *Figure* window, click it with the mouse or use the figure(n) command to make it active, and then use the print command.

```
EDU» print % prints the current plot to your printer
```

The orient command changes the print orientation mode. The default ***portrait*** mode prints vertically in the middle of the page. ***landscape*** mode prints horizontally and fills the page. ***tall*** mode prints vertically, but fills the page. The chosen printing mode remains the same until you change it or end your MATLAB session.

```
EDU» orient % what is the current orientation?

ans =
    portrait

EDU» orient landscape % print sideways on the page

EDU» orient tall % stretch to fill the vertical page
```

For further information regarding printing, see on-line help or reference for print.

17.7   Manipulating Plots

You can add lines to an existing plot using the hold command. When you set hold on, MATLAB does not remove the existing axes when new plot commands are issued; instead, it adds new curves to the current axes. However, if the new data does not fit within the current axes limits, the axes are rescaled. Setting hold off releases the current *Figure* window for new plots. The hold command without arguments toggles the hold setting. Going back to our previous example:

```
EDU» x=linspace(0,2*pi,30);

EDU» y=sin(x);

EDU» z=cos(x);

EDU» plot(x,y)
```

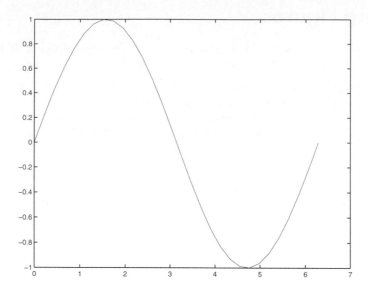

Figure 17.14

Now, hold the plot and add a cosine curve.

```
EDU» hold on
EDU» ishold  % this logical function returns 1 (True) if hold is ON
ans =
    1
EDU» plot(x,z,'m')
EDU» hold off
EDU» ishold  % hold is no longer ON
ans =
    0
```

Notice that this example specified the color of the second curve. Since there is only one set of data arrays in each plot command, the line color for each plot command would otherwise default to the first color in the list, resulting in two lines plotted in the same color on the plot. Note also that ishold provides a means for testing the hold state.

If you want two or more plots in different *Figure* windows, use the figure command in the *Command* window, or the **New Figure** selection from the **File** menu in the *Command* or *Figure* windows. figure with no arguments creates

Two-Dimensional Graphics   Chapter 17

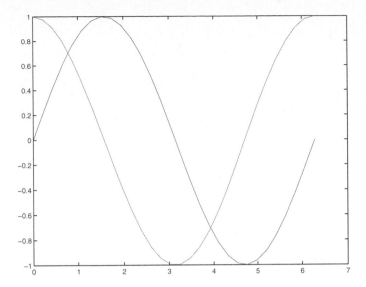

Figure 17.15

a new *Figure* window. You can choose a specific *Figure* window to be the default by selecting it with the mouse, or by using figure(n), where n is the number of the window to be made active for subsequent plotting commands.

One *Figure* window, on the other hand, can hold more than one set of axes. The subplot(m,n,p) command subdivides the current *Figure* window into an m-by-n matrix of plotting areas, and chooses the pth area to be active. The subplots are numbered left to right along the top row, then the second row, and so on. For example:

```
EDU» x=linspace(0,2*pi,30);

EDU» y=sin(x);

EDU» z=cos(x);

EDU» a=2*sin(x).*cos(x);

EDU» b=sin(x)./(cos(x)+eps);

EDU» subplot(2,2,1) % pick the upper left of a 2-by-2 grid of subplots

EDU» plot(x,y),axis([0 2*pi −1 1]),title('sin(x)')

EDU» subplot(2,2,2) % pick the upper right of the 4 subplots

EDU» plot(x,z),axis([0 2*pi −1 1]),title('cos(x)')
```

```
EDU» subplot(2,2,3) % pick the lower left of the 4 subplots
EDU» plot(x,a),axis([0 2*pi -1 1]),title('2sin(x)cos(x)')
EDU» subplot(2,2,4) % pick the lower right of the 4 subplots
EDU» plot(x,b),axis([0 2*pi -20 20]),title('sin(x)/cos(x)')
```

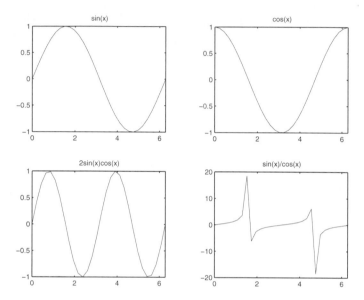

Figure 17.16

Note that when a particular subplot is active, it is the only subplot or axis that is responsive to `axis`, `hold`, `xlabel`, `ylabel`, `title`, `grid`, and `box` commands. The other subplots are not affected. In addition, the active subplot remains active until another `subplot` or `figure` command is issued. If the new `subplot` command changes the number of subplots in the *Figure* window, previous subplots are erased to make room for the new orientation. To return to the default mode and use the entire *Figure* window for a single set of axes, use the command `subplot(1,1,1)`. If you print a *Figure* window containing multiple plots, all of them will be printed on the same page. For example, if the current *Figure* window contains four subplots and the orientation is landscape mode, each of the plots will use one-quarter of the printed page.

MATLAB provides an interactive tool to expand sections of a two-dimensional plot to see more detail, or to ***zoom in*** on a region of interest. The command `zoom on` turns on zoom mode. Clicking the mouse button on a Macintosh, or the left mouse button on a Windows computer, within the *Figure* window expands the plot by a factor of two centered around the point under the mouse pointer. Each time you click, the plot expands. Click the right mouse button on a Windows computer, or shift-click on the Macintosh, to zoom out by a factor of two. You can also click-and-drag a rectangular area to zoom into a specific area. zoom(n) zooms in by a factor of n. zoom out returns the plot to its initial state. zoom off turns off zoom mode. zoom with no arguments toggles the zoom state of the active *Figure* window.

Try zooming in and out on a plot created using the M-file called peaks.m. This is an interesting function that generates a square matrix of data. The data are based on a function of two variables, and contain data points for x and y in the range –3 to 3. The function is:

$$f(x,y) = 3\,(1 - x)^2 e^{-x^2} - 10\left(\frac{x}{5} - x^3 - y^5\right)e^{-x^2} - y^2 - \frac{1}{3}e^-(x + 1)^2 - y^2$$

You can specify the size of the square matrix peaks generates by passing it an argument. If you omit the argument, it defaults to [[31]]. Try this example:

```
EDU» M=peaks(25)        % create a 25-by-25 matrix of data

EDU» plot(M)            % plot the columns of M

EDU» title('Peaks Plot for ZOOM Practice')

EDU» zoom on
```

The command plot(M), where M is a matrix, plots each column of M versus its index. The prior example plotted 25 lines on the plot. Zoom in and out with the mouse to experiment with zooming.

Since both the legend and zoom commands respond to mouse clicks in the *Figure* window, they interfere with each other. Therefore, if zoom is to be used, legend first must be turned off.

17.8   Other Two-Dimensional Plotting Features

- loglog is the same as plot, except that logarithmic scales are used for both axes.
- semilogx is the same as plot, except that the x-axis uses a logarithmic scale, and the y-axis uses a linear scale.
- semilogy is the same as plot, except that the y-axis uses a logarithmic scale, and the x-axis uses a linear scale.
- area(x,y) is the same as plot(x,y), except that the area between 0 and y is filled in. The base y-value may be specified, but defaults to zero.
- Standard pie charts can be created using pie(a,b) command, where a is a vector of values, and b is an optional logical vector describing a slice or slices to be pulled out of the pie chart.

```
EDU» a=[.5 1 1.6 1.2 .8 2.1];
EDU» pie(a,a==max(a));    % chart a and pull out the biggest slice
EDU» title('Example Pie Chart')
```

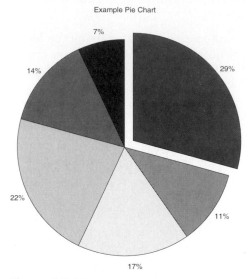

Figure 17.17

- Another way to visualize the same data is with a Pareto chart, where the values in the vector argument are drawn as bars in descending order along with an associated accumulated-value line plot. Using the vector a from the previous example, we get:

```
EDU» pareto(a);
EDU» title('Example Pareto Chart')
```

- Sometimes, you may want to plot two different functions on the same axes using different *y*-axis scales. plotyy can do that for you:

```
EDU» x=-2*pi:pi/10:2*pi;
EDU» y=sin(x); z=2*cos(x);
EDU» subplot(2,1,1), plot(x,y,x,z),
EDU» title('Two plots on the same scale.');
EDU» subplot(2,1,2), plotyy(x,y,x,z)
EDU» title('Two plots on different scales.');
```

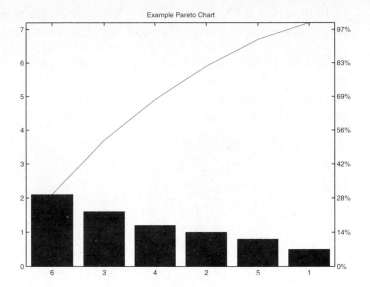

Figure 17.18

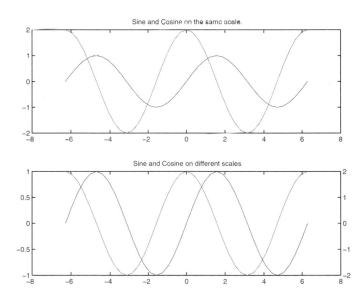

Figure 17.19

Note that both `pareto` and `plotyy` actually create two sets of axes in the same *Figure* window. Any command that affects the current axes (like `axis`, `zoom`, or `legend`) will affect only one set of axes, and may lead to unintended results. So, in general, it is best to avoid these commands when using `pareto` and `plotyy` functions.

- Bar and stair plots can be generated using the `bar`, `bar3`, `barh`, and `stairs` plotting commands. Here are examples of a bell curve:

```
EDU» x=-2.9:0.2:2.9;

EDU» y=exp(-x.*x);

EDU» subplot(2,2,1)

EDU» bar(x,y)

EDU» title('Bar Chart of a Bell Curve')

EDU» subplot(2,2,2)

EDU» bar3(x,y)

EDU» title('3-D Bar Chart of a Bell Curve')

EDU» subplot(2,2,3)

EDU» stairs(x,y)

EDU» title('Stair Chart of a Bell Curve')

EDU» subplot(2,2,4)

EDU» barh(x,y)

EDU» title('Horizontal Bar Chart')
```

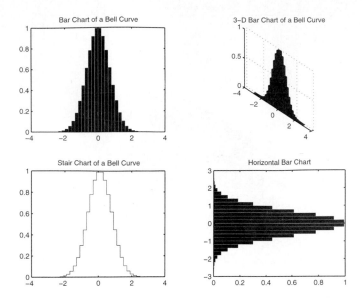

Figure 17.20

- hist(y) draws a 10-bin histogram for the data in vector y. hist(y,n), where n is a scalar, draws a histogram with n bins. hist(y,x), where x is a vector, draws a histogram using the bins specified in x. Here is an example of a bell-curve histogram from Gaussian data:

```
EDU» x=-2.9:0.2:2.9; % specify the bins to use

EDU» y=randn(5000,1); % generate 5000 random data points

EDU» hist(y,x) % draw the histogram

EDU» title('Histogram of Gaussian Data')
```

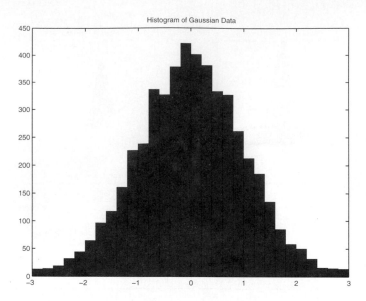

Figure 17.21

- Discrete sequence data can be plotted using the `stem` function. `stem(z)` creates a plot of the data points in vector `z` connected to the horizontal axis by a line. An optional character string argument can be used to specify line style. `stem(x,z)` plots the data points in `z` at the values specified in `x`.

```
EDU» z=randn(50,1); % create some random data

EDU» stem(z,':') % draw a stem plot using dotted linestyle

EDU» title('Stem Plot of Random Data')
```

- A plot can include error bars at the data points. `errorbar(x,y,e)` plots the graph of vector `x` versus vector `y` with error bars specified by vector `e`. All vectors must be the same length. For each data point (x_i, y_i), an error bar is drawn a distance e_i above and e_i below the data point.

```
EDU» x=linspace(0,2,21); % create a vector

EDU» y=erf(x); % y is the error function of x

EDU» e=rand(size(x))/10; % e contains random error values

EDU» errorbar(x,y,e) % create the plot

EDU» title('Errorbar Plot')
```

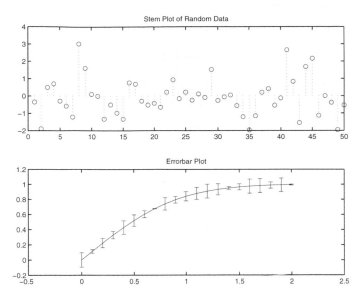

Figure 17.22

- Plots in polar coordinates can be created using the `polar(t,r,S)` command, where t is the angle vector in radians, r is the radius vector, and S is an optional character string describing color, marker symbol, or line style. See `plot` for a description of appropriate string values.

  EDU» t=linspace(0,2*pi);

  EDU» r=sin(2*t).*cos(2*t);

  EDU» polar(t,r)

  EDU» title('Polar Plot of sin(2t)cos(2t)')

- Complex data can be plotted using `compass` and `feather`. `compass(z)` draws a plot that displays the angle and magnitude of the complex elements of z as arrows emanating from the origin. `feather(z)` plots the same data using arrows emanating from equally spaced points on a horizontal line. `compass(x,y)` and `feather(x,y)` are equivalent to `compass(x+i*y)` and `feather(x+i*y)`.

  EDU» z=eig(randn(20,20));

  EDU» compass(z)

  EDU» title('Compass Plot of Eigenvalues of a Random Matrix')

17.8 Other Two-Dimensional Plotting Features

```
EDU» fplot('sin(x)./x',[-20 20 -.4 1.2])
EDU» title('Fplot of f(x)=sin(x)/x')
EDU» xlabel('x')
EDU» ylabel('f(x)')
```

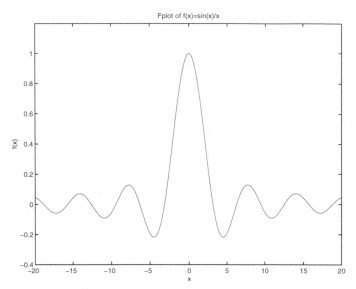

Figure 17.25

- `fill(x,y,'c')` fills the two-dimensional polygon defined by the column vectors x and y with the color specified by c. The vertices of the polygon are specified by the pairs (x_i, y_i). If necessary, the polygon is closed by connecting the last vertex to the first. Consult on-line help for more information. Try this example:

```
EDU» t=(1/8:2/8:15/8)'*pi; % column vector [π/8;3π/8;...;15π/8]'
EDU» x=sin(t);
EDU» y=cos(t);
EDU» fill(x,y,'r') % a filled red circle using only 8 data points
EDU» axis square
EDU» text(0,0,'STOP','FontSize',96,'HorizontalAlignment','center')
EDU» title('Red Stop Sign')
```

Two-Dimensional Graphics   Chapter 17

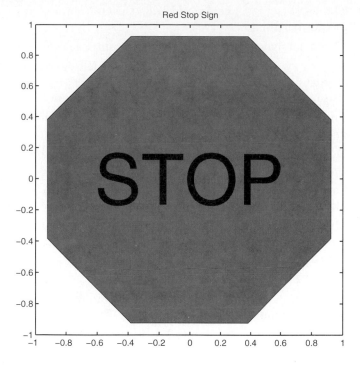

Figure 17.26

This example uses the `text(x,y,'string')` command with extra arguments. The `FontSize` and `HorizontalAlignment` arguments tell MATLAB to use Handle Graphics® to modify the text. Handle Graphics is the name of MATLAB's underlying graphics architecture. Some Handle Graphics features will be discussed later.

- Scatter plots can be created with the `plotmatrix` command. See on-line help for more information on `plotmatrix`.

17.9   Summary

- The `plot` command creates a plot of vectors or columns of matrices. The form of the command is $plot(x_1,y_1,S_1,x_2,y_2,S_2,...)$, where (x_n,y_n) are data sets and S_n are optional strings specifying color, marker symbols, or line styles.
- `grid` toggles the grid at the tick marks of your plot.
- `box` toggles the axes box.
- Titles and axis labels can be added using `title`, `xlabel`, and `ylabel`.

- The text(x,y,S) command adds the character string S to the current plot at the coordinates (x,y).
- gtext lets you place text on your plot interactively using the mouse.
- axis([xmin xmax ymin ymax]) scales the current plot to the values given as arguments. axis('string'), where 'string' is one of a number of specific options, changes axis limits or the appearance of the plot in many ways.
- The print command prints the plot in the current *Figure* window to your printer, to the clipboard, or to a file.
- Orientation of printed plots can be changed with the orient command. The three orientations are portrait, landscape, and tall.
- You can add plots to your current plot by setting hold on. Setting hold off allows the next plot command to clear the *Figure* window before plotting.
- Multiple *Figure* windows can be generated by the figure command. figure(n) chooses *Figure* window n to be the active *Figure* window.
- A *Figure* window may be subdivided, and any subdivision made active with the subplot command.
- If you set zoom on, the active *Figure* window can be expanded interactively using the mouse.
- Scaled plots can be created using loglog, semilogx, semilogy, and plotyy.
- Many specialized two-dimensional plots can be created with area, pie, pareto, polar, bar, stairs, hist, stem, errorbar, compass, feather, rose, fill, and plotmatrix.
- Plotting utilities include ginput, fplot, and legend.
- The commands legend, zoom, and ginput interfere with each other, so only one can be used at a time.

Three-Dimensional Graphics

MATLAB provides a variety of functions to display three-dimensional data. Some functions plot lines in three dimensions, while others draw surfaces and wire frames. Color may be used to represent a fourth dimension.

18.1 Line Plots

The `plot` command from the two-dimensional world can be extended into three dimensions with `plot3`. The format is the same as the two-dimensional `plot`, except the data are in triples rather than in pairs. The generalized format of `plot3` is `plot3(x₁,y₁,z₁,S₁,x₂,y₂,z₂,S₂,...)`, where x_n, y_n, and z_n are vectors or matrices, and S_ns are optional character strings specifying color, marker symbol, or line style. Here is an example of a three-dimensional helix:

```
EDU» t=linspace(0,10*pi);
EDU» plot3(sin(t),cos(t),t)
EDU» title('Helix'), xlabel('sin(t)'), ylabel('cos(t)'),
EDU» zlabel('t')
```

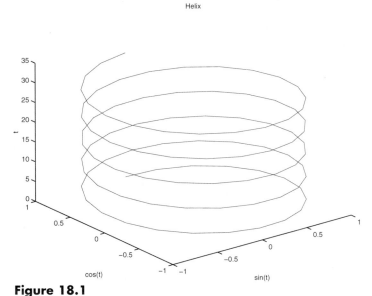

Figure 18.1

Notice that there is a `zlabel` function corresponding to the two-dimensional `xlabel` and `ylabel` functions. In the same way, the `axis` command has a three-dimensional form: `axis([xmin xmax ymin ymax zmin zmax])` sets the limits of all three axes. Other axis commands also work in three-dimensions. Let's change the plot origin:

```
EDU» axis('ij')     % change the y-axis to increase back-to-front
```

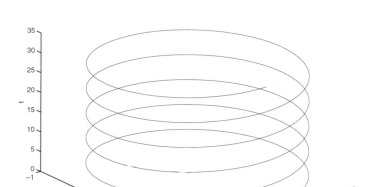

Figure 18.2

The `text` function also has a three-dimensional form: `text(x,y,z, 'string')` will place the text `'string'` beginning at the coordinate (`x,y,z`) on the current plot. As opposed to two-dimensional plots, `grid on` and `box off` are the default states for three-dimensional plots. Subplots and multiple *Figure* windows apply directly to three-dimensional graphics functions.

18.2 Mesh and Surface Plots

MATLAB defines a ***mesh*** surface by the z-coordinates of points above a rectangular grid in the *x–y* plane. It forms a plot by joining adjacent points with straight lines. The result looks like a fishing net with the knots at the data points. Mesh plots are very useful for visualizing large matrices or for plotting functions of two variables.

The first step in generating the mesh plot of a function of two variables, $z = f(x,y)$, is to generate X and Y matrices consisting of repeated rows and columns, respectively, over some range of the variables x and y. MATLAB provides the function meshgrid for this purpose. [X,Y]=meshgrid(x,y) creates

a matrix X whose rows are copies of the vector x, and a matrix Y whose columns are copies of the vector y. This pair of matrices may then be used to evaluate functions of the two variables using MATLAB's array mathematics features.

Here is an example using meshgrid to generate evenly spaced data points in the x–y plane between −7.5 and 7.5 in both x and y.

```
EDU» x=−7.5:.5:7.5;

EDU» y=x;

EDU» [X,Y]=meshgrid(x,y);
```

X and Y are a pair of matrices representing a rectangular grid of points in the x–y plane. Any function $z = f(x,y)$ may be generated using these points.

```
EDU» R=sqrt(X.^2+Y.^2)+eps;  % find the distance from the origin (0,0)

EDU» Z=sin(R)./R;            % calculate sin(r)/r
```

The matrix R contains the radius of each point in [X,Y]. This is the distance from each point to the center of the matrix, which is the origin. Adding eps prevents dividing by zero, and generating NaNs (not-a-numbers) in the data. The matrix Z now contains the sine of the radius divided by the radius for each point in the plane. The following command generates a mesh plot:

```
EDU» mesh(X,Y,Z)
```

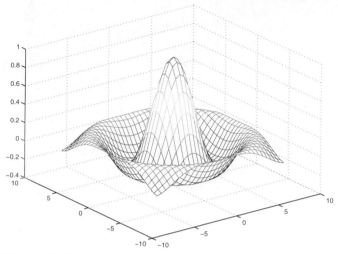

Figure 18.3

The plots in Figure 18.2 are in monochrome, but please note on your monitor how the line colors are related to the height of the mesh above the x–y plane. mesh will accept an optional argument to control the colors and color ranges used in the plot. This ability to change how MATLAB uses color will be discussed later in the sections on **colormaps**.

In this example, mesh mapped the values of the matrix elements to the points (X_{ij}, Y_{ij}, Z_{ij}) in three-dimensional space. mesh can also take a single matrix as an argument; mesh(Z) uses the points (i, j, Z_{ij}). That is, Z is plotted versus its subscripts or indices. In this case, mesh(Z) simply changes the scale of the x and y axes to the indices of matrix Z. Try it for yourself.

A **_surface_** plot of the same matrix Z looks like the mesh plot previously generated, except that the spaces between the lines (called **_patches_**) are filled in. Plots of this type are generated using the surf function, which has all of the same arguments as the mesh function. Here is an example:

```
EDU» surf(X,Y,Z)
```

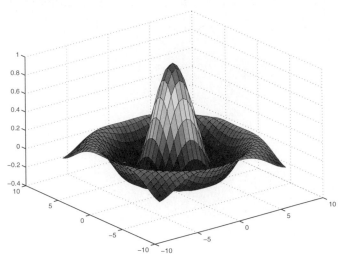

Figure 18.4

To help illustrate the next several topics, let's return to the `peaks` function discussed earlier. A three-dimensional mesh plot of this function can be generated by:

```
EDU» mesh(peaks)
EDU» title('Mesh Plot of the Peaks Function')
```

Contour plots show lines of constant elevation or height. Maybe you've seen these before. Certainly, if you've ever seen a topographical map, you know what a contour plot looks like. In MATLAB, contour plots in two-dimensional and three-dimensional are generated using the `contour` and `contour3` functions respectively. Plots using the following commands are illustrated in **Color Plate 1.** (Color Plate 1 replaces Figure 18.5.)

```
EDU» [x,y,z]=peaks;
EDU» contour(x,y,z,20)        % generate 20 2-D contour lines
EDU» title('Peaks Contour Plot')
EDU» contour3(x,y,z,20)       % the same contour plot in 3-D
EDU» axis([-3 3 -3 3 -6 8]    % use a better-looking scale
EDU» title('Peaks Contour3 Plot')
```

Another interesting way to visualize contour information is to use color to represent height. The `pcolor` function maps height to a set of colors and presents

Three-Dimensional Graphics   Chapter 18

the same information as the contour plot at the same scale. Here is the peaks function again:

```
EDU» [x,y,z]=peaks;
EDU» pcolor(x,y,z)
EDU» title('Peaks Pseudocolor Plot')
```

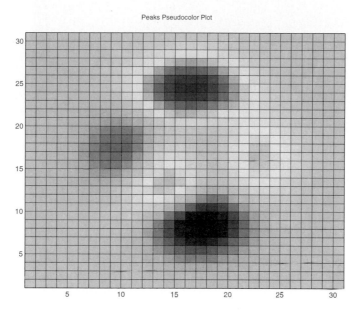

Figure 18.8

Since both pcolor and contour show the same information at the same scale, it is often useful to superimpose the two. The next example uses shading to change the appearance of the plot. shading will be discussed later in this tutorial.

```
EDU» [x,y,z]=peaks;
EDU» pcolor(x,y,z)     % generate the pseudocolor plot
EDU» shading interp   % remove the grid lines
EDU» hold on
EDU» contour(x,y,z,20,'k') % plot 20 contour lines in black
EDU» hold off
EDU» title('Peaks Pseudocolor Plot with Contours')
```

Refer to **Color Plate 1** for illustrations of the above examples.

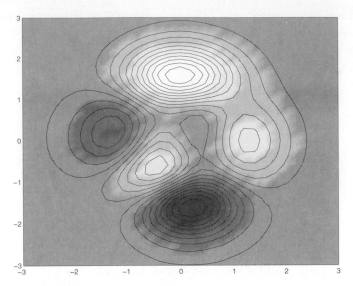

Figure 18.9

18.3 Manipulating Plots

MATLAB allows you to specify the angle from which to view a three-dimensional plot. The function `view(azimuth,elevation)` sets the angle of view by specifying your ***azimuth*** and ***elevation***. "Elevation" describes the location of the observer as an angle in degrees above the x–y plane. "Azimuth" describes the angle within the x–y plane where the observer stands. These concepts are illustrated in Fig. 18.10.

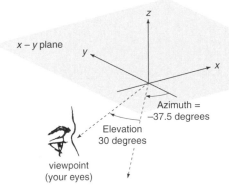

Figure 18.10

Three-Dimensional Graphics   Chapter 18

Azimuth is measured in degrees from the negative y-axis, with Fig. 18.9 showing the default MATLAB azimuth of -37.5 degrees, i.e., the negative y-axis is rotated counterclockwise away from you by 37.5 degrees. Elevation is the angle at which your eyes view the x–y plane. Figure 18.11 attempts to illustrate the default MATLAB elevation of 30 degrees, i.e., you are looking down at the x–y plane at an angle of 30 degrees. Using `view` to set various viewpoints allows you to inspect a figure from any direction. For example, if elevation is set negative, you view the figure from the bottom. If azimuth is set positive, the figure turns clockwise from its default view. You can even look at the figure from directly above by setting view to `view(0,90)`. In fact, this is the default two-dimensional viewpoint, where the x-axis increases from left to right and the y-axis increases from bottom to top. The form `view(2)` is equivalent to `view(0,90)`, the default two-dimensional view, and `view(3)` produces the default three-dimensional view, `view(-37.5,30)`.

A few examples of the `peaks` mesh from different viewpoints are illustrated in **Color Plate 2.** (Color Plate 2 replaces Figure 18.6.)

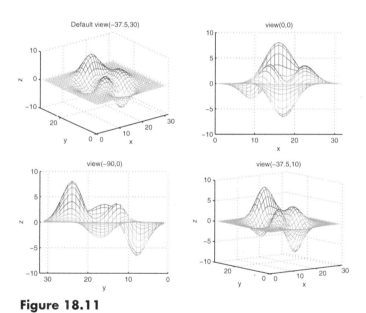

Figure 18.11

The `view` command has another form that may be more useful in some instances. `view([x y z])` places your view on a vector containing the Cartesian coordinate `(x,y,z)` in three-dimensional space. The distance you are from the origin is not affected. For example, view([0 -10 0]), view([0 -1 0]), and view(0,0) all produce the same view. In addition, the azimuth and elevation of the current view may be obtained using [az,el]=view. For example:

```
EDU» view([-7 -9 7]) % on a line from the origin through (-7,-9,7)
EDU» [az,el]=view % find the azimuth and elevation of this viewpoint
az =
    -37.8750
el =
    31.5475
```

Another useful tool for viewing three-dimensional plots is the rotate3d function. The azimuth and elevation may be set interactively using the mouse. rotate3d on turns on mouse-based view rotation, rotate3d off turns it off, and rotate3d with no arguments toggles the state.

The hidden command controls hidden line removal. When you plot a mesh that overlaps itself from your viewpoint (like peaks, or the sombrero plotted earlier), the part of the mesh that is behind another part, i.e., the hidden lines, are removed. You see only the parts that are in your line of sight. If you turn hidden off, you can look right through the mesh. Here is an example:

```
EDU» mesh(peaks(20)+7) % coarse (20) mesh, shifted up

EDU» hold on

EDU» pcolor(peaks(20)) % add a pseudocolor plot

EDU» hold off

EDU» title('Mesh With Hidden On')
```

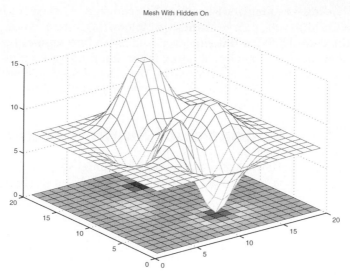

Figure 18.12

Now, turn off hidden line removal and see the difference:

```
EDU» hidden off
EDU» title('Mesh With Hidden Off')
```

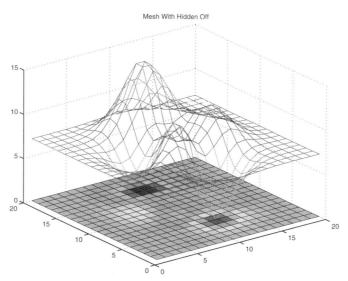

Figure 18.13

Shading was mentioned earlier. You can choose between three kinds of shading for mesh, surf, pcolor, and fill plots: flat, interpolated, and faceted shading (the default). With flat shading, each mesh line segment or surface patch has a constant color. Faceted shading is flat shading with superimposed black mesh lines. Interpolated shading varies the color of the patch or line segment linearly. Try shading flat, shading interp, and shading faceted on mesh and surf plots to see the effects.

18.4 Other Three-Dimensional Plotting Features

- The function ribbon(x,y) is the same as plot(x,y), except that the columns of y are plotted as separated ribbons in three dimensions. Here is the sine curve:

```
EDU» x=linspace(0,2*pi,30);
EDU» y=sin(x);
EDU» ribbon(x,y)
EDU» title('Ribbon Plot of a Sine Curve')
```

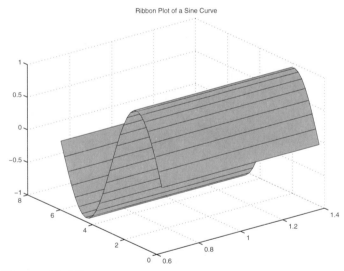

Figure 18.14

- The `clabel` function adds height labels to contour plots. There are three forms: `clabel(cs)`, `clabel(cs,V)`, and `clabel(cs,'manual')`. `clabel(cs)`, where `cs` is the contour structure returned from a `contour` command, i.e., `cs=contour(z)`, labels all plotted contours with their heights. The label positions are selected randomly. `clabel(c,V)` labels just those contour levels given in vector `V`. `clabel(c,'manual')` places contour labels at the locations clicked with a mouse, similar to the `ginput` command described earlier. Pressing the **Return** key terminates labeling.

- The `contourf` function will draw a filled contour plot; the areas between contour lines are filled with color.

- Two alternative forms of the `mesh` command add to the mesh plot. `meshc` plots the mesh and adds a contour plot beneath it. `meshz` plots the mesh and draws a *curtain plot*, or reference plane, beneath the mesh. Try `meshc(peaks)` and `meshz(peaks)` to see the result.

- The function `waterfall` is identical to `mesh`, except that the mesh lines appear only in the x-direction.

- There are two alternative forms of the `surf` command, as well. `surfc` draws a `surf` plot and adds a contour plot beneath it. `surfl` draws a `surf` plot, but adds surface highlights from a light source. The general form is `surfl (X,Y,Z,S,K)`, where `X`, `Y`, and `Z` are the same as `surf`. `S` is an optional vector in Cartesian (`S=[Sx Sy Sz]`) or spherical (`S=[az,el]`) coordinates that specifies the direction of the light source. If not specified, `S` defaults to 45 degrees counter-clockwise from the current view direction. `K` is an optional vector that specifies the contribution due to ambient light, diffuse reflection, specular reflection, and the specular spread coefficient (`K=[ka,kd,ks, spread]`).

```
EDU» colormap(gray)

EDU» surfl(peaks), shading interp

EDU» title('Surfl Plot of Peaks With Default Lighting')
```

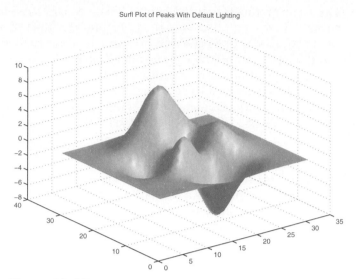

Surfl Plot of Peaks With Default Lighting

Figure 18.15

- fill3, the three-dimensional version of fill, draws filled three-dimensional polygons in three-dimensional space. The general form is fill3(x,y,z,c), where the vertices of the polygon are specified by triples of the components of x, y, and z. If necessary, the polygon is closed by connecting the last vertex to the first. If c is a character, the polygon is filled with the specified color as shown in the table for plot. c can also be an RGB row vector triple ([r g b]), where r, g, and b are values between 0 and 1 that represent the amount of red, green, and blue in the resulting color. If c is a vector or matrix, it is used as an index into a colormap (discussed next). Multiple polygons may be specified by adding more arguments: fill3(x1,y1,z1,c1,x2,y2,z2,c2,...). The following exercise will fill four random triangles with color:

  ```
  EDU» colormap(cool)

  EDU» fill3(rand(3,4),rand(3,4),rand(3,4),rand(3,4))
  ```

- The bar3 and bar3h are the three-dimensional versions of bar and barh, and pie3 is the three-dimensional version of pie.

18.5 Understanding Colormaps

Colors and colormaps were mentioned a number of times in this tutorial. This section is a brief exploration of the subject of color and colormaps. MATLAB defines a colormap as a three-column matrix. Each row of the matrix defines a particular color using numbers in the range 0 to 1. These numbers specify the RGB values: the intensity of the red, green, and blue components of a color. Some representative samples are given in the following table:

Red	Green	Blue	Color
0	0	0	black
1	1	1	white
1	0	0	red
0	1	0	green
0	0	1	blue
1	1	0	yellow
1	0	1	magenta
0	1	1	cyan
.5	.5	.5	medium gray
.5	0	0	dark red
1	.62	.40	copper
.49	1	.83	aquamarine

Here are some MATLAB functions that generate predefined colormaps:

Function	Color Map Description
hsv	Hue-saturation-value (HSV)
hot	Black-red-yellow-white
gray	Linear gray-scale
bone	Gray-scale with a tinge of blue
copper	Linear copper-tone
pink	Pastel shades of pink
white	All-white color map
flag	Alternating red, white, blue, and black
jet	A variant of HSV
prism	Prism color map
cool	Shades of cyan and magenta
lines	Color map using plot line colors
colorcube	Enhanced color-cube color map
summer	Shades of green and yellow
autumn	Shades of red and yellow
winter	Shades of blue and green
spring	Shades of magenta and yellow

By default, each of the colormaps in the table will generate a 64-by-3 matrix specifying the RGB descriptions of 64 colors. Each of these functions can be given an argument specifying the number of rows to generate. For example, hot(m) will generate an m-by-3 matrix containing the RGB values of colors that range from black, through shades of red, orange, and yellow, to white.

Most computers can display up to 256 colors in an 8-bit color lookup table, although some have display cards that can handle many more colors simultaneously. This means that, normally, up to three or four 64-by-3 colormaps may be in use at one time in different figures. If more colormap entries are used, the computer must usually swap out entries in its hardware lookup table. As a result, it is usually prudent to keep the total number of different colormap entries used at any one time below 256.

18.6 Using Colormaps

The statement `colormap(M)` installs the matrix `M` as the colormap to be used by the current figure. For example, `colormap(cool)` installs a 64-entry version of the `cool` colormap.

The `plot` and `plot3` functions do not use colormaps; they use the colors listed in the `plot` color, marker, and line-style table. Most other plotting functions, such as `mesh`, `surf`, `contour`, `fill`, `pcolor`, and their variations, use the current colormap.

Functions that take a color argument usually accept the argument in one of three forms: a character string representing one of the colors in the `plot` color, marker, and line-style table, e.g., `'r'`; a 3-entry row vector representing a single RGB value (`[.25 .50 .75]`); or a column vector or matrix. If the color argument is a column vector or matrix, the elements are scaled and used as indices into the current colormap matrix.

Here is an example that uses the color argument to `surf` to show the angle of view as a color:

```
EDU» [X,Y,Z]=peaks(30);
EDU» surf(X,Y,Z,atan2(X,Y))
EDU» colormap(hsv), shading flat
EDU» axis([-3 3 -3 3 -6.5 8.1]), axis off
EDU» title('Using a Color Argument to surf')
```

Using a Color Argument to surf

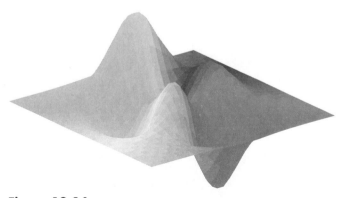

Figure 18.16

Another interesting angle is to view the surface from above. Try this:

```
EDU» view(2)
```

18.7   Using Color to Add Information

Color may be used to add information to three-dimensional plots if it is used to display a fourth dimension. Functions such as mesh and surf vary the color along the z-axis, unless a color argument is given, e.g., surf(X,Y,Z) is equivalent to surf(X,Y,Z,Z), where the fourth argument is used as an index into the colormap. This makes for a colorful plot, but does not add information, since the z-axis already exists.

Here are some ways to use the color argument to add new information or to emphasize information already in the plot. Refer to **Color Plate 3** for illustrations of the following plots. (Color Plate 3 replaces Figure 18.7a.)

```
EDU» x=-7.5:.5:7.5; y=x;     % create a data set

EDU» [X,Y]=meshgrid(x,y);     % create plaid data

EDU» R=sqrt(X.^2 + Y.^2)+eps;   % create radial data

EDU» Z=sin(R)./R;  % create a sombrero

EDU» subplot(2,2,1), surf(X,Y,Z),

EDU» title('Color Varies with the Z-Axis')

EDU» subplot(2,2,2), surf(X,Y,Z,R),

EDU» title('Color Varies with the Radius')

EDU» subplot(2,2,3), surf(X,Y,Z,del2(Z)),

EDU» title('Color Varies with Curvature')

EDU» [dZdx,dZdy]=gradient(Z);  % compute the slope

EDU» dZ=sqrt(dZdx.^2 + dZdy.^2);  % compute the slope's
magnitude

EDU» subplot(2,2,4), surf(X,Y,Z,dZ)

EDU» title('Color Varies with Slope Magnitude')
```

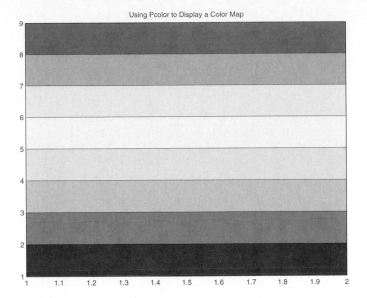

Figure 18.17

18.8   Displaying Colormaps

You can display a colormap in a number of ways. One way is to view the elements in a colormap matrix directly:

```
EDU» hot(8)
ans =
    0.3333        0             0
    0.6667        0             0
    1.0000        0             0
    1.0000        0.3333        0
    1.0000        0.6667        0
    1.0000        1.0000        0
    1.0000        1.0000        0.5000
    1.0000        1.0000        1.0000
```

In addition, the pcolor function can be used to display a colormap. Try this example a few times, using different colormap functions and varying the parameter n:

```
EDU» n=8;
EDU» colormap(jet(n))
EDU» pcolor([1:n+1;1:n+1]')
EDU» title('Using Pcolor to Display a Colormap')
```

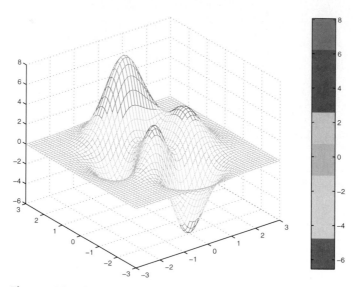

Figure 18.18

The `colorbar` function adds a vertical or horizontal colorbar (color scale) to your current *Figure* window showing the color mappings for the current axis. `colorbar('h')` places a colorbar horizontally beneath your current plot. `colorbar('v')` places a vertical colorbar to the right of your plot. `colorbar` without arguments either adds a vertical colorbar, if no colorbars exist, or updates any existing colorbar.

```
EDU» [X,Y,Z]=peaks;
EDU» mesh(X,Y,Z);
EDU» colormap(hsv)
EDU» axis([-3 3 -3 3 -6 8])
EDU» colorbar
```

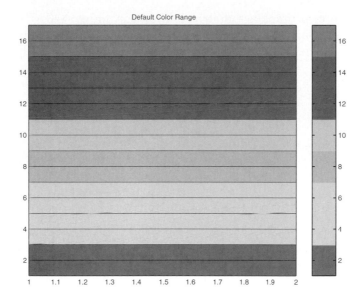

Figure 18.19

18.9 Creating and Altering Colormaps

The fact that colormaps are matrices means that you are able to manipulate them just like any other matrices. The function `brighten` takes advantage of this fact to adjust a given colormap to increase or decrease the intensity of the dark colors. `brighten(n)` brightens ($0 < n \leq 1$) or darkens ($-1 \leq n < 0$) the current colormap. `brighten(n)` followed by `brighten(-n)` restores the original colormap. The command `newmap=brighten(n)` creates a brighter or darker version of the current colormap without changing the current map. The command `newmap=brighten(cmap,n)` creates an adjusted version of the specified colormap without affecting either the current colormap or `cmap`. The form `brighten(gcf,n)` brightens all the objects in the current *Figure* window.

You can create your own colormap by generating an m-by-3 matrix mymap and installing it with colormap(mymap). Each value in a colormap matrix must be between 0 and 1, inclusive. If you try to use a matrix with more or fewer than 3 columns or containing any values less than zero or greater than one, colormap will report an error.

You can combine colormaps arithmetically, although the results are sometimes unpredictable. For example, the map called pink is simply:

```
EDU» pinkmap=sqrt(2/3*gray+1/3*hot);
```

Since colormaps are matrices, they can be plotted. The rgbplot command plots colormap matrix values just the way plot would, but uses the colors red, green, and blue for the line colors. Try rgbplot(hot). This shows that the red component increases first, then the green, then the blue. rgbplot(gray) shows that all three columns increase linearly and equally (all three lines overlap). Try rgbplot with some of the other colormaps, such as jet, hsv, and prism.

Normally, a colormap is scaled to extend from the minimum to the maximum values of your data; that is, the entire colormap is used to render your plot. You may occasionally wish to change the way colors are used. The caxis function allows you to use the entire colormap for a subset of your data range, or use only a portion of the current colormap for your entire data plot.

The current values of cmin and cmax are returned by caxis without arguments. These will normally be the minimum and maximum values of your data. caxis([cmin cmax]) uses the entire colormap for data in range between cmin and cmax; data points greater than cmax will be rendered with the color associated with cmax, and data points smaller than cmin will be rendered with the color associated with cmin. If cmin is less than min(data) or cmax is greater than max(data), the colors associated with cmin or cmax will never be used; only a portion of the colormap will be used. caxis('auto') will restore the default values of cmin and cmax.

The following examples are illustrated in **Color Plate 4.** (Color Plate 4 replaces Figure 18.7b.)

```
EDU» pcolor([1:17;1:17]')
EDU» title('Default Color Range')
EDU» colormap(hsv(8))
EDU» caxis('auto')
EDU» colorbar
```

```
EDU» caxis
ans =
      1    17
```

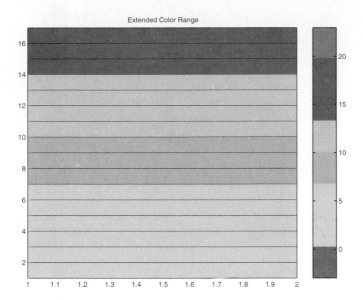

Figure 18.20

As you can see, all eight colors in the current colormap are used for the entire data set, two bars for each color. If the colors are mapped to values from −3 to 23, only five colors will be used in the plot, as shown:

```
EDU» title('Extended Color Range')

EDU» caxis([−3 23]) % extend the color range

EDU» colorbar    % redraw the color scale
```

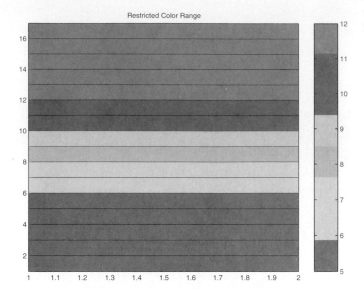

Figure 18.21

If the colors are mapped to values from 5 to 12, all colors are used. However, the data less than 5 or greater than 12 get the colors associated with 5 and 12, respectively:

```
EDU» title('Restricted Color Range')
EDU» caxis([5 12])  % restrict the color range
EDU» colorbar    % redraw the color scale
```

18.10 Summary

- plot3 is the three-dimensional version of the plot command, and is used in the same way. plot(x,y,z) plots a line in three-dimensional space.

- zlabel is used to label the z-axis on three-dimensional plots.

- The axis([xmin xmax ymin ymax zmin zmax]) command sets limits for all three axes. axis('ij') moves the origin of a three-dimensional plot, and changes the y-axis to increase left-to-right in the default view.

- The three-dimensional form of the text function, text(x,y,z,S), will place the character string S at the location (x,y,z) on the current plot.

- A rectangular grid of evenly spaced points in the x–y plane may be easily generated using meshgrid. [X,Y]=meshgrid(x,y), where x and y are vectors, generates a matrix X, whose rows are copies of the vector x, and matrix Y, whose columns are copies of the vector y. The coordinates (X_{ij}, Y_{ij}) represent a regular rectangular grid in the x–y plane.

- mesh(Z), where Z is a matrix, plots a mesh in three dimensions with intersections at the points (i, j, Z_{ij}). mesh(X,Y,Z) plots a mesh with intersections at the points (X_{ij}, Y_{ij}, Z_{ij}). An additional color argument is optional.

- surf is the surface version of mesh, and uses the same arguments. surf draws a mesh plot and fills in the patches (holes between line segments) with appropriate colors.

- Contour plots may be generated with contour. This function uses the general form contour(X,Y,Z,n,S), where X and Y are optional vectors specifying the x and y axes, Z is the matrix of data points, n is an optional number of contour lines to draw, and S is a character string specifying color or line type, as in the plot command. contour3 draws contours in three-dimensional space, and contourf draws filled contours.

- Pseudocolor plots may be generated using pcolor. pcolor(C) generates a *checkerboard* plot of matrix C, where the values of the elements of C determine the color of each cell of the plot. pcolor(X,Y,C), where X and Y are vectors or matrices, draws a pseudocolor plot on the grid defined by X and Y. pcolor is really surf with its view set to directly above the x–y plane.

- The angle of view of a three-dimensional plot may be set with the view command. The usual format is view(az,el), where az is the azimuth (angle in degrees from the y-axis), and el is the angle of elevation (in degrees above the x–y plane). An alternative form is view([x y z]), where (x,y,z) is the Cartesian coordinate of the observer. view(2) sets the default two-dimensional view (view(0,90)), and view(3) sets the default three-dimensional view (view(−37.5,30)).

- Azimuth and elevation may be set interactively, with the mouse using rotate3d.

- Hidden line removal may be controlled with hidden off and hidden on.

- bar3, bar3h, pie3, and fill3 are the three-dimensional equivalents of bar, barh, pie, and fill, respectively.

- Three types of shading are available using shading flat, shading interp, and shading faceted.

- A colormap is a 3-column matrix whose rows contain the RGB values of a color in the form [r g b].

- MATLAB supplies functions to create different colormaps, including hsv, cool, summer, jet, copper, and many others.

- colormap(M) installs the matrix M as the current colormap. M must have 3 columns and contain only values between 0 and 1.

- Functions that take a color argument usually accept either a character representing one of the colors in the `plot` color, marker, and line-style table; a single RGB value in the form `[r g b]`; or a column vector or matrix whose elements are scaled and used as indices into the current colormap.

- Color can add information to three-dimensional plots. The color argument to functions such as `mesh` and `surf` may be used to describe some property of the data that is not reflected by the three axes, i.e., color may be used to describe a fourth dimension.

- Colormaps may be displayed by viewing the elements of the colormap matrix, using `pcolor` to display colorbars or using the `colorbar` function to add a color scale to an existing plot.

- `brighten` adjusts the brightness of the current colormap, or creates a new colormap from an existing one.

- Colormaps may be created by any array operation, and may be installed and used as long as they consist of 3 columns, and contain only values between 0 and 1.

Cell Arrays and Structures

MATLAB 5 introduces two new data types called **Cell Arrays** and **Structures.** Cell arrays may be visualized as an array of bins or containers that can hold different kinds of other MATLAB data. Think of a collection of post-office boxes in a Post Office: Each post-office box holds mail of differing types and amounts. In the same way, each cell in a cell array holds data of potentially differing types and amounts. Structures are array-oriented data constructs with named fields that can contain any kind of data, including cell arrays and other structures. Structures provide a convenient way to group related data of different types. These new data types, cell arrays and structures, give you the ability to organize MATLAB data into convenient packages.

19.1 Cell Arrays

Cell arrays are MATLAB arrays whose elements are *cells*. Each cell in a cell array can hold any MATLAB data type, including numeric arrays, text, symbolic objects, cell arrays, and structures. For example, one cell of a cell array might contain a numeric array, another an array of text strings, and another a vector of complex values. Cell arrays can be created with more than two dimensions; for convenience, however, the examples in this section will be limited to two dimensions.

19.2 Creating and Displaying Cell Arrays

Cell arrays can be created by using assignment statements, or by preallocating the array using the `cells` function and then assigning data to the cells. If you have trouble with these examples, it is likely that you have another variable in the workspace of the same name. If you assign a cell to an existing numeric array, MATLAB will complain. If any examples give unexpected results, clear the cell array from the workspace and try again.

Like other kinds of arrays, cell arrays can be built by assigning data to individual cells, one at a time. There are two different way to access cells. If you use standard array syntax to index the array, you must enclose the cell contents in curly braces { }. For example:

```
EDU» A(1,1)={[1 2 3; 4 5 6; 7 8 9]};
EDU» A(1,2)={2+3i};
EDU» A(2,1)={'A text string'};
EDU» A(2,2)={12:-2:0};
```

The curly braces on the right side of the equal sign indicate that the expression represents a cell. This is called *cell indexing*. Alternatively, the following statements create the same cell array:

```
EDU» A{1,1}=[1 2 3; 4 5 6; 7 8 9];
EDU» A{1,2}=2+3i;
EDU» A{2,1}='A text string';
EDU» A{2,2}=12:-2:0;
```

Here, the curly braces on the left side of the assignment indicate that A is a cell array, and the expression is put "inside" the specified cell. This is called *content addressing*. You can use both methods interchangeably.

MATLAB displays the cell array A as:

```
EDU» A
A =
        [3x3 double]      2.0000+ 3.0000i
    'A text string'          [1x7 double]
```

Here, [3x3 double] indicates that A(1,1) is a cell that holds a 3-by-3 double array. To display the *contents* of each cell in a cell array, use the celldisp function.

```
EDU» celldisp(A)
A{1,1} =
        1       2       3
        4       5       6
        7       8       9

A{2,1} =
    A text string

A{1,2} =
    2.0000+ 3.0000i

A{2,2} =
    12      10      8       6       4       2       0
```

To display the contents of a single cell, access the cell using curly braces.

```
EDU» A{2,2}
ans =
    12      10      8       6       4       2       0
```

MATLAB displays a graphical structure map of a cell array in a *Figure* window using the cellplot function. Filled rectangles are used to represent the number of elements in each cell. Scalars and string data are displayed as values, as well.

```
EDU» cellplot(A)
```

Curly braces work the same way as square brackets for numeric arrays, except that cells can be nested. Use comma and semicolon syntax for column and row breaks.

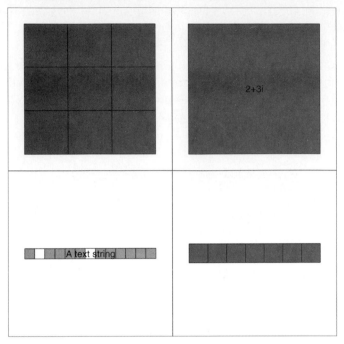

Figure 19.1

```
EDU» B={[1 2] 'John Smith'; 2+3i, 5}
B =
        [1x2 double]    'John Smith'
    [2.0000+ 3.0000i]    [        5]
```

The `cell` function makes working with cell arrays more efficient by preallocating an empty array of the specified size. `cell` actually creates the cell array and fills it with empty numeric matrices.

```
EDU» C=cell(2,3)
C =
    []      []      []
    []      []      []
```

Once the cell array has been defined, use the preceding assignment syntax to populate the new array.

19.3   Combining and Reshaping Cell Arrays

If you assign data to a cell that is outside the dimensions of the current array, MATLAB automatically expands the array and fills the intervening cells with the empty *numeric* matrix [ ]. Note that the notation { } represents the empty cell array, just as [ ] represents the empty matrix for numeric arrays.

Use square brackets to concatenate cell arrays.

```
EDU» C=[A B]
C =
        [3x3 double]     2.0000+  3.0000i            [1x2 double]      'John Smith'
    'A text string'          [1x7 double]    [2.0000+  3.0000i]     [          5]
EDU» C=[A;B]
C =
        [3x3 double]     2.0000+  3.0000i
    'A text string'          [1x7 double]
        [1x2 double]       'John Smith'
    [2.0000+  3.0000i]     [          5]
```

A subset of cells can be extracted into a new cell array. If D is a 3-by-3 cell array, a 2-by-2 portion can be extracted into a new cell array F, as follows:

```
EDU» F=D(2:3,2:3);
```

An entire row or column of a cell array can be deleted using the empty matrix:

```
EDU» C(3,:)=[];
```

Notice that curly braces do not appear in either of the preceding expressions.

The reshape function can be used to change the configuration of a cell array, but cannot be used to add or remove cells.

```
EDU» X=cells(3,4);
EDU» size(X)
ans =
     3    4
EDU» Y=reshape(X,6,2);
EDU» size(Y)
ans =
     6    2
```

19.4   Accessing Cell Array Contents

To access data contained in elements of a cell array, use curly braces. Use parentheses to access an element as a cell. To access the contents of any sub-element of a cell array, concatenate appropriate indexing expressions as shown.

```
EDU» x=B{2,2}        % access the contents of the cell
x =
     5

EDU» class(x)
ans =
     double

EDU» y=B(2,2)        % access the cell itself
y =
     [5]

EDU» class(y)
ans =
     cell

EDU» B{1,1}(1,2)     % access the second element of the vector
                     % inside the cell
ans =
     2
```

To access elements of a range of cells in a cell array, use the deal function:

```
EDU» [a,b]=deal(B{2,:})
a =
     2.0000+    3.0000i
b =
     5
```

This brings up an interesting point. The deal function expects a list of values separated by commas as arguments to distribute to the output variables. The expression B{2,:} can be used anywhere a comma-separated list of values can be used. That is, B{2,:} is equivalent to B(2,1),B(2,2). Because of this property of cell addressing, content indexing can be used only to access a single cell in assignment statements. For example, the statements A{1,:}=value and B=A{1,:} are both invalid. However, you can use a subset of cells in any expression that expects a comma-separated list of values. For example, using A from above, we get:

```
EDU» [D{1:2}]=eig(A{1,1});
D =
     [3x3 double]    [3x3 double]

EDU» celldisp(D)
D{1} =
     0.2320     0.7858     0.4082
     0.5253     0.0868    −0.8165
     0.8187    −0.6123     0.4082
```

```
         D{2} =
          16.1168            0            0
               0      -1.1168            0
               0            0      -0.0000
```

19.5   Cell Arrays of Character Strings

One of the most common applications of cell arrays is the creation of text arrays. Standard arrays of character strings require that all strings have the same length. Because cell arrays can contain different types of data in each element, text strings in cell arrays do not have this limitation. For example,

```
EDU» T={'Tom'; 'Dick';' Harry Smith'; 'Mohamad'; 'Suzanne'}
T =
    'Tom'
    'Dick'
    'Harry Smith'
    'Mohamad'
    'Suzanne'
```

T and its elements can now be used anywhere a text string or multi-line text is desired. For more information on cell arrays of strings, see Chapter 9.

19.6   Structures

Structures are MATLAB objects with named "data containers" called *fields*. Like the elements of a cell array, the fields of a structure can contain any type of data. They differ in that structure fields are accessed by a name rather than an index, and there are no additional restrictions on the number or configuration of structure fields. Like cell arrays, structures can be nested and collected into arrays and cell arrays. Like all MATLAB objects, structures are inherently array-oriented. A single structure is a 1-by-1 structure array, just as the number 3.25 is a 1-by-1 numeric array.

19.7   Building Structures

Structures use dot-notation to access the fields. Building a structure can be as simple as assigning data to individual fields. This example builds a client record for a testing laboratory.

```
EDU» client.name = 'John Doe';
EDU» client.cost = 86.50;
EDU» client.test.A1C = [6.3 6.8 7.1 7.0 6.7 6.5 6.3 6.1 6.4];
EDU» client.test.CHC = [2.8 3.4 3.6 4.1 3.5];
```

```
EDU» client
client =
    name: 'John Doe'
    cost: 86.50
    test: [1x1 struct]

EDU» client.test
ans =
    A1C: 6.3000 6.8000 7.1000 7.0000 6.7000 6.5000 6.3000 6.1000 6.4000
    CHC: 2.8000 3.4000 3.6000 4.1000 3.5000
```

Now, create a second client record.

```
EDU» client(2).name = 'Alice Smith';
EDU» client(2).cost = 112.35;
EDU» client(2).test.A1C = [5.3 5.8 7.0 6.5 6.7 5.5 6.0 5.9 6.1];
EDU» client(2).test.CHC = [3.8 3.6 3.2 3.1 2.5];

EDU» client
client =
1x2 struct array with fields
    name
    cost
    test
```

As you expand the structure array, MATLAB fills in unspecified fields with the empty numeric matrix so that all structures in the array have the same number of fields and the same field names. Note that field sizes do not have to match. The name fields can have different lengths, and the test fields can be arrays of different sizes.

Structures can also be built using the struct function to preallocate an array of structures. The syntax is struct('field1',V1,'field2',V2,...) where field1, field2, etc. are field names, and arrays V1, V2, etc. must be cell arrays of the same size, scalar cells, or single values. For example, a structure array can be created as follows:

```
EDU» N={'John Doe', 'Alice Smith'};
EDU» C={86.50, 112.35};
EDU» P={[10.00 20.00 45.00],[100.00 12.35]};

EDU» bills=struct('name',N,'cost',C,'payment',P)
bills =
1x2 struct array with fields
    name
    cost
    payment
```

Cell Arrays and Structures   Chapter 19

19.8 Accessing Structure Fields

Because structure containers are named rather than indexed, as is the case with cell arrays, the names of the fields in a structure must be known to access the data contained within them. Field names can be found in the *Command* window simply by typing the name of the structure. In an M-file, however, a function is needed to obtain the field names. The `fieldnames` function returns a cell array containing the names of the fields in a structure.

```
EDU» T=fieldnames(bills)
T =
    'name'
    'cost'
    'payment'
```

There are two methods for accessing structure fields. Direct indexing uses the appropriate indexing mechanism, e.g., a period to access a structure field and the appropriate array index to access a numeric or a cell array. Here is an example based on the `bills` and `client` structures just shown.

```
EDU» bills.name
ans =
    John Doe
ans =
    Alice Smith

EDU» bills(2).cost
ans =
    112.3500

EDU» bills(1)
ans =
      name: 'John Doe'
      cost: 86.5000
   payment: 10.0000   20.0000   45.0000

EDU» baldue=bills(1).cost - sum(bills(1).payment)
baldue =
    6.5000

EDU» bills(2).payment(2)
ans =
    12.3500

EDU» client(2).test.A1C(3)
ans =
    7.0000
```

Symbolic Math Toolbox

20.40 Interactive Symbolic Tools

20.41 Function Calculator

Symbolic Math Toolbox Function List

In previous chapters, you learned how MATLAB can be used like a powerful, programmable, top-of-the-line calculator. Even a powerful calculator, however, has its limitations. Like a calculator, *basic* MATLAB uses numbers. It takes numbers (123/4) or variables ($x = [1\ 2\ 3]$) and acts upon them using the commands and functions you specify ($y = \cos(\mathrm{pi}/4)$ or $r = \log(4/3)$) to produce numerical results. What most calculators and *basic* MATLAB lack is the ability to manipulate mathematical expressions without actually using numbers. *Basic* MATLAB must have numbers to work with. For example, asking for the sine of a variable that has not been assigned a numerical value results in:

```
EDU» y=sin(x)  % take the sine of x
???  Undefined function or variable x.
```

The commands and functions introduced in this section change all that. Now, you can tell MATLAB to manipulate *expressions* that let you compute with mathematical symbols rather than numbers. This process is often called *symbolic math*. Here are some examples of symbolic expressions:

$$\cos(x^2) \qquad 3x^2 - 5x - 1 \qquad v = \frac{d}{dx}2x^2 \qquad f = \int \frac{x^2}{\sqrt{1-x}}\,dx$$

The *Symbolic Math Toolbox* is a collection of *tools* (functions) for MATLAB that are used for manipulating and solving symbolic expressions. There are tools to combine, simplify, differentiate, integrate, and solve algebraic and differential equations. Other tools are used in linear algebra to derive exact results for inverses, determinants, and canonical forms, and to find the eigenvalues of symbolic matrices without the error introduced by numerical computations. Variable precision arithmetic, which calculates symbolically and returns a result to any specified accuracy, is also supported. If some of these topics are foreign to you, don't worry. As with *basic* MATLAB, you don't need to know everything to make MATLAB help you solve problems.

The tools in the Symbolic Math Toolbox are built upon portions of the powerful software program called Maple®, originally developed at the University of Waterloo in Ontario, Canada and now the product of Waterloo Maple Software, Inc. When you ask MATLAB to perform a symbolic operation, it uses *Symbolic Math Toolbox* functions to do the operation and returns the answer to the MATLAB command window. As a result, performing symbolic manipulations in MATLAB is a natural extension of the way you use MATLAB to crunch numbers.

20.1 Symbolic Objects and Expressions

Basic MATLAB uses a number of different object types to store values. Numeric variables are used to store numeric values, e.g., x=2, and character arrays are used to store text strings, e.g., t='A text string'. The *Symbolic Math Toolbox* uses *symbolic objects* to represent variables and operators, e.g., x=sym('x'). Symbolic objects are used by MATLAB in much the same way that numeric variables and strings are used. *Symbolic expressions* are expressions containing symbolic objects that represent numbers, functions, operators, and variables. The variables are not required to have predefined numeric values. *Symbolic arithmetic* is the practice of solving these symbolic equations by applying known rules and identities to the given symbols, exactly the way you learned to solve them in algebra and calculus. *Symbolic matrices* are arrays whose elements contain symbolic objects or expressions.

20.2   Creating and Using Symbolic Objects

Symbolic objects are created from character strings or numeric values using the sym function. For example, x=sym('x') creates a symbolic variable x. y=sym('1/3') creates a symbolic variable y containing the value 1/3. Once the symbolic variable is defined, it can be used in expressions in the same way that numeric variables are used in MATLAB. Given that x and y are symbolic variables, the command z=(x+y)/(x-2) creates a symbolic variable z because the expression that it represents contains one or more symbolic variables (x and y).

A numeric object can be converted into a symbolic object, as well. Here is an example:

```
EDU» m=magic(3)            % create a numeric matrix
m =
     8    1    6
     3    5    7
     4    9    2

EDU» M=sym(m)              % create a symbolic matrix from m
M =
     [ 8, 1, 6]
     [ 3, 5, 7]
     [ 4, 9, 2]

EDU» det(M)        % find the determinant of the symbolic matrix M
ans =
     -360
```

This example creates a 3-by-3 magic square, converts it to a symbolic matrix, and finds the determinant of the matrix.

Remember that the floating-point representation of a number is accurate only to around 16 digits. If you use the number 1/3, MATLAB divides 1 by 3 and stores the result as a double-precision floating-point number. The ideal floating-point representation is a decimal point and an infinite number of 3s. The difference between the ideal and actual representations is the roundoff error.

Repeated numeric operations can introduce significant error in the result, whereas symbolic operations generally introduce no error.

The `sym` function lets you choose a format for the symbolic representation of a numeric value. The form is `S=sym(A,fmt)`, where `A` is a numeric value or matrix and `fmt` is an optional format specification, which may be `'f'`, `'r'`, `'e'`, or `'d'`. The default format is `'r'`. *Floating point* format (`'f'`) represents values as a hexadecimal number times two to an integer power. *Rational* format (`'r'`) represents values as the ratio of modest-sized integers, if possible; otherwise, the format will be p^q with large integers p and q. *Estimate error* format (`'e'`) is similar to the `'r'` format but the result is supplemented by a term involving the variable `eps`, which estimates the difference between the theoretical rational expression and its actual floating point value; a roundoff error fudge factor. *Decimal* format (`'d'`) is represented to 32 digits (or the value of `'Digits'` used by `vpa`, as discussed later). See the on-line documentation for `sym`, or use the `help` command for more details.

Here are examples of each of the numeric and symbolic display format options:

Command	Representation of 1/3	Class
`format short`	`0.3333`	`double`
`format long`	`0.333333333333333`	`double`
`format short e`	`3.3333e−001`	`double`
`format long e`	`3.333333333333333e−001`	`double`
`format short g`	`0.33333`	`double`
`format long g`	`0.333333333333333`	`double`
`format hex`	`3fd5555555555555`	`double`
`format bank`	`0.33`	`double`
`format rat`	`1/3`	`double`
`format +`	`+`	`double`
`sym(1/3,'f')`	`'1.5555555555555'*2^(−2)`	`sym`
`sym(1/3,'r')`	`1/3`	`sym`
`sym(1/3,'e')`	`1/3−eps/12`	`sym`
`sym(1/3,'d')`	`.33333333333333331482961625624739`	`sym`

The differences between the symbolic formats can create some confusion. For example:

```
EDU» sym(1/3)−sym(1/3,'e')        % rational result minus error-
                                  % estimate result
ans =
    1/12*eps
EDU» double(ans)                  % decimal format
ans =
    1.8504e−17
```

Here is another example:

```
EDU» sym(1/3,'d')−sym(1/3,'e')    % decimal result minus error-
                                  % estimate result
ans =
    −.1850371707708594e−16+1/12*eps

EDU» double(ans)                  % decimal format
ans =
    2.3404e−33
```

The differences in the results are very small, but very real. Since MATLAB interprets any numeric value (or numeric variable) used on the command line and introduces some roundoff error, it is usually prudent to use the string form of a constant such as sym('1/3') to create a symbolic constant, rather than the numeric form sym(1/3).

20.3   MATLAB Representation of Symbolic Expressions

MATLAB represents symbolic expressions internally as expressions containing symbolic objects to differentiate them from numeric variables, expressions, or operations; otherwise, they look almost exactly like basic MATLAB expressions. Here are some examples of symbolic expressions, along with their MATLAB equivalents:

Symbolic Expression	MATLAB Representation
$\dfrac{1}{2x^3}$	x = sym('x')
$y = \dfrac{1}{\sqrt{2x}}$	x=sym('x')
$\cos(x^2) - \sin(2x)$	x = sym('x')
$M = \begin{bmatrix} a & b \\ c & d \end{bmatrix}$	syms('a','b','c','d');
$f = \displaystyle\int_a^b \dfrac{x^3}{\sqrt{1-x}}\,dx$	syms x a b
	f = int(x^3/sqrt(1-x),a,b)

MATLAB symbolic functions let you manipulate these expressions in many ways. For example:

```
EDU» x = sym('x')      % create a symbolic variable x
EDU» diff(cos(x))      % differentiate cos(x) with respect to x
ans =
    -sin(x)

EDU» syms('a','b','c','d')    % create symbolic variables a, b, c, and d
EDU» M=[a,b;c,d]              % create a symbolic matrix M
M =
    [ a, b]
    [ c, d]

EDU» det(M)            % find the determinant of the symbolic matrix M
ans =
    a*d-b*c
```

In the first example just given, x is defined as a symbolic variable before it is used in an expression, in the same way that numeric variables must be given a value before they are used. This allows MATLAB to determine that cos(x) is a symbolic expression, and therefore diff(cos(x)) is a symbolic operation rather than a numeric operation. In the second example, the syms function was used to define a number of symbolic variables at once. syms('a','b') is the equivalent of a = sym('a'); b = sym('b');. MATLAB knows that M=[a,b;c,d] is a symbolic matrix because it contains symbolic variables, and that det(M) is, therefore, a symbolic operation.

In MATLAB, the command form `func arg` is equivalent to `func('arg')`, where `func` is a function and `arg` is a character-string argument. For example, MATLAB can figure out that `syms a b c d` and `syms('a','b', 'c','d')` are equivalent; but, as you can see, the first form is certainly easier to type.

Let's take a closer look at the second example given above:

```
EDU» a=1; b=2; c=3; d=4;    % define numeric variables a through d
EDU» M=[a,b;c,d]            % M is a numeric matrix
M =
     1    2
     3    4

EDU» size(M)                % M is a 2x2 matrix
ans =
     2    2

EDU» class(M)               % What kind of object is M?
ans =
     double

EDU» M='[a,b;c,d]'          % M is a character string
M =
     [a,b;c,d]

EDU» size(M)                % M is a row vector of 9 characters
ans =
     1    9

EDU» class(M)
ans =
     char

EDU» M=sym('[a,b;c,d]')     % a symbolic object, but not a matrix
M =
     [   a, b;c,    d]

EDU» size(M)                % M is a 3-element vector (two commas)
ans =
     1    3

EDU» class(M)
ans =
     sym

EDU» syms a b c d           % define symbolic variables a through d
EDU» M=[a,b;c,d]            % M is a symbolic matrix
```

```
M =
    [ a, b]
    [ c, d]
EDU» size(M)
ans =
    2    2

EDU» class(M)
ans =
    sym

EDU» a=1; b=2; syms c d    % define a mix of variables a through d
EDU» M=[a,b;c,d]           % M is a symbolic matrix
M =
    [ 1, 2]
    [ c, d]
EDU» size(M)
ans =
    2    2

EDU» class(M)
ans =
    sym
```

In this example, M was defined five ways: numerically; as a character string; as a symbolic object; and, twice, as a symbolic matrix. The first form is the familiar numeric 2-by-2 double-precision matrix. The second form is a plain character string, and can be passed to `eval` or used in a title or some other text string. The third form is a valid symbolic object, but it cannot be used in any useful way. This shows that **any** string can be converted into a symbolic object. The fourth form is a symbolic 2-by-2 matrix. The final form shows how numeric and symbolic variables can be combined in a symbolic expression to create a symbolic matrix.

Symbolic expressions without variables are called *symbolic constants*. When symbolic constants are displayed, they are sometimes difficult to distinguish from integers. For example:

```
EDU» f=sym(3)              % create a symbolic constant
f =
    3

EDU» class(f)              % what kind of object is f?
ans =
    sym
```

```
EDU» g=sym(pi)              % create a symbolic constant from pi
g =
    pi
EDU» class(g)              % what kind of object is g?
ans =
    sym
EDU» h=sym(sin(pi/4))      % create a symbolic constant from an expression
h =
    sqrt(1/2)
EDU» class(h)              % what kind of object is h?
ans =
    sym
```

In this example, f represents the symbolic constant 3, not the number 3. In the same fashion, g represents the symbolic constant pi rather than the numeric version of pi, and h represents a symbolic constant, as well.

20.4   Symbolic Variables

When working with symbolic expressions containing more than one variable, exactly one variable is the *independent* variable. If MATLAB is not told which variable is the independent variable, it usually selects the one closest to x alphabetically.

The default independent variable, sometimes known as the *free* variable, in the symbolic expression 1/(5+cos(x)) is x; the free variable in the expression 3*y+z is y; and the free variable in the expression a+sin(t) is t. There is no free symbolic variable in the expression sin(pi/4)−cos(3/5) because this expression is a symbolic constant, containing no symbolic variables. You can ask MATLAB to tell you which variable in a symbolic expression it thinks is the independent variable by using the findsym function:

```
EDU» syms a s t u omega ij   % define some symbolic variables
EDU» findsym(a*t+s/(u+3),1)  % u is closest to x
ans =
    u
EDU» findsym(sin(a+omega),1) % omega is closest to x
ans =
    omega
EDU» findsym(3*i+4*j)        % i and j are equal to sqrt(−1)
ans =
    ' '
```

If findsym cannot find any symbolic variables, it will return the empty string. This will be true for expressions containing i and j, as well as symbolic constants that contain no variables. Note that most symbolic operations will accept an argument specifying the independent variable, but will use 'x' as the default independent variable if findsym returns the empty string.

20.5   Things to Try on Your Own

Here are some expressions to practice on. Given each symbolic expression, use MATLAB syntax to create the equivalent MATLAB symbolic expressions:

$$f = ax^2 + bx + c \qquad g' = \frac{d}{dx}\sqrt{3x^2 + 2x + 5} \qquad z = \frac{3\cos(w)}{\sin\left(\dfrac{2w}{w+1}\right)}$$

$$A = \begin{bmatrix} 3\sin(t) & -\cos(t^2) \\ \cos(2t) & -\sin(t) \end{bmatrix} \qquad p = \frac{3s^2 + 2s + 1}{4s - 2} \qquad r = e^{-2t}$$

Here are answers to the foregoing expressions:

```
EDU» syms a b c x
EDU» f=a*x^2+b*x+c
f =
    a*x^2+b*x+c

EDU» g_prime=diff(sqrt(3*x^2+2*x+5))
g_prime =
    1/2/(3*x^2+2*x+5)^(1/2)*(6*x+2)

EDU» w=sym('w');
EDU» z=3*cos(w)/sin(2*w/(w+1))
z =
    3*cos(w)/sin(2*w/(w+1))

EDU» t=sym('t');
EDU» A=[3*sin(t) -cos(t^2); cos(2*t) -sin(t)]
A =
    [ 3*sin(t), -cos(t^2)]
    [ cos(2*t),   -sin(t)]

EDU» s=sym('s');
EDU» p=(3*s^2-2*s+1)/(4*s-2)
p =
    (3*s^2-2*s+1)/(4*s-2)
```

```
EDU» r=exp(-2*t)
r =
    exp(-2*t)
```

20.6   Summary

- *Basic* MATLAB commands and functions operate on numeric values and predefined variables that represent numeric values or numeric matrices.

- Symbolic commands and functions operate on symbolic variables and expressions that have no predefined numeric value.

- In MATLAB, the form `func arg` is equivalent to `func('arg')` in all cases except those that return a value. For example, the commands `colorbar vert` and `colorbar('vert')` are equivalent, and `cb=colorbar('vert')` will work, but `cb=colorbar vert` will result in an error.

- The `sym` function is used to explicitly define a symbolic variable or expression, or to convert a numeric expression into a symbolic expression with an optional format specification argument. The default format specification is `'r'`.

- The `syms` function may be used to define several symbolic expressions at once: `syms a b` or `syms('a','b')` is a shortcut for `a=sym('a'); b=sym('b');`.

- Remember, some symbolic constants may look like integers. The `class` function returns 'sym' if its argument is a symbolic expression.

- The `findsym` function may be used to find the symbolic variables in a symbolic expression, and the variable that will be used by MATLAB symbolic functions as the default independent variable.

- Most symbolic functions let you specify the independent variable in one or more of their forms.

20.7   Operations on Symbolic Expressions

Once you have created a symbolic expression, you will probably want to change it in some way. You may wish to extract part of an expression, combine two expressions, or find the numeric value of a symbolic expression. There are many symbolic tools that let you accomplish these tasks.

All symbolic functions (with a few specific exceptions discussed later) act on symbolic expressions and symbolic arrays, and return symbolic expressions or arrays. The result may sometimes look like a number, but it is a symbolic expression. As we discussed earlier, you can find out if what looks like a number is an integer, a character string, or a symbolic object by using the `class` function from *basic* MATLAB.

20.8 Extracting Numerators and Denominators

If your expression is a *rational polynomial* (a ratio of two polynomials), or can be expanded to a rational polynomial (including those with a denominator of 1), you can extract the numerator and denominator using numden. For example, given the expressions:

$$m = x^2 \qquad f = \frac{ax^2}{b - x} \qquad g = \frac{3}{2}x^2 + \frac{2}{3}x - \frac{3}{5} \qquad h = \frac{x^2 + 3}{2x - 1} + \frac{3x}{x - 1}$$

$$K = \begin{bmatrix} \dfrac{3}{2} & \dfrac{2x + 1}{3} \\ \dfrac{4}{x^2} & 3x + 4 \end{bmatrix}$$

numden combines and rationalizes the expression if necessary, and returns the resulting numerator and denominator. The MATLAB statements to do this are:

```
EDU» syms x a b  % create some symbolic variables

EDU» m=x^2       % create a simple expression
m =
    x^2

EDU» [n,d]=numden(m)  % extract the numerator and denominator
n =
    x^2
d =
    1

EDU» f=a*x^2/(b—x)  % create a rational expression
f =
    a*x^2/(b—x)

EDU» [n,d]=numden(f)  % extract the numerator and denominator
n =
    —a*x^2
d =
    —b+x
```

The first two expressions gave the expected result.

```
EDU» g=3/2*x^2+2*x—3/4  % create another expression
g =
    3/2*x^2+2*x—3/4

EDU» [n,d]=numden(g)  % rationalize and extract the parts
n =
    6*x^2+8*x—3
```

```
d =

     4

EDU» h=(x^2+3)/(2*x-1)+3*x/(x-1)   % the sum of rational polynomials
h =

     (x^2+3)/(2*x-1)+3*x/(x-1)

EDU» [n,d]=numden(h)  % rationalize and extract
n =

     x^3+5*x^2-3
d =

     (2*x-1)*(x-1)

EDU» h2=n/d               % recreate the expression for h
h2 =

     (x^2+3)/(2*x-1)+3*x/(x-1)
```

The two expressions for g and h were *rationalized*, or turned into a single expression with a numerator and denominator, before the parts were extracted. Dividing the numerator by the denominator recreates the original expression.

```
EDU» K=[3/2, (2*x+1)/3; 4/x^2, 3*x+4]  % try a symbolic matrix
K =

     [   3/2, 2/3*x+1/3]
     [ 4/x^2,     3*x+4]

EDU» [n,d]=numden(K)
n =

     [ 3,  2*x+1]
     [ 4,  3*x+4]
d =

     [   2, 3]
     [ x^2, 1]

EDU» K2=n./d             % recreate the matrix K
K2 =

     [   3/2, 2/3*x+1/3]
     [ 4/x^2,     3*x+4]
```

In this example, K is a symbolic matrix. numden returns two new arrays, n and d, where n is an array of the numerators and d is an array of the denominators. If you use the form s=numden(f), numden returns only the numerator into the variable s. The element-by-element form of the division operator (./) must be used to recreate the original matrix from the numerator and denominator.

20.9 Standard Algebraic Operations

A number of standard algebraic operations can be performed on symbolic expressions using familiar operators. For example, given two functions:

$$f = 2x^2 + 3x - 5 \qquad g = x^2 - x + 7$$

```
EDU» x=sym('x');                % define a symbolic variable

EDU» f=2*x^2+3*x−5              % define symbolic expressions f and g
f =
    2*x^2+3*x−5

EDU» g=x^2−x+7
g =
    x^2−x+7

EDU» f+g                        % find an expression for f + g
ans =
    3*x^2+2*x+2

EDU» f−g                        % find an expression for f − g
ans =
    x^2+4*x−12

EDU» f*g                        % find an expression for f * g
ans =
    (2*x^2+3*x−5)*(x^2−x+7)

EDU» f/g                        % find an expression for f / g
ans =
    (2*x^2+3*x−5)/(x^2−x+7)

EDU» f^(3*x)                    % find an expression for f³ˣ
ans =
    (2*x^2+3*x−5)^(3x)
```

The fact that an operation on any expression containing at least one symbolic variable will result in a symbolic expression lets you combine mixed expressions to create new symbolic expressions. For example:

```
EDU» a=1; b=3/2; x=sym('x');  % create some numeric and symbolic variables
EDU» f=sin(a−x)                % create some expressions
ans =
    −sin(x−1)
EDU» g=sin(b*x^2)
ans =
    sin(3/2*x^2)
```

```
EDU» b*f/(g-5)+x              % combine them
ans =
    -3/2*sin(x-1)/(sin(3/2*x^2)-5)+x
```

All of these operations work with array arguments, as well. They will be discussed again later in this tutorial.

20.10   Advanced Operations

MATLAB has the capability to perform more advanced operations on symbolic expressions. The compose function combines $f(x)$ and $g(x)$ into $f(g(x))$, the finverse function finds the functional inverse of an expression, and the symsum function finds the symbolic summation of an expression.

Given the expressions:

$$f = \frac{1}{1 + x^2} \qquad g = \sin(x) \qquad h = \frac{x}{1 + u^2} \qquad k = \cos(x + v)$$

```
EDU» syms x u v;        % define three symbolic variables
EDU» f=1/(1+x^2);       % create the four expressions
EDU» g=sin(x);
EDU» h=x/(1+u^2);
EDU» k=cos(x+v);

EDU» compose(f,g)       % find an expression for f(g(x))
ans =
    1/(1+sin(x)^2)

EDU» compose(g,f)       % find an expression for g(f(x))
ans =
    sin(1/(1+x^2))
```

compose may also be used on functions that have different independent variables:

```
EDU» compose(h,k)               % given h(x), k(x), find h(k(x))
ans =
    cos(x+v)/(1+u^2)

EDU» compose(h,k,u,v)           % given h(u), k(v), find h(k(v))
ans =
    x/(1+cos(2*v)^2)
```

The functional inverse of an expression, say $f(x)$, is the expression $g(x)$ that satisfies the condition $g(f(x)) = x$. For example, the functional inverse of e^x is $ln(x)$, since $ln(e^x) = x$. The functional inverse of $\sin(x)$ is $\arcsin(x)$, and the functional inverse of $1/\tan(x)$ is $\arctan(1/x)$. The finverse function returns a functional inverse of an expression. Note that finverse returns only one solution, even if that solution is not unique.

```
EDU» syms x a b c d z        % define some symbolic variables
EDU» finverse(1/x)           % the inverse of 1/x is 1/x since 1/(1/x)=x
ans =
    1/x

EDU» finverse(x^2)           % find one of the solutions to g(x^2)=x
ans =
    x^(1/2)

EDU» finverse(a*x+b)         % find the solution to g(f(x))=x
ans =
    -(b-x)/a

EDU» finverse(a*b+c*d-a*z, a)   % find solution to g(f(a))=a
ans =
    -(c*d-a)/(b-z)
```

The `symsum` function finds the symbolic summation of an expression. There are four forms of the function: `symsum(f)` returns $\sum_0^{x-1} f(x)$; `symsum(f,s)` returns $\sum_0^{s-1} f(s)$; `symsum(f,a,b)` returns $\sum_a^b f(x)$; and the most general form, `symsum(f,s,a,b)`, returns $\sum_a^b f(s)$.

Let us try $\sum_0^{x-1} x^2$, which should return $x^3/3 - x^2/2 + x/6$:

```
EDU» syms x n
EDU» symsum(x^2)
ans =
    1/3*x^3-1/2*x^2+1/6*x
```

How about $\sum_1^n (2n - 1)^2$, which should return $[n(2n - 1)(2n + 1)]/3)$:

```
EDU» symsum((2*n-1)^2,1,n)
ans =
    11/3*n+8/3-4*(n+1)^2+4/3*(n+1)^3

EDU» factor(ans)  % change the form (we will revisit 'factor' later on)
ans =
    1/3*n*(2*n-1)*(2*n+1)
```

Finally, let's try $\sum_1^\infty [1/(2n - 1)^2]$, which should return $(\pi^2/8)$:

```
EDU» symsum(1/(2*n-1)^2,1,inf)
ans =
    1/8*pi^2
```

20.11 Conversion Functions

This section presents tools to convert from symbolic expressions to numeric values, and back again. These are some of the very few symbolic functions that can return numeric values.

The `sym` function can convert a string or numeric argument into symbolic representation; the `double` function does the opposite. `double` converts a symbolic constant (a symbolic expression with no variables) into a double-precision numeric value.

```
EDU» phi=sym('(1+sqrt(5))/2')    % the 'golden' ratio
phi =
    (1+sqrt(5))/2

EDU» double(phi)                 % convert to a numeric value
ans =
    1.6180
```

Notice, in the previous example, that the argument is presented to `sym` as a string. If the argument is numeric, MATLAB evaluates the numeric argument before converting the result to a symbolic constant. A string argument is converted directly. This is what happens if the argument is numeric:

```
EDU» phi=sym((1+sqrt(5))/2)      % the 'golden' ratio
phi =
    7286977268806824*2^(−52)

EDU» double(phi)                 % convert to a numeric value
ans =
    1.6180
```

The two forms produce the same final result.

You have already worked with polynomials in *basic* MATLAB, using vectors whose elements are the coefficients of the polynomials. The symbolic function `sym2poly` converts a symbolic polynomial to its *basic* MATLAB equivalent coefficient vector. The function `poly2sym` does the reverse, and lets you specify the variable to use in the resulting expression.

```
EDU» x=sym('x');
EDU» f=x^3+2*x^2−3*x+5  % f is the symbolic polynomial
f =
    x^3+2*x^2−3*x+5

EDU» n=sym2poly(f)        % extract the numeric coefficient vector
n =
    1   2  −3   5
```

```
EDU» poly2sym(n)              % recreate the polynomial in x (the default)
ans =
    x^3+2*x^2-3*x+5

EDU» s=sym('s');              % define s as a symbolic variable
EDU» poly2sym(n,s)            % recreate the polynomial in s
ans =
    s^3+2*s^2-3*s+5
```

20.12   Variable Substitution

Suppose you have a symbolic expression in *x*, and you want to change the variable to *y*. MATLAB gives you a tool to make substitutions in symbolic expressions, called subs. The format is subs(f,old,new), where f is a symbolic expression, old is a symbolic variable or expression, and new is a symbolic variable, expression, or matrix, or a numeric value or matrix. The contents of new will replace each occurrence of old in the expression f. Here are some examples:

```
EDU» syms a alpha b c s x   % define some symbolic variables
EDU» f=a*x^2+b*x+c          % create a function f(x)
f =
    a*x^2+b*x+c

EDU» subs(f,x,s)            % replace x by s in the expression f
ans =
    a*s^2+b*s+c

EDU» subs(f,a,[alpha;s])    % replace a by a symbolic matrix
ans =
    [alpha*x^2+b*x+c]
    [    s*x^2+b*x+c]

EDU» g=3*x^2+5*x-4          % create another function
g =
    3*x^2+5*x-4

EDU» h=subs(g,x,2)          % new is a numeric value
h =
    18

EDU» class(h)              % show that the result is a symbolic constant
ans =
    sym
```

The previous example shows how subs makes the substitution, and then tries to simplify the expression. Since the result of the substitution is a symbolic constant, MATLAB can reduce it to a single symbolic value. Notice that since subs is a symbolic function, it returns a symbolic expression, actually a symbolic constant, even though it looks like a number. To get a number, we need to use the `double` function to convert the string.

```
EDU» double(h)    % convert a symbolic expression to a number
ans =
    18

EDU» class(ans)   % show that the result is a numeric value
ans =
    double
```

If the result of a symbolic operation is a complicated symbolic expression, `subexpr` can help make it readable. `subexpr` will parse a symbolic expression, replace repeated common sub-expressions with a variable (`sigma` by default), and place `sigma` in the workspace. For example:

```
EDU» syms a x
EDU» t=solve(a*x^3+b*x^2+c*x+d); % find roots of a cubic polynomial
EDU» t(2)                         % look at a single root
ans =
-1/12/a*(36*b*c*a-108*d*a^2-8*b^3+12*3^(1/2)
*(4*c^3*a-c^2*b^2-18*b*c*a*d+27*d^2*a^2+4*d*b^3)^(1/2)*a)^(1/3)
+1/3*(3*c*a-b^2)/a/(36*b*c*a-108*d*a^2-8*b^3+12*3^(1/2)
*(4*c^3*a-c^2*b^2-18*b*c*a*d+27*d^2*a^2+4*d*b^3)^(1/2)*a)^(1/3)
-1/3*b/a+1/2*i*3^(1/2)*(1/6/a*(36*b*c*a-108*d*a^2-
8*b^3+12*3^(1/2)
*(4*c^3*a-c^2*b^2-18*b*c*a*d+27*d^2*a^2+4*d*b^3)^(1/2)*a)^(1/3)
+2/3*(3*c*a-b^2)/a/(36*b*c*a-108*d*a^2-8*b^3+12*3^(1/2)
*(4*c^3*a-c^2*b^2-18*b*c*a*d+27*d^2*a^2+4*d*b^3)^(1/2)*a)^(1/3))
```

```
EDU» r=subexpr(t(2))    % find a simpler expression
        1/3                 2
      %1               3 c a - b
 - 1/12 ----- + 1/3 ----------- - 1/3 b/a
        a                1/3
                      a %1

                   /       1/3                2\
              1/2 |      %1             3 c a - b  |
    + 1/2 i 3     |1/6 ----- + 2/3 -----------|
                  |     a                1/3    |
                  \                   a %1      /
                       2      3
```

```
%1 := 36 b c a − 108 d a − 8 b
          1/2    3    2 2                        2 2       3 1/2
   + 12 3     (4 c a − c b  − 18 b c a d + 27 d a  + 4 d b ) a

sigma =

36*b*c*a−108*d*a^2−8*b^3+12*3^(1/2)
*(4*c^3*a−c^2*b^2−18*b*c*a*d+27*d^2*a^2+4*d*b^3)^(1/2)*a

r =

−1/12/a*sigma^(1/3)+1/3*(3*c*a−b^2)/a/sigma^(1/3)−1/3*b/a+1/2*i*
3^(1/2)
*(1/6/a*sigma^(1/3)+2/3*(3*c*a−b^2)/a/sigma^(1/3))
```

The variable %1 in the preceding expression corresponds to the subexpression sigma. The form [r,lambda]=subexpr(t(2)) will use the variable lambda rather than the default variable sigma to contain the subexpression.

20.13   Summary

- All symbolic functions return symbolic expressions, with the exception of those few functions (like sym2poly and double) that are intended to convert from symbolic notation to numeric values.

- The function numden extracts the numerator and denominator of a symbolic expression, and rationalizes the expression before extracting, if necessary. The usual form is [n,d]=numden(f). If f is an array, n and d will be arrays of numerators and denominators, respectively. The original expression can be recreated by dividing d into n using element-by-element division.

- Standard arithmetic operators (+ − * / ^) are used to combine and manipulate symbolic expressions. Numeric variables or constants may be used, as well.

- Given two symbolic expressions $f(x)$ and $g(x)$, the composite function $f(g(x))$ can be found by using compose(f,g). Functions of other variables use the compose(f,g,n), compose(f,g,u,v), or compose(f,g,u,v,w) forms.

- The functional inverse of a function $f(x)$ is defined as the function $g(x)$ such that $g(f(x)) = x$. The functional inverse can be found using finverse. The form finverse(f,n) is used to specify the independent variable.

- Symbolic summation can be performed using the symsum function. Given a function $f(n)$, symsum(f) finds an expression for $\sum_0^{n-1} f(n)$. The form symsum(f,a,b) finds an expression for $\sum_a^b f(n)$.

- The symbolic function sym2poly converts a symbolic polynomial to its *basic* MATLAB form, which is a row vector of its numeric coefficients in descending order. poly2sym will do the reverse, and let you choose the independent variable in the resulting expression.

- Variable substitution in symbolic expressions can be performed with the subs function. This tool substitutes one variable for each occurrence of a second variable within an expression, using the format subs(f,old,new).

- The appearance of some complicated symbolic expressions can be simplified using subexpr.

20.14 Differentiation

Differentiation of a symbolic expression uses the diff function in one of four forms:

```
EDU» syms a b c d x s    % define some symbolic variables
EDU» f=a*x^3+x^2-b*x-c   % define a symbolic expression
f =
    a*x^3+x^2-b*x-c

EDU» diff(f)  % differentiate f with respect
              % to the default variable x
ans =
    3*a*x^2+2*x-b

EDU» diff(f,a)  % differentiate f with respect to a
ans =
    x^3

EDU» diff(f,2)  % differentiate f twice with respect to x
ans =
    6*a*x+2

EDU» diff(f,a,2)  % differentiate f twice with respect to a
ans =
    0
```

The diff function also operates on arrays. If F is a symbolic vector or matrix, diff(F) differentiates each element in the array:

```
EDU» F=[a*x,b*x^2;c*x^3,d*s]  % create a symbolic array
F =
    [   a*x,  b*x^2]
    [ c*x^3,    d*s]

EDU» diff(F)  % differentiate the elements with respect to x
ans =
    [     a, 2*b*x]
    [ 3*c*x^2,    0]
```

Note that the diff function is also used in *basic* MATLAB to compute the numerical differences of a numeric vector or matrix. For a numeric vector or matrix M, diff(M) computes the numerical differences M(2:m,:)—M(1:m—1,:) as shown:

```
EDU» M=[(1:8).^2]  % create a vector
M =
     1    4    9   16   25   36   49   64
EDU» diff(M)  % find the differences between elements
ans =
     3    5    7    9   11   13   15
```

If the expression or variable argument to diff is numeric, MATLAB is smart enough to compute the numerical difference; if the argument is a symbolic expression or a variable, MATLAB differentiates the expression.

20.15 Integration

The integration function int(f), where f is a symbolic expression, attempts to find another symbolic expression F such that diff(F)=f. As you probably found in your study of calculus, integration is more complicated than differentiation. The integral or antiderivative may not exist in closed form; or, it may exist but the software can't find it; or, the software could find it eventually but runs out of memory or time. When MATLAB cannot find the antiderivative, it returns a warning and the symbolic representation of the integral that can be used with pretty.

```
EDU» x=sym('x');
EDU» p=int(log(x)/exp(x^2))  % attempt to integrate
   Warning: Explicit integral could not be found.
> In c:\matlab\toolbox\symbolic\@sym\int.m at line 58

p = int(....

EDU» pretty(p)
ans =
    output from pretty
```

The integration function, like differentiation, has more than one form. The form int(f) attempts to find an antiderivative with respect to the default independent variable. The form int(f,s) attempts to find an antiderivative with respect to the symbolic variable s. The forms int(f,a,b) and int(f,s,a,b), where a and b are numeric values, attempt to find symbolic expressions for the definite integral from a to b. The forms int(f,m,n) and int(f,s,m,n), where m and n are symbolic variables, attempt to find symbolic expressions for the definite integral from m to n.

```
EDU» syms x s m n  % define some variables

EDU» f=sin(s+2*x)  % create a symbolic function
```

```
f =
    sin(s+2*x)

EDU» int(f)  % integrate with respect to x
ans =
    -1/2*cos(s+2*x)

EDU» int(f,s)  % integrate with respect to s
ans =
    -cos(s+2*x)

EDU» int(f,pi/2,pi)  % integrate with respect to x from pi/2 to pi
ans =
    -cos(s)

EDU» int(f,s,pi/2,pi)  % integrate with respect to s from pi/2 to pi
ans =
    2*cos(x)^2-1-2*sin(x)*cos(x)

EDU» g=simple(int(f,m,n))   % integrate with respect to x from m to n
g =
    -1/2*cos(s+2*n)+1/2*cos(s+2*m)
```

In this example, the `simple` function was used to simplify the result of the integration. We'll learn more about `simple` later.

Like the `diff` function, the integration function `int` operates on each element of a symbolic array:

```
EDU» syms a b c d x s     % define some symbolic variables
EDU» f=[a*x,b*x^2;c*x^3,d*s]  % create a symbolic array
f =
    [    a*x,  b*x^2]
    [  c*x^3,    d*s]

EDU» int(f)  % integrate the array elements with respect to x
ans =
    [ 1/2*a*x^2, 1/3*b*x^3]
    [ 1/4*c*x^4,     d*s*x]
```

Example: Symbolic Solution of a Classic Calculus Problem

In this section, we will use the symbolic capabilities of MATLAB to find answers to a classic calculus problem.

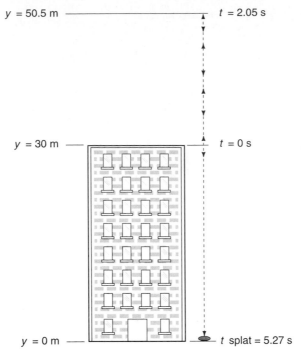

y = 50.5 m — t = 2.05 s

y = 30 m — t = 0 s

y = 0 m — t splat = 5.27 s

Figure 20.1

Fox Mulder, while on a stakeout on the roof of a tall building in Roswell, New Mexico, is eating his lunch when he spots a strange shape in the air at an altitude of about 50 meters. He takes a ripe tomato out of his lunch bag, leans over the edge of the roof, and hurls the tomato up into the air. The tomato is thrown straight up, with an initial speed of v_0 = 20 meters per second. The roof is y_0 = 30 meters above the ground. Where is the tomato some arbitrary t seconds later? When does it reach its maximum height? How high above the ground does the tomato rise? When does the tomato hit the ground? Assume that there is no air resistance and that the acceleration due to gravity is a constant a = −9.7536 feet per second.

Let's choose ground level to be zero height, i.e., y = 0 is the ground, and y = 30 is the top of the building. The velocity is $v = dy/dt$, and the acceleration is $a = d^2y/dt^2$. Therefore, if we integrate acceleration once, we get velocity; if we integrate velocity we get position or height y.

```
EDU» t=sym('t');      % define a symbolic variable t for time
EDU» digits(5);       % use 5 digits of accuracy
```

```
EDU» a=sym('-9.7536')  % acceleration in meters/second/second
a =
   -9.7536
EDU» v=int(a,t)   % find the velocity as a function of time
v =
   -9.7536*t
EDU» v=v+20        % at time t=0, the velocity is 20 meters/second
v =
   -9.7536*t+20
EDU» y=int(v,t)   % find the height y at time t by integration
y =
   -4.8768*t^2+20.*t
EDU» y=y+30        % the height at t=0 is 30 meters
y =
   -4.8768*t^2+20.*t+30
```

Let's check that the result is correct. If we replace t by 0 in the prior expression, we get:

```
EDU» y0=subs(y,t,0)  % the height at t=0 should be 30 meters
y0 =
   30
```

which is the correct height of the tomato before it is thrown.

We now have expressions for the velocity and position (height) as a function of time. The maximum height is reached when the tomato stops rising and starts downward. To find this point, we will find the value of t when $v = 0$ by using the solve function. This function finds a zero of a symbolic expression. In other words, solve(f), where f is a function of x, solves for x when $f(x) = 0$.

```
EDU» t_top=solve(v)   % Find the value of t when v(t)=0
t_top =
   2.0505
```

Since solve is a symbolic function, it returns a symbolic constant (even though it looks like a number). Now, we will find the maximum height, which occurs at $t = 2.0505$ seconds:

```
EDU» y_max=subs(y,t,t_top)   % substitute t_top for t in y
y_max =
   50.505
```

Notice that the subs function does the same thing we did before, when we checked the expression for y. subs substitutes the symbolic value 2.0505 for each t in the expression, simplifies if it can, and returns the resulting expression.

Now, find the time when the tomato hits the ground

```
EDU» t_splat=solve(y)   % the tomato hits the ground when y=0
t_splat =
    [ −1.1676]
    [  5.2686]
```

Since the first result is negative and the tomato cannot hit the ground before it is thrown, the second solution is the only meaningful solution. Thus, the height of the tomato at t seconds is given by $y = -9.7536t^2+20t+30$, the tomato rises to a maximum height of 50.505 meters above the ground at time $t = 2.0505$ seconds, and the tomato hits the ground at $t = 5.2686$ seconds.

Let's introduce another factor into this problem.

Dana Scully, who is on her way to join Mulder, is walking down the street. If the falling tomato hits Scully, who happens to be directly beneath it when it arrives, and Scully is 1.7 meters tall, when will the tomato hit her on the head?

For this, we need to find the time t at $y = 1.7$. This can be done as follows:

```
EDU» y_bonk=y−sym('1.7')   % create a symbolic expression for
                           % y=1.7 or y−1.7=0
y_bonk =
    −4.8768*t^2+20.*t+28.3
EDU» t_bonk=solve(y_bonk)  % find the time t when y=1.7
t_bonk =
    [ −1.1130]
    [  5.2140]
```

Again, Scully cannot be hit before the tomato is thrown, so the only meaningful solution is $t = 5.2140$ seconds.

This example raises some interesting points about using the Symbolic Math Toolbox to solve problems. First, whenever a floating-point constant is used in a symbolic expression, it should be defined using sym. As you may have noticed in the previous example, acceleration was defined as a symbolic value:

```
EDU» a=sym('−9.7536')
or
sym(−97536,'d')
a =
    −9.7536
EDU» v=int(a,t)
v =
    −9.7536*t
```

rather than a numeric value:

```
EDU» a=−9.7536
a =
     −9.7536
EDU» v=int(a,t)
v =
     −6096/625*t
```

In the former case, `int` was given symbolic arguments, and it preserved their forms. In the latter case, `int` was given a numeric value that was automatically converted to a symbolic value using the default `sym(num,'r')` conversion format.

The second point raised in this example is the use of the `digits` function. Symbolic functions do their calculations out to 32 digits by default. This example reduced the accuracy to five digits to make the results more readable and because the input data was accurate only to five digits anyway. Now that this problem has been solved, the default accuracy should be restored by:

```
EDU» digits(32)  % return to the default accuracy
```

Remember that the `solve` function solves a symbolic expression in one variable by setting the expression equal to zero and solving it for the free variable. This implies that an expression like $3x^2 + 2x + 1 = 5x + 12$ can be solved for x with a little rearranging:

```
EDU» x=sym('x');
EDU» g=solve((3*x^2+2*x+1)−(5*x+12))  % solve an expression with 2 roots
g =
     [ 1/2+1/6*141^(1/2)]
     [ 1/2−1/6*141^(1/2)]
EDU» double(g)  % convert to numeric values
ans =
      2.4791
     −1.4791
```

We'll learn more about both `solve` and `digits` later in this tutorial.

20.16 Summary

- Use the `diff` function to differentiate a symbolic expression or the elements of a symbolic array. The symbolic variable to use and the number of differentiations to perform, can be specified.

- If the expression or variable argument to `diff` is numeric, it computes the numerical difference; if the argument is a symbolic expression or variable, it differentiates the expression.

- The `int` function is used to integrate a symbolic expression or the elements of a symbolic array. Optional arguments can be used to specify the symbolic variable and the limits of a definite integral.
- Symbolic solutions of algebraic expressions are generated by the `solve` function. For one expression in one unknown, `solve(f)` solves the symbolic equation $f = 0$, for its default variable as determined by `findsym`. Other forms of `solve` will be discussed later.

20.17   Plotting Symbolic Expressions

To get a better idea of what happened to the tomato, let's plot the result of the tomato toss. Recall that the tomato position (or height) was described by the expression $y = (-4.8768)*t^2 + 20*t + 30$.

```
EDU» ezplot(y)   % plot the height of the tomato
```

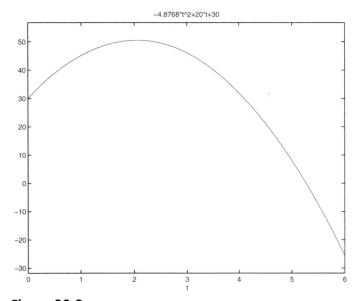

Figure 20.2

As you can see, `ezplot` graphs the given symbolic function over the domain $-2\pi \le t \le 2\pi$ and scales the y-axis accordingly. It also adds grids and labels. In this case, we are interested only in times between 0 and 6. Let's try again and specify the time range:

```
EDU» ezplot(y,[0 6])   % plot y for 0<t<6
```

Symbolic Math Toolbox   Chapter 20

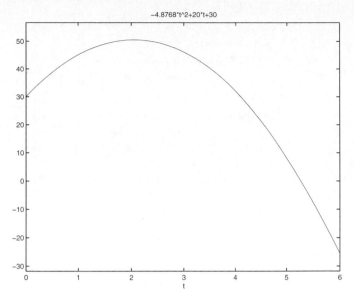

Figure 20.3

Now the region of interest shows up a little better, but part of the plot is still below ground. The plot could be fixed by changing the time range and reissuing the `ezplot` command, e.g., `ezplot(y,[0 5.1623])`, but you have more control with some other MATLAB plotting commands. Once the plot is in the *Figure* window, it can be modified like any other plot. Let's scale both axes of the current plot and change the title and labels:

```
EDU» axis([0 5.5 0 55])  % scale to show the region of interest
EDU» title('Plot of Tomato Height vs. Time')  % change the title
EDU» ylabel('Height in Meters')
EDU» xlabel('Time in Seconds')
```

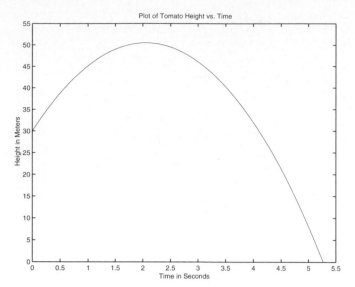

Figure 20.4

The other MATLAB plotting commands are also available to customize your plots. For example, the command `zoom on` will let you use the mouse to zoom in on any desired area of a two-dimensional plot, such as the one we just generated. For more information, type `help zoom`. Other MATLAB commands to add text, identify specific points, and change scaling are also available.

20.18   Formatting and Simplifying Expressions

Sometimes MATLAB will return a symbolic expression that is too complicated to read easily. A number of tools are available to help make the expression more readable. The first is the `pretty` function. This command attempts to display a symbolic expression in a form that resembles typeset mathematics. Let's look at a Taylor series expansion:

```
EDU» x=sym('x');
EDU» f=taylor(log(x+1)/(x-5))
f =
-1/5*x+3/50*x^2-41/750*x^3+293/7500*x^4-1207/37500*x^5

EDU» pretty(f)
                     2     41   3      293   4      1207   5
   -  1/5  x  + 3/50 x   - ---  x  + ----  x  -  -----  x
                          750        7500        37500
```

Symbolic expressions can be presented in many equivalent forms. Some forms may be preferable to others in different situations. MATLAB uses a number of commands to simplify or change the form of symbolic expressions.

```
EDU» x=sym('x');
EDU» f=(x^2−1)*(x−2)*(x−3)   % create a function
f =
     (x^2−1)*(x−2)*(x−3)

EDU» collect(f)   % collect all like terms
ans =
     x^4−5*x^3+5*x^2+5*x−6

EDU» horner(ans)   % change to Horner or nested representation
ans =
     −6+(5+(5+(x−5)*x)*x)*x

EDU» factor(ans)   % express as a product of polynomials
ans =
     (x−1)*(x−2)*(x−3)*(x+1)

EDU» expand(f)   % distribute products over sums
ans =
     x^4−5*x^3+5*x^2+5*x−6
```

simplify is a powerful, general-purpose tool that attempts to simplify an expression by the application of many different kinds of algebraic identities involving sums; integral and fractional powers; trig, exponential, and log functions; and Bessel, hypergeometric, and gamma functions. A few examples will reveal the power of this function:

```
EDU» syms x y a

EDU» simplify(log(2*x/y))
ans =
     log(2)+log(x/y)

EDU» simplify(sin(x)^2+3*x+cos(x)^2−5)
ans =
     −4+3*x

EDU» simplify((−a^2+1)/(1−a))
ans =
     a+1
```

The last function to be discussed here is one of the most powerful, but the least orthodox, of all the simplification tools. The function simple tries several different simplification tools (including some symbolic math tools not available directly), and then selects the form that has the fewest number of *characters* in the resulting symbolic expression. Let's try a cube root:

$$f = \sqrt[3]{\frac{1}{x^3} + \frac{6}{x^2} + \frac{12}{x} + 8}$$

```
EDU» x=sym('x');

EDU» f=(1/x^3+6/x^2+12/x+8)^(1/3)  % create the expression
f =
    (1/x^3+6/x^2+12/x+8)^(1/3)

EDU» g=simple(f)  % simplify it
g =
    (2*x+1)/x

EDU» g=simple(g)  % try it once again — another method may help
g =
    2+1/x
```

simple tries a number of simplification techniques that may help reduce the expression, and returns the shortest answer. Sometimes it helps to apply simple more than once to try a different simplification technique on the result of the first, as it did above. simple is especially useful for expressions containing trig functions. Let's try one:

$$\cos(x) + \sqrt{-\sin(x)^2}$$

This time, however, we will not assign the output to a variable so that we can see the intermediate steps:

```
EDU» simple(cos(x)+sqrt(−sin(x)^2)) % simplify a trig expression
simplify:
    cos(x)+(−sin(x)^2)^(1/2)
radsimp:
    cos(x)+i*sin(x)
combine(trig):
    cos(x)+1/2*(−2+2*cos(2*x))^(1/2)
factor:
    cos(x)+(−sin(x)^2)^(1/2)
expand:
    cos(x)+(−sin(x)^2)^(1/2)
convert(exp):
    1/2*exp(i*x)+1/2/exp(i*x)+1/2*((exp(i*x)−1/exp(i*x))^2)
    ^(1/2)
convert(sincos):
    cos(x)+(−sin(x)^2)^(1/2)
convert(tan):
(1−tan(1/2*x)^2)/(1+tan(1/2*x)^2)+(−4*tan(1/2*x)^2/(1+tan(1/2*x)
^2)^2)^(1/2)
collect(x):
    cos(x)+(−sin(x)^2)^(1/2)
```

```
ans =
    cos(x)+i*sin(x)
EDU» g=simple(ans)  % one more time for luck...
ans =
    exp(i*x)
```

20.19   Summary and Other Features

- A complex symbolic expression in MATLAB syntax can be presented in a form that may be easier to read by using the `pretty` function.
- There may be many equivalent forms of a symbolic expression, some of which are more useful than others in different situations. MATLAB gives you many tools to change the form of these expressions. Among these tools are:

Tool	Description
collect	Collect like terms
horner	Change to Horner or nested representation
factor	Attempt to factor the expression
expand	Expand all terms
simplify	Simplify the expression using identities
simple	Attempt to find the equivalent expression yielding the shortest character string

- It is sometimes useful to apply `simple` more than once; the result of the first try may, in itself, be a candidate for further simplification.
- MATLAB symbolic functions may be used to convert a symbolic expression to its partial fraction representation. Given a rational polynomial f, `int(f)` will integrate the function, and will usually separate terms. Then `diff(ans)` will differentiate each term to produce the original expression f in a sum-of-terms form that is the partial fraction representation of f. For example:

```
EDU» s=sym('s');
EDU» Y=(10*s^2+40*s+30)/(s^2+6*s+8)
Y =
    (10*s^2+40*s+30)/(s^2+6*s+8)

EDU» diff(int(Y))  % find the partial fraction representation of Y
ans =
    10-15/(s+4)-5/(s+2)
```

```
EDU» pretty(ans)
```

$$10 - \frac{15}{s + 4} - \frac{5}{s + 2}$$

This technique is also useful for reducing a rational polynomial where the numerator is of a higher order than the denominator:

```
EDU» x=sym('x');
EDU» g=(x^3+5)/(x^2−1)
g =
    (x^3+5)/(x^2−1)

EDU» diff(int(g))  %
ans =
    x+3/(x−1)−2/(x+1)

EDU» pretty(ans)
```

$$x + \frac{3}{x - 1} - \frac{2}{x + 1}$$

It is left as an exercise for you to create a function M-file, called `pfd.m`, that will return the partial fraction representation of an expression argument.

- Another tool that may be useful, if you use the LaTeX program for word processing or publishing, is `latex`. This function returns the LaTeX code required to recreate the expression you supply, and can even save the LaTeX code to a file. See on-line help for more information.

20.20 Variable Precision Arithmetic

Round-off error may be introduced in any operation on numeric values, since numeric precision is limited by the number of digits preserved by each numeric operation. Repeated or multiple numeric operations can, therefore, accumulate error. Operations on symbolic expressions, however, are highly accurate, since they do not perform numeric computations and there is no round-off error. Using `double` on the result of a symbolic operation can introduce round-off error only in the converted result.

Basic MATLAB relies exclusively on the computer's floating-point arithmetic for number crunching. Although fast and easy on the computer's memory, floating-point operations are limited by the number of digits supported, and they can introduce round-off error in each operation; they cannot produce exact results. The relative accuracy of individual arithmetic operations in MATLAB is about 16 digits. The symbolic functions, on the other hand, can carry out operations to any arbitrary number of digits. As the default number of digits is increased, however, more time and computer storage are required for each computation.

The *Symbolic Math Toolbox* functions default to 32 digits of accuracy unless told otherwise. The function `digits` returns the current value of the global `Digits` parameter. The default number of digits of accuracy for symbolic functions can be changed using `digits(n)`, where n is the number of digits of accuracy desired. The downside of increasing accuracy this way is that every symbolic function will subsequently carry out computations to the new accuracy, increasing computation time. The display of results will not change; only the default accuracy of the underlying symbolic functions will be affected.

Another function is available, however, that will let you perform a single computation to any arbitrary accuracy while leaving the global `Digits` parameter unchanged. The variable precision arithmetic function, or `vpa`, evaluates a single symbolic expression or character string to the default or to any specified accuracy, and displays a symbolic result to the same accuracy:

```
EDU» format long  % let's see all the usual digits

EDU» pi  % how about pi to numeric accuracy
ans =
    3.14159265358979

EDU» digits  % display the default 'Digits' value
Digits = 32

EDU» vpa(pi)  % how about pi to 'Digits' accuracy
ans =
    3.1415926535897932384626433832795

EDU» digits(50)  % change the default to 50 digits

EDU» vpa(pi)  % evaluate pi to 'Digits' digits
ans =
    3.1415926535897932384626433832795028841971693993751

EDU» digits(32)  % restore the default

EDU» vpa(pi,639)  % pi to 639 digits
ans =

3.141592653589793238462643383279502884197169399375105820974944592
3078164062862089986280348253421170679821480865132823066470938446
0955058223172535940812848111745028410270193852110555964462294895
4930381964428810975665933446128475648233786783165271201909145648
5669234603486104543266482133936072602491412737245870066063155881
7488152092096282925409171536436789259036001133053054882046652138
4146951941511609433057270365759591953092186117381932611793105118
5480744623799627495673518857527248912279381830119491298336733624
4065664308602139494639522473719070217986094370277053921717629317
6752384674818467669405132000568127145263560827785771342757789609
```

The vpa function applied to a symbolic matrix evaluates each element to the number of digits specified as well:

```
EDU» A=[sym('1/4'),sym('sqrt(2)');sym('exp(1)'),sym('3/7')]
A =
    [    1/4, sqrt(2)]
    [ exp(1),     3/7]
EDU» vpa(A,20)  % evaluate to 20 digits
ans =
    [ .25000000000000000000, -1.4142135623730950488]
    [ 2.7182818284590452354,  .42857142857142857143]
```

20.21 Things to Try on Your Own

Find the value of $e^{\pi\sqrt{163}}$ to 18, 29, 30, and 31 digits. Notice that the result is close to an integer value, but is not exactly an integer.

```
EDU» vpa('exp(pi*sqrt(163))',18)
```

Use the hilb(3) function to display the 3-by-3 Hilbert matrix to 20 digits of accuracy.

```
EDU» vpa(hilb(3),20)
```

20.22 Summary

- The accuracy of any numeric calculation is limited by the number of digits of precision used by your computer and software. If a calculation has intermediate steps, each step has the potential for introducing round-off error.

- MATLAB symbolic operations can be carried out to any desired accuracy. The global Digits parameter, normally set at 32, can be changed to any value; however, increasing it will trade off time and resources for additional accuracy.

- The vpa function evaluates a symbolic expression to any desired accuracy without affecting any other operation. The format is vpa('expression'), which uses the Digits parameter, or vpa('expression',d) to specify the number of digits desired.

- If you remember that func arg and func('arg') mean the same thing, and that all symbolic functions return symbolic expressions, you may not be surprised to learn that the forms vpa pi/2 23 and vpa('pi/2','23') both return an expression for $\pi/2$ to 23 digits of accuracy.

- The vpa function applied to a symbolic array acts upon each element of the array.

20.23 Solving Equations

Symbolic equations can be solved using symbolic tools available in MATLAB. Some of them have been introduced earlier; more will be examined in the next section.

20.24 Solving a Single Algebraic Equation

We saw earlier in the tutorial that MATLAB contains tools for solving symbolic expressions. The `solve` function sets the symbolic expression equal to zero before solving it:

```
EDU» syms a b c x
EDU» solve(a*x^2+b*x+c)  % solve for the roots of the quadratic equation
x =
    [ 1/2/a*(−b+(b^2−4*a*c)^(1/2)]
    [ 1/2/a*(−b−(b^2−4*a*c)^(1/2)]
```

The result is a symbolic vector whose elements are the two solutions. To solve an equation containing an equal sign (=), solve a string containing the expression:

```
EDU» solve('a*x^2+b*x=(−c)')  % solve a symbolic equation
x =
    [ 1/2/a*(−b+(b^2−4*a*c)^(1/2)]
    [ 1/2/a*(−b−(b^2−4*a*c)^(1/2)]
```

If you wish to solve for something other than the default variable x, `solve` will let you specify it:

```
EDU» solve(a*x^2+b*x+c,b)  % solve for b
b =
    −(a*x^2+c)/x
```

Equations may be solved by setting them equal to zero. Here, we solve $\cos(x) = \sin(x)$ and $\tan(x) = \sin(2x)$ for x, and capture the result in the variables f and t:

```
EDU» f=solve(cos(x)−sin(x))  % solve for x
f =
    1/4*pi
EDU» t=solve(tan(x)−sin(2*x))
t =
    [        0]
    [       pi]
    [   1/4*pi]
    [  −3/4*pi]
```

and numeric solutions found:

```
EDU» double(f)
ans =
    0.7854

EDU» double(t)
ans =
          0
     3.1416
     0.7854
    -2.3562
```

Notice that when solving equations of periodic functions, there are an infinite number of solutions. solve restricts its search for solutions in these cases to a limited range near zero, and returns a non-unique subset of solutions.

```
EDU» solve(sin(x)-cos(x))
ans =
    1/4*pi
```

If a symbolic solution cannot be found, a variable precision one will be computed, if possible:

```
EDU» solve(cos(x)-sin(x^2))
x =
    2.3467493099980692005782210464841
```

Otherwise, an empty matrix will be returned.

An alternate syntax is available for solving expressions without defining symbolic objects. If the arguments to solve are character strings, MATLAB will solve the expression and return the result without creating any new symbolic variables. Notice that the expression to be solved **can** include an equals sign using this syntax.

```
EDU» clear
EDU» solve('z*sin(x)=3*y','y')     % solve for y
ans =
    1/3*z*sin(x)

EDU» who

Your variables are:

    ans
```

20.25 Several Algebraic Equations

Several algebraic equations may be solved at the same time. A statement of the form [a1,a2,...,aN]=solve(f1,f2,...,fN) solves N equations for the default variables and returns the results in a1...aN. Note, however, that the default variables will be sorted and returned in lexicographic order. For example:

```
EDU» syms x y
EDU» [a1 a2]=solve(x^2+x*y+y−3, x^2−4*x+3)
X =        [XY] =
    [ 1]
    [ 3]
Y =
    [   1]
    [ −3/2]
```

In this example, the default variables are X and Y. Since the solutions for the default variables are sorted before being returned, X represents the solutions for X and Y represents the solutions for Y.

A statement of the form [a1,a2,...aN]=solve(f1,f2,...,fN,v1,v2, ...,vN]) solves the N equations for the N unknowns specified by v1...vN, and places the (sorted) solutions in aN. The form S=solve(f1,f2,f3,...,fN) or S=solve(f1,f2,...,fN,v1,v2,...,vN]) returns the solutions in the structure S whose named fields hold the solutions for each variable.

```
EDU» S=solve(x^2+x*y+y−3, x^2−4*x+3)
S =
    x: [ 2x1 sym ]
    y: [ 2x1 sym ]

EDU» S.x
ans =
    [ 1]
    [ 3]

EDU» S.y
ans =
    [    1]
    [ −3/2]
```

You can access these symbolic values using the standard structure syntax discussed in Chapter 19.

If an analytic solution cannot be found, solve returns a variable precision solution.

```
EDU» S=solve(sin(x+y)−exp(x)*y, x^2−y−2)
S =
    x: [ 1x1 sym ]
    y: [ 1x1 sym ]
EDU» S.x
ans =
    1.4909277316389787589318613366183
EDU» S.y
ans =
    .22286550097015066383124586678807
```

Example: Solving a Symbolic Equation

The implicit function $(x - 3)^2 + (y - 2)^2 = 5^2$ is the standard form for the equation of a circle of radius 5 with origin at (3, 2). Solve the expression for y in terms of x.

```
EDU» syms x y
EDU» f=(x−3)^2+(y−2)^2−5^2  % create the function f=0
f =
    (x−3)^2+(y−2)^2−25
EDU» y=solve(f,y)  % solve f=0 for y
y =
    [ 2+(16−x^2+6*x)^(1/2)]
    [ 2−(16−x^2+6*x)^(1/2)]
```

There are two functions for y. The solutions are: $y = 2 \pm \sqrt{16 - x^2 + 6x}$.

Example: Symbolic Solutions to a System of Linear Equations

In this example, we will solve a system of linear equations with four equations in four unknowns. Given the following equations, solve for d, n, p, and q.

$$d + \frac{n}{2} + \frac{p}{2} = q \qquad n + d + q - p = 10 \qquad q + d - \frac{n}{4} = p \qquad q + p - n - 8d = 1$$

```
EDU» syms d n p q
EDU» eq1=d+n/2+p/2−q;
EDU» eq2=n+d+q−p−10;
EDU» eq3=q+d−n/4−p;
EDU» eq4=q+p−n−8*d−1);
EDU» S=solve(eq1,eq2,eq3,eq4)
S =
    d: [ 1x1 sym ]
    n: [ 1x1 sym ]
    p: [ 1x1 sym ]
    q: [ 1x1 sym ]
```

```
EDU» S.d
ans =
    3
EDU» S.n
ans =
    8
EDU» S.p
ans =
   16
EDU» S.q
ans =
   15
```

When there are more equations than unknowns, the *overdetermined* case, MATLAB will let you know about it and continue to generate the correct solutions.

```
EDU» eq5=2*n−q+5*d−p;
EDU» S=solve(eq1,eq2,eq3,eq4,eq5)
Warning: 5 equations in 4 variables.
S =
    d: [1x1 sym]
    n: [1x1 sym]
    p: [1x1 sym]
    q: [1x1 sym]
```

In the *underdetermined* case, where there are fewer equations than unknowns, Matlab will consider the first variable alphabetically to be a parameter and return symbolic expressions that include this variable.

```
EDU» S=solve(eq1,eq2,eq3) % solve in terms of d
S =
    n: [1x1 sym]
    p: [1x1 sym]
    q: [1x1 sym]
EDU» S.n
ans =
    8
EDU» S.p
ans =
    4*d+4
EDU» S.q
ans =
    3*d+6
```

20.26 Single Differential Equation

Ordinary differential equations are sometimes difficult to solve. MATLAB gives you a powerful tool to help you find solutions to differential equations.

The function `dsolve` computes symbolic solutions to ordinary differential equations. The syntax of `dsolve` is somewhat different than most other functions. Arguments to `dsolve` **must** be character strings representing equations, i.e., strings containing an equal sign (=). This is clearly different from the syntax of the `solve` function, whose arguments must be symbolic expressions without an equal sign.

Since we are working with differential equations, we also need a way to include differentials in an expression. The equations are specified by using the capital letter D to denote differentiation, and D2, D3, and so on, to denote repeated differentiation. Any letters following Ds are dependent variables. The equation $(d^2y/dt^2) = 0$ is represented by the character string 'D2y=0'. The independent variable may be specified, or will otherwise default to t. For example, the general solution to the first-order equation $(dy,dt) = 1 + y^2$ can be found by:

```
EDU» clear                % clear the workspace
EDU» dsolve('Dy=1+y^2')   % find the general solution
ans =
    tan(t-C1)
```

where C1 is a constant of integration. Solving the same equation with the initial condition $y(0) = 1$ will produce:

```
EDU» dsolve('Dy=1+y^2, y(0)=1')  % add an initial condition
ans =
    tan(t+1/4*pi)
```

The independent variable can be specified using this form:

```
EDU» dsolve('Dy=1+y^2, y(0)=1', 'x')  % find solution to dy/dx
ans =
    tan(x+1/4*pi)
```

Let's try a second-order differential equation with two initial conditions:

$$\frac{d^2y}{dt^2} = \cos(2t) - y \qquad \frac{dy}{dt}(0) = 0 \qquad y(0) = 1$$

```
EDU» y=dsolve('D2y=cos(2*t)-y, Dy(0)=0, y(0)=1')
y =
    -2/3*cos(t)^2+1/3+4/3*cos(t)

EDU» y=simple(ans)   % y looks like it can be simplified
y =
    -1/3*cos(2*t)+4/3*cos(t)
```

Notice that the string arguments given to dsolve (the differential equation to be solved and the initial conditions, if any) can be given as a single-character string with the elements separated by commas (,) as just shown, or by comma-separated character strings as shown in the following, or any combination.

Often, a differential equation to be solved contains terms of more than one order, and is presented in the following form:

$$\frac{d^2y}{dt^2} - 2\frac{dy}{dt} - 3y = 0$$

The general solution is:

```
EDU» y=dsolve('D2y-2*Dy-3*y=0')
y =
    C1*exp(3*t)+C2*exp(-t)
```

Applying the initial conditions $y(0) = 0$ and $y(1) = 1$ gives:

```
EDU» y=dsolve('D2y-2*Dy-3*y=0','y(0)=0', 'y(1)=1')
y =
    (-1/(-exp(3)+exp(-1))*(exp(3*t)*exp(t)+1/(-exp(3)+exp(-1)))/
    exp(t)

EDU» y=simple(y)   % this looks like a candidate for simplification
y =
    exp(-3+3*t)*(-1+exp(-4*t))/(-1+exp(-4))

EDU» pretty(y)   % pretty it up

           exp(-3 + 3 t) (-1 +exp(-4 t))
           ------------------------------
                  -1 + exp(-4)
```

Now, plot the result in an interesting region:

```
EDU» ezplot(y,[-6 2])
```

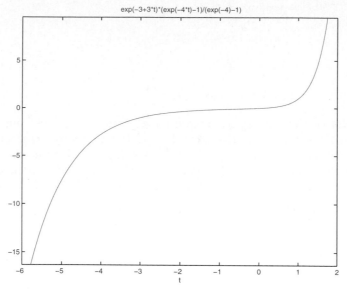

Figure 20.5

20.27   Several Differential Equations

The function `dsolve` can also handle several differential equations at once. When solving multiple differential equations, `dsolve` returns values into a structure or vector in the same way that `solve` does. Note that, like `solve`, `dsolve` sorts the independent variables before returning them; the first output variable will be assigned the solution to the independent variable that is nearest to the beginning of the alphabet.

Here is a pair of linear, first-order equations:

$$\frac{df}{dt} = 3f + 4g \qquad \frac{dg}{dt} = -4f + 3g$$

The general solutions are:

```
EDU» [f,g]=dsolve('Df=3*f+4*g, Dg=−4*f+3*g')
f =
    exp(3*t)*cos(4*t)*C1+exp(3*t)*sin(4*t)*C2
g =
    −exp(3*t)*sin(4*t)*C1+exp(3*t)*cos(4*t)*C2
```

Adding initial conditions $f(0) = 0$ and $g(0) = 1$, we get:

```
EDU» S=dsolve('Df=3*f+4*g, Dg=−4*f+3*g, f(0)=0, g(0)=1')
```

```
S =
    f: [1x1 sym]
    g: [1x1 sym]
EDU» S.f
f =
    exp(3*t)*sin(4*t)
EDU» S.g
g =
    exp(3*t)*cos(4*t)
```

Example: Symbolic Solution of a Second-Order Differential Equation

Solve the initial value problem:

$$x^2 \frac{d^2y}{dx^2} + 7x\frac{dy}{dx} + 5y = 10 - \left(\frac{4}{x}\right) \qquad y(1) = 1, \qquad \frac{dy}{dx}(1) = 0.$$

```
EDU» y=dsolve('x^2*D2y+7*x*Dy+5*y=10-4/x, y(1)=1, Dy(1)=0','x')
y =
    1/4*(8*x^5-4*x^4*log(x)-4*x^4)/x^5
EDU» y=simple(y)
ans =
    2+(-log(x)-1)/x
```

20.28   Summary and Other Features

- The `solve` function generates symbolic solutions to algebraic equations. For one expression in one unknown, `solve(f)` solves the symbolic equation `f=0` for its default variable as determined by `findsym`. The form `solve(f,v)` solves the symbolic equation `f` for the symbolic variable `v`.

- A symbolic equation (containing an equal sign) may be solved by enclosing the equation in single quotes. The `solve` function generates the solution(s) without creating additional symbolic variables in the workspace.

- Several symbolic expressions can be solved simultaneously. The form `solve(f1,f2,...,fn)` solves the n symbolic expressions for the default independent variables. The form `solve(f1,f2,...,fn,v1,v2,..., vn])` solves the system of symbolic equations for the variables v1..vn.

- Sometimes MATLAB cannot find a symbolic or numeric solution, and it will return an empty symbolic variable. Note that an empty `sym` may be created by using `sym([])`.

```
EDU» x=sym('x');
EDU» q=solve(x^5+x^4+2)      % solve an expression in x
```

```
q =
    [empty sym]
```

- The `dsolve` function computes symbolic solutions to ordinary differential equations, with or without initial conditions. Arguments to `dsolve` must be character strings representing equations and containing equal signs. MATLAB uses the convention that D represents

$$\frac{d}{dt}$$

  D2 represents

$$\frac{d^2}{dt^2}$$

  and D2y represents

$$\frac{d^2y}{dt^2}$$

  The solution will contain constants of integration C1..Cn when initial conditions are not specified.

- Several differential equations may be solved simultaneously. The form is `dsolve('F,G')` or `dsolve('F,G,k1,k2')`, where F and G are a pair of differential equations, and k1 and k2 are initial conditions. As before, initial conditions are not required for general solutions containing constants of integration.

- The `dsolve` function uses t as the default independent variable if none is specified. When t is a dependent variable, you **must** specify an independent variable, or MATLAB will return an error. For example,

```
EDU» dsolve('Dt=1+t^2')  % t is a dependent variable
??? Error using ==> dsolve
Error, (in dsolve/diffeq) not a differential equation in
specified variables
```

20.29   Linear Algebra and Matrices

Linear algebra is the study and application of the properties of matrices and vectors. In this section, we present an introduction to symbolic matrices and the tools MATLAB supplies for solving problems using linear algebra.

Symbolic matrices and vectors are arrays whose elements are symbolic expressions. They can be generated with the `sym` function:

```
EDU» syms a b c s t   % define some symbolic variables
EDU» A=[a,b,c;b,c,a;c,a,b]
```

```
A =
    [ a, b, c]
    [ b, c, a]
    [ c, a, b]
EDU» G=[cos(t),sin(t);-sin(t),cos(t)]
G =
    [  cos(t), sin(t)]
    [ -sin(t), cos(t)]
```

The `sym` function can also convert a numeric matrix to its symbolic form:

```
EDU» M=[1.1,1.2,1.3;2.1,2.2,2.3;3.1,3.2,3.3]  % a numeric matrix
M =
    1.1000   1.2000   1.3000
    2.1000   2.2000   2.3000
    3.1000   3.2000   3.3000

EDU» S=sym(M)   % convert to symbolic form using default format
S =
    [ 11/10,  6/5, 13/10]
    [ 21/10, 11/5, 23/10]
    [ 31/10, 16/5, 33/10]
```

If the elements of the numeric matrix can be specified as the ratio of small integers, the `sym` function will use the rational (fractional) representation. If the elements are irrational, `sym` will represent the elements as floating-point numbers in symbolic form:

```
EDU» E=[exp(1) 2^(1/3)]
E =
    2.7183     1.2599

EDU» sym(E)
ans =
    [ 6121026514868073*2^(-51), 5674179970822795*2^(-52)]

EDU» double(ans)
ans =
    2.7183     1.2599
```

The size (number of rows and columns) of a symbolic matrix can be found using the standard functions `size` and `length`, which return a numeric value or vector, not a symbolic expression. `size` and `length` are illustrated as follows.

```
EDU» syms a b c d e f       % define some variables
EDU» S=[a,b,c;d,e,f]        % create a symbolic matrix
S =
    [ a, b, c]
    [ d, e, f]
```

```
EDU» h=size(S)          % returns the size of S as the 2-element vector h
h =
    2    3
EDU» [m,n]=size(S)      % return the number of rows in m, and columns in n
m =
    2
n =
    3
EDU» length(S)          % return the largest dimension of S
ans =
    3
```

Symbolic-array elements are accessed in the same way as numeric-array elements.

```
EDU» syms ab cd ef gh
EDU» G=[ab,cd;ef,gh]      % create a 2x2 symbolic matrix
G =
    [ ab, cd]
    [ ef, gh]

EDU» G(1,2)               % access the element in row 1, column 2
G =
    cd

EDU» G(2,2)=sym('pq')   % change the (2,2) element in G from
                             'gh' to 'pq'
G =
    [ ab, cd]
    [ ef, pq]

EDU» G(3,3)=sym('rs')   % expand G by placing an element in G(3,3)
G =
    [ ab, cd,  0]
    [ ef, pq,  0]
    [ 0,   0, rs]
```

Three other matrix operators work on symbolic matrices, as well as on numeric matrices. A diagonal may be extracted from a symbolic matrix using diag(M,d), and the upper or lower triangular portion of a matrix may be extracted using triu(M,d) and tril(M,d). In each case, M is the symbolic matrix, and the optional parameter d is the diagonal to work with or from. The default is d=0, or the main diagonal. Here are some examples.

```
EDU» syms a b c d e f g h k
EDU» M=[a,b,c;d,e,f;g,h,k]  % create a symbolic matrix
M =
    [ a, b, c]
    [ d, e, f]
    [ g, h, k]

EDU» triu(M)      % upper triangular part
ans =
    [ a, b, c]
    [ 0, e, f]
    [ 0, 0, k]

EDU» tril(M)      % lower triangular part
ans =
    [ a, 0, 0]
    [ d, e, 0]
    [ g, h, k]

EDU» diag(M)      % main diagonal
ans =
    [ a]
    [ e]
    [ k]

EDU» diag(M,1)    % +1 diagonal
ans =
    [ b]
    [ f]

EDU» tril(M,-1)   % lower triangular part starting with -1 diagonal
ans =
    [ 0, 0, 0]
    [ d, 0, 0]
    [ g, h, 0]
```

Most common algebraic operations can be performed on symbolic matrices using the standard arithmetic and array operators.

```
EDU» t=sym('t');
EDU» G=[cos(t),sin(t);-sin(t),cos(t)] % create a symbolic matrix
G =
    [  cos(t), sin(t)]
    [ -sin(t), cos(t)]
```

```
EDU» G+t              % add 't' to each element
ans =
    [  cos(t)+t,  sin(t)+t]
    [ -sin(t)+t,  cos(t)+t]

EDU» G+G              % add G to itself
ans =
    [  2*cos(t),  2*sin(t)]
    [ -2*sin(t),  2*cos(t)]

EDU» G*G              % matrix multiplication; same as G^2
ans =
    [ cos(t)^2-sin(t)^2,    2*cos(t)*sin(t)]
    [  -2*cos(t)*sin(t), cos(t)^2-sin(t)^2]

EDU» GG=simple(ans)  % try to simplify
GG =
    [  cos(2*t),  sin(2*t)]
    [ -sin(2*t),  cos(2*t)]

EDU» G.*G              % element-by-element multiplication, same as G.^2
ans =
    [ cos(t)^2,  sin(t)^2]
    [ sin(t)^2,  cos(t)^2]
```

Next, we'll show that G is an orthogonal matrix by showing that the transpose of G is its inverse:

```
EDU» I=G*G.'          % multiply G by its transpose
I =
    [ cos(t)^2+sin(t)^2,                   0]
    [                  0, cos(t)^2+sin(t)^2]
EDU» simplify(I)      % there appears to be a trig identity here
ans =
    [1, 0]
    [0, 1]
```

which is the identity matrix, as expected.

20.30   Linear Algebra Operations

The inverse and determinant of symbolic matrices are computed by the functions inv and det.

```
EDU» H=sym(hilb(3))   % the symbolic form of the numeric 3x3 Hilbert matrix
```

```
H =

     [  1,   1/2,  1/3]
     [ 1/2,  1/3,  1/4]
     [ 1/3,  1/4,  1/5]

EDU» det(H)  % find the determinant of H
ans =
     1/2160

EDU» J=inv(H)  % find the inverse of H
J =

     [  9,   -36,    30]
     [-36,   192,  -180]
     [ 30,  -180,   180]

EDU» det(J)  % find the determinant of the inverse
ans =
     2160
```

20.31   Other Features

- The function `poly` finds the characteristic polynomial of a matrix:

```
EDU» G=sym([1,1/2;1/3,1/4])   % create a symbolic matrix
G =

     [    1, 1/2]
     [ 1/3, 1/4]

EDU» poly(G)   % find the characteristic polynomial of G
ans =
     x*2-5/4*x+1/12
```

- Eigenvalues and eigenvectors of symbolic matrices can be found using the `eig` function. E=eig(X) is a vector containing the eigenvalues of a square matrix X. [V,D]=eig(X) produces a diagonal matrix D of eigenvalues and a full matrix V whose columns are the corresponding eigenvectors so that X*V=V*D.

```
EDU» F=sym([1/2,1/4,1/2;1/4,1/2,1/4;1/2,1/4,1/2])
F =

     [ 1/2, 1/4, 1/2]
     [ 1/4, 1/2, 1/4]
     [ 1/2, 1/4, 1/2]

EDU» eig(F)  % find the eigenvalues of F
ans =
     [                0]
     [3/4+1/4*3^(1/2)]
     [3/4-1/4*3^(1/2)]
```

```
EDU» [V,D]=eig(F)   % find eigenvectors V and eigenvalue matrix
                      D
V =
    [                  -1,   1/2+1/2*3^(1/2),   1/2+1/2*3^(1/2)]
    [                   0,                 1,                 1]
    [                   1,   1/2−1/2*3^(1/2),   1/2−1/2*3^(1/2)]
D =
    [                   0,                 0,                 0]
    [                   0,   3/4+1/4*3^(1/2),                 0]
    [                   0,                 0,   3/4−1/4*3^(1/2)]

EDU» simple(F*V)==simple(V*D)   % verify the result
ans =
     1   1   1
     1   1   1
     1   1   1
```

- The Jordan canonical form of a matrix is the diagonal matrix of eigenvalues; the columns of the transformation matrix are eigenvectors. For a
  given matrix A, jordan(A) attempts to find a non-singular matrix V, such
  that inv(V)*A*V is the Jordan canonical form. The jordan function has
  two forms:

```
EDU» K=sym([1/2,1/4;1/4,1/2])
K =
    [ 1/2, 1/4]
    [ 1/4, 1/2]

EDU» jordan(K)   % find the Jordan form of K, above
ans =
    [ 1/4,   0]
    [   0, 3/4]

EDU» [V,J]=jordan(K)   % find the Jordan form and eigenvectors
V =
    [  1/2, 1/2]
    [ −1/2, 1/2]
J =
    [ 1/4,   0]
    [   0, 3/4]
```

The columns of V, in the foregoing, are some of the possible eigenvectors of K.

- Since K, in the foregoing, is non-singular, the null-space basis of K is the
  empty matrix, and the column-space basis is the identity matrix.

```
EDU» K              % look at K again
K =
    [ 1/2, 1/4]
    [ 1/4, 1/2]
EDU» null(K)        % the nullspace of K is the empty matrix
ans =
    [ empty sym ]
EDU» colspace(K)  % find the column space of K
ans =
    [ 1, 0]
    [ 0, 1]
```

- Singular values of a matrix can be found by using the svd function. For more information and for other forms and uses of svd, see the on-line help.

```
EDU» A=sym(magic(3))   % generate a 3x3 matrix
A =
    [ 8, 1, 6]
    [ 3, 5, 7]
    [ 4, 9, 2]
EDU» svd(A)              % find the singular values
ans =
    [          15]
    [ 2*3^(1/2)]
    [ 4*3^(1/2)]
```

- The function jacobian(w,v) computes the Jacobian of w with respect to v. The (i,j)th entry of the result is (df(i)/dv(j)). Note that when f is a scalar, the Jacobian of f is the gradient of f. See the on-line help for more information.

```
EDU» syms u v
EDU» jacobian(u*exp(v),[u,v])
ans =
    [   exp(v), u*exp(v)]
```

20.32 Summary

- Symbolic matrices and vectors are arrays whose elements are symbolic objects or expressions. Notice that since single symbolic expressions are matrices consisting of a single element, all of the functions discussed here also apply to single expressions.
- The sym function may be used to create a symbolic matrix or expression, or to convert a numeric matrix or expression to symbolic form.

- The size of a symbolic matrix may be found by using the `size` and `length` functions, which return numeric values.
- Other arithmetic operations may be performed on symbolic matrices and expressions using standard arithmetic and array functions.
- The inverse of a symbolic matrix may be found using the `inv` function. The symbolic determinant of a symbolic matrix uses the `det` function.

20.33 Transforms

Transforms are used extensively in engineering to change the frame of reference between the time domain and the s-domain, the frequency domain, or the z-domain. Many techniques exist for analyzing steady-state and smoothly changing systems in the time domain, but complex systems often can be more easily analyzed in other domains.

One word of caution before we start. All of the transforms discussed in this section will use `findsym` to figure out the default independent variable if none is supplied. Since `findsym` finds the variable closest to `x` alphabetically, and transforms traditionally use other variables (such as `t`, `s`, and `w`), it is prudent to supply the variable names to the transforms.

20.34 Step and Impulse Functions

Engineering problems often make use of the step function $u(t)$ and the impulse function $\delta(t)$ when describing systems. The step function $Ku(t-a)$, where K is a constant, is defined as $Ku(t - a) = 0$ for $t < a$, and $Ku(t - a) = K$ for $t > a$. Here is a plot of the step function $Ku(t - a)$:

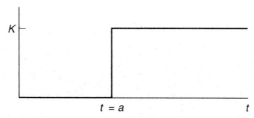

Figure 20.6

The impulse function $\delta(t)$ is the derivative of the step function $u(t)$. The impulse function $K\delta(t - a)$ is defined as $K\delta(t - a) = 0$ for $t \neq a$, and $\int_{-\infty}^{\infty} K\delta(t - a)\, dt = K$ for $t = a$. When graphed, it is commonly drawn as an arrow of amplitude K at $t = a$. Here is a plot of $K\delta(t - a)$:

Symbolic Math Toolbox   Chapter 20

Figure 20.7

The step and impulse function notation uses the names of famous mathematicians who used these functions extensively in their work. The step function $u(t)$ is called Heaviside(t), and the impulse function $\delta(t)$ is called Dirac(t).

```
EDU» syms k a t
EDU» u=k*sym('Heaviside(t-a)') % create a step function
u =
    k*Heaviside(t-a)

EDU» d=diff(u)  % find the derivative of the step function
d =
    k*Dirac(t-a)

EDU» int(d)  % integrate the impulse function
ans =
    k*Heaviside(t-a)
```

20.35   The Laplace Transform

The Laplace transform performs the operation

$$L(s) = \int_0^\infty f(t)e^{-st}\,dt$$

to transform $f(t)$ in the time domain to $L(s)$ in the s-domain.

The Laplace transform of the damped cosine function $e^{-at}\cos(wt)$ is found using the laplace function:

```
EDU» syms a s t w
EDU» f=exp(-a*t)*cos(w*t) % create an expression f(t)
f =
    exp(-a*t)*cos(w*t)

EDU» L=laplace(f,t,s)  % perform the Laplace transform f(t) => L(s)
L =
    (s+a)/((s+a)^2+w^2)
```

```
EDU» pretty(L)
```

$$
\frac{s + a}{(s + a)^2 + w^2}
$$

```
EDU» laplace(sym('Dirac(t)'))  % the transform of the impulse function
ans =
    1

EDU» laplace(sym('Heaviside(t)'))  % the transform of the step function
ans =
    1/s
```

Expressions can be transformed back to the time domain by using the inverse Laplace transform, ilaplace, which performs the operation:

$$
f(t) = \frac{1}{2\pi j} \int_{c+j0}^{c+j\infty} L(s)e^{st}\, ds
$$

Using L from above, we get:

```
EDU» ilaplace(L,s,t)  % transform L(s) => f(t)
ans =
    exp(-a*t)*cos(w*t)
```

20.36   The Fourier Transform

The Fourier transform and inverse Fourier transform are used extensively in circuit analysis to determine the characteristics of a system in both the time and frequency domains. MATLAB uses the fourier and ifourier functions to transform expressions between domains. The Fourier and inverse Fourier transforms are defined as:

$$
F(\omega) = \int_{-\infty}^{\infty} f(t)e^{-j\omega t}\, dt \qquad f(t) = \frac{1}{2\pi} \int_{-\infty}^{\infty} F(\omega)e^{j\omega t}\, dt
$$

MATLAB uses a 'w' to represent ω in symbolic expressions.

```
EDU» syms t w
EDU» f=t*exp(-t^2)     % create a function
f =
    t*exp(-t^2)/t

EDU» F=fourier(f,t,w)  % transform using the usual t and w parameters
```

```
F =
    -1/2*i*pi^(1/2)*w*exp(-1/4*w^2)
EDU» ifourier(F,w,t)  % find the inverse Fourier transform
ans =
    1/2*4^(1/2)*t*exp(-t^2)
EDU» simplify(ans)       % find a simpler form
ans =
    t*exp(-t^2)
```

Since both i and j represent $\sqrt{(-1)}$, MATLAB has to choose between them when returning an expression containing this value. By default, MATLAB will return i, as just shown.

Often, when we use the Fourier transform to solve engineering problems, expressions can include a step function $u(t)$ or an impulse function $\delta(t)$.

Consider the function $f(t) = -e^{-t}u(t) + 3\delta(t)$. The Fourier transform can be found by:

```
EDU» syms w t
EDU» fourier(sym('-exp(-t)*Heaviside(t)+3*Dirac(t)'))
ans =
    -1/(1+i*w)+3
EDU» ifourier(ans,t)  % find the inverse
ans =
    -exp(-t)*Heaviside(t)+3*Dirac(t)
```

20.37 Things to Try on Your Own

The Fourier and inverse Fourier transforms convert between the time domain and the frequency domain as $f(t) <=> F(\omega)$, where t represents time and ω represents frequency in radians per second. Some engineering fields and some instructors tend to use the transform pair $g(t) <=> G(f)$, where t represents time and f represents frequency in cycles per second (Hz). The relationship used is $\omega = 2\pi f$ or $f = \omega/2\pi$. It would be convenient to have functions that would do the conversion for you so that you could work with either convention. For example, to convert $g = e^{-t2}$ to the frequency domain using ω, and then to do the same using f, you could:

```
EDU» syms t w f
EDU» g=exp(-t^2)  % create the function
g =
    exp(-t^2)
EDU» Gw=fourier(g,t,w)  % get the transform in terms of w
Gw =
    pi^(1/2)*exp(-1/4*w^2)
```

```
EDU» ifourier(Gw,w,t)  % get the inverse
ans =
    1/2*4^(1/2)*exp(-t^2)

EDU» simplify(ans)      % check the result
ans =
    exp(-t^2)

EDU» Gf=ftf(g)  % get the transform in terms of f
Gf =
    pi^(1/2)*exp(-pi^2*f^2)

EDU» iftf(Gf)  % get the inverse to check it out
ans =
    exp(-t^2)
```

This was done using a function M-file called ftf.m for the $g(t) => G(f)$ transform, and another function M-file called iftf.m for the inverse. Here is an example of an M-file for ftf.m:

```
function G = ftf(g)
%FTF Fourier transform g(t) => G(f) where f = w/(2*pi)
%
G=fourier(g,'t','w');          % get the transform
G=subs(G,'w','(2*pi*f)');      % change of variable
```

20.38 The *Z*-Transform

The Laplace and Fourier transforms are used to analyze continuous-time systems. *Z*-transforms, on the other hand, are used to analyze discrete-time systems. The *Z*-transform is defined as:

$$F(z) = \sum_{n=0}^{\infty} f(n)z^{-n}$$

where z is a complex number.

Z-transforms and inverse *Z*-transforms are obtained using the ztrans and iztrans functions. The format is similar to the fourier and laplace transform functions:

```
EDU» syms n z
EDU» f=2^n/7-(-5)^n/7  % create a function
f =
    1/7*2^n-1/7*(-5)^n
```

```
EDU» G=ztrans(f,n,z)  % transform using the usual n and z
                              parameters
G =
    z/(z-2)/(z+5)
EDU» pretty(G)
                    z
            ------------------
            (z - 2) (z + 5)
EDU» iztrans(G,z,n)  % find the inverse Z-transform
ans =
    1/7*2^n-1/7*(-5)^n
```

The default variables in all transforms are the variables found by findsym. Note that all of these transforms, including the Laplace, Fourier, and Z-transform pairs, have forms that let you specify different independent variables.

20.39 Summary

- The step function $u(t)$ is represented in MATLAB symbolic notation by Heaviside(t); the impulse function $\delta(t)$ is represented by Dirac(t). These functions often will appear in transforms.
- Laplace transforms and inverse Laplace transforms laplace and ilaplace, transform $f(t) <=> L(s)$. Use laplace(f,t,s) to transform $f(t) => L(s)$, and ilaplace(L,s,t) to transform $L(s) => f(t)$.
- Fourier transforms are found using fourier and ifourier. These functions are used to transform $f(t) <=> F(\omega)$, and have the same forms as the laplace transform pair.
- Z-transforms are found using ztrans and iztrans. These functions are used to transform $f(n) <=> F(z)$, and they have the same forms as the laplace and fourier functions.

20.40 Interactive Symbolic Tools

As you saw as you worked your way through this tutorial, the MATLAB *Symbolic Math Toolbox* contains many powerful functions to solve both simple and complex problems by using symbolic expressions. As a reward for all your hard work, we will now study two unique 'fun' tools that are included in MATLAB.

The integral of a function can represent the area under the curve of the function, and may be approximated over a closed interval using Riemann sums. MATLAB supplies an interactive tool that lets you look at different approximations of the integral using this technique.

The form of the function is rsums(f), where f is a symbolic function. This will bring up a graphics window where the area under the curve of the function from 0 to 1 will be approximated by 10 rectangles. The title displays the function and the total calculated area of the rectangles. Underneath the graph is a horizontal slider that lets you change the number of rectangles used to approximate the curve from as little as 2 to as many as 256 by using the mouse. Here is an example:

```
EDU» x=sym('x');
EDU» f=10*x*exp(-5*x^2)          % create an interesting function
f =
      10*x*exp(-5*x^2)

EDU» ezplot(f)  % look at the graph from -2pi to 2pi
```

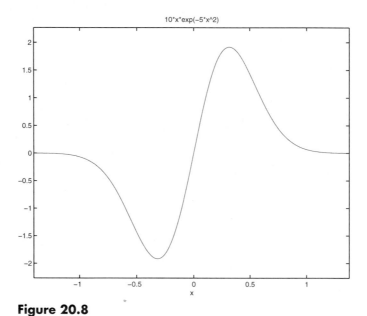

Figure 20.8

```
EDU» vpa(int(f,0,1),6)  % find the value of the integral from 0 to 1
ans =
      .993262

EDU» rsums(f)  % the Riemann approximation of the function from 0 to 1
```

Symbolic Math Toolbox   Chapter 20

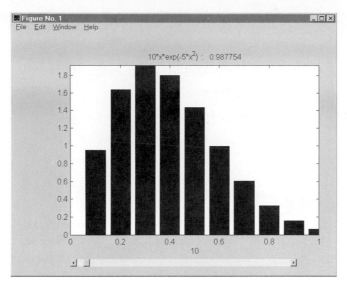

Figure 20.9

Use the mouse to change the setting of the slider, and notice how the total area under the rectangles (shown to the right of the title) approaches the value that we just obtained from the symbolic integral. It will never match, because the maximum number of rectangles that can be used is 256, while the integral is calculated in the limit.

Try some other functions on your own.

20.41   Function Calculator

This tool is an interactive graphical function calculator, called `funtool`, that uses mouse clicks to perform operations on symbolic expressions. `funtool` manipulates two functions of a single variable, $f(x)$ and $g(x)$, and graphs them in two windows. A third window controls the calculator, and contains the symbolic functions f and g, the domain of the graphs x, and a constant expression a that you can change by typing in the text boxes. There are three rows of buttons under the text boxes that invoke MATLAB symbolic functions, and a fourth row of buttons to control the calculator itself.

The first row of buttons operate on f alone. There are buttons to differentiate, integrate, simplify, extract the numerator or denominator, calculate $1/f$, and

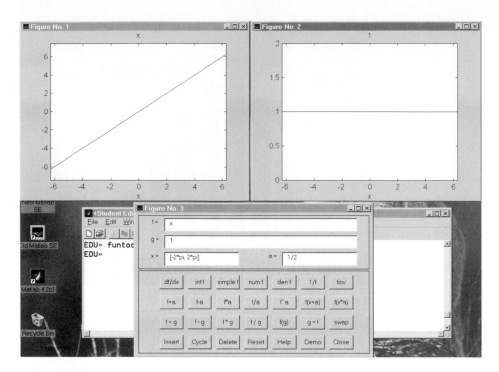

Figure 20.10

replace f by its inverse function. The second row of buttons translate and scale f by the parameter a. There are buttons to add, subtract, multiply, and divide f by a, and to raise f^a. The last two buttons replace f(x) by f(x+a) or f(x*a). The third row of buttons operate on both f(x) and g(x). The first four buttons add, subtract, multiply and divide f(x) by g(x). The fifth button replaces f(x) by f(g(x)), and the last two buttons copy f(x) to g(x), or swap f(x) and g(x).

The last row of buttons controls the calculator itself. The funtool calculator maintains a list of functions called fxlist. The first three buttons add the active function to the list, cycle through the list, and delete the active function from the list. The **Reset** button sets f, g, x, a, and fxlist to their initial values. The **Help** button gives you some more detailed information about funtool. The **Demo** button shows how to generate f=sin(x) from the initial values in nine clicks, and the **Close** button closes all funtool windows.

Try out funtool. Experience the possibilities of many of MATLAB's symbolic functions. You deserve a break.

20.42 Symbolic Math Toolbox Function List

Calculus	
diff	Differentiate
int	Integrate
taylor	Taylor series
jacobian	Jacobian matrix
symsum	Summation of series

Linear Algebra	
diag	Create or extract diagonals
triu	Upper triangle
tril	Lower triangle
inv	Matrix inverse
det	Determinant
rank	Rank
rref	Reduced row echelon form
null	Basis for null space
colspace	Basis for column space
eig	Eigenvalues and eigenvectors
svd	Singular values and singular vectors
poly	Characteristic polynomial
expm	Matrix exponential

Simplification	
simplify	Simplify
expand	Expand
factor	Factor
collect	Collect
simple	Search for shortest form
numden	Numerator and denominator
horner	Nested polynomial representation
allvalues	Find all values for RootOf expression
subexpr	Rewrite in terms of subexpressions
subs	Symbolic substitution

Solution of Equations	
solve	Symbolic solution of algebraic equations
dsolve	Symbolic solution of differential equations
finverse	Functional inverse
compose	Functional composition

Variable Precision Arithmetic	
vpa	Variable precision arithmetic
digits	Set variable precision accuracy

Integral Transforms	
fourier	Fourier transform
laplace	Laplace transform
ztrans	Z-transform
ifourier	Inverse Fourier transform
ilaplace	Inverse Laplace transform
iztrans	Inverse Z-transform

Conversions	
double	Convert symbolic matrix to double
poly2sym	Coefficient vector to symbolic polynomial
sym2poly	Symbolic polynomial to coefficient vector
char	Convert symbolic object to string

Basic Operations	
sym	Create symbolic object
syms	Short cut for constructing symbolic objects
findsym	Determine symbolic variables
pretty	Pretty print a symbolic expression
latex	LaTeX representation of a symbolic expression
ccode	C code representation of a symbolic expression
fortran	Fortran representation of a symbolic expression

Specisl Functions	
`sinint`	Sine integral
`cosint`	Cosine integral
`zeta`	Riemann zeta function
`lambertw`	Lambert W function

Pedagogical and Graphical Applications	
`rsums`	Riemann sums
`ezplot`	Easy-to-use function plotter
`funtool`	Function calculator

Demonstrations	
`symintro`	Introduction to the Symbolic Math Toolbox
`symcalcdemo`	Calculus demonstration
`symlindemo`	Demonstrate symbolic linear algebra
`symvpademo`	Demonstrate variable precision arithmetic
`symrotdemo`	Study plane rotations
`symeqndemo`	Demonstrate symbolic equation solving

21

Control System Toolbox

In addition to the general features and functions that have been described in the preceding chapters, MATLAB offers collections of function M-files, called **Toolboxes**, that solve problems in specific disciplines. This chapter introduces the *Control System Toolbox* for solving control system problems.

If you are not involved in the study of control systems, the functions in this toolbox probably will not be useful to you. In addition, the material and the functions may be confusing or have no meaning for you. Either way, you can just skip the material in this chapter, knowing that if you ever do study control systems, you can come back to this chapter for information. On the other hand, if you are studying control systems, you will find that the power of the *Control System Toolbox* simplifies many of the computations required to solve common problems.

Because of the broad scope of functions available, it is impractical to illustrate each function. The utility of individual toolbox functions becomes obvious when the underlying academic material is understood. As a result, we will describe how MATLAB represents systems, illustrate basic concepts by creating examples, and organize the available functions for easy reference. For more complete documentation, see the on-line help.

21.1 System Representations

Continuous and discrete (or digital) systems are represented in a consistent manner in MATLAB. Systems may be written in transfer function, zero-pole-gain, or state-space forms. Since transfer functions are described by ratios of polynomials, they are described in MATLAB by row vectors of their coefficients. The zero-pole-gain form is closely associated with the transfer function form. In this form, the roots of the numerator and denominator polynomials and the overall gain of the system are described with MATLAB arrays. The state-space form is perhaps the most natural form for MATLAB, since the state-space representation is described by the matrices $\mathbf{A}$, $\mathbf{B}$, $\mathbf{C}$, and $\mathbf{D}$. The following tables illustrate these forms.

Most of the tools in the *Control System Toolbox* transparently handle both the transfer function and state-space representations. In addition, multiple-input, multiple-output (MIMO) systems can be handled. In the case of the state-space representation, MIMO systems are generated by creating $\mathbf{B}$, $\mathbf{C}$, and $\mathbf{D}$ matrices of the required dimensions. MIMO transfer function representations are produced by using cell arrays to store the corresponding transfer functions polynomials. For example,

```
EDU» num={10, [1 10]; −1, [3 0]};  % 2-by-2 cell array

EDU» den={[1 10], [1 6 10];[1 0],[1 3 3]};  % 2-by-2 cell array
```

represents the system having two inputs and two outputs

Transfer Function		
Continuous	$H(s) = \dfrac{N(s)}{D(s)} = \dfrac{N_1 s^m + N_2 s^{m-1} + \ldots + N_m s + N_{m+1}}{D_1 s^n + D_2 s^{n-1} + \ldots + D_n s + D_{n+1}}$	$m \leq n$
	MATLAB: `num = [N₁ N₂ ... Nₘ₊₁]`, `den = [D₁ D₂ ... Dₙ₊₁]`	
Discrete (z^1 form)	$H(z) = \dfrac{N(z)}{D(z)} = \dfrac{N_1 z^m + N_2 z^{m-1} + \ldots + N_m z + N_{m+1}}{D_1 z^n + D_2 z^{n-1} + \ldots + D_n z + D_{n+1}}$	$m \leq n$
	MATLAB: `num = [N₁ N₂ ... Nₘ₊₁]`, `den = [D₁ D₂ ... Dₙ₊₁]`	
(z^{-1} form)	$H(z) = \dfrac{N(z)}{D(z)} = \dfrac{N_1 + N_2 z^{-1} + \ldots + N_n z^{-n+1} + N_{n+1} z^{-n}}{D_1 + D_2 z^{-1} + \ldots + D_n z^{-n+1} + D_{n+1} z^{-n}}$	
	MATLAB: `num = [N₁ N₂ ... Nₙ₊₁]`, `den = [D₁ D₂ ... Dₙ₊₁]`	

Zero-Pole-Gain		
Continuous	$H(s) = \dfrac{N(s)}{D(s)} = K \dfrac{(s - z_1)(s - z_2)\ldots(s - z_m)}{(s - p_1)(s - p_2)\ldots(s - p_n)}$	$m \leq n$
	MATLAB: `K, Z = [z₁; z₂; ... ;zₘ] P = [p₁; p₂; ... ;pₙ]`	
Discrete	$H(z) = \dfrac{N(z)}{D(z)} = K \dfrac{(z - z_1)(z - z_2)\ldots(z - z_m)}{(z - p_1)(z - p_2)\ldots(z - p_n)}$	$m \leq n$
	MATLAB: `K, Z = [z₁; z₂; ... ;zₘ] P = [p₁; p₂; ... ;pₙ]`	

State-Space	
Continuous	$\dot{x} = \mathbf{A}x + \mathbf{B}u$ $y = \mathbf{C}x + \mathbf{D}u$
	MATLAB: `A, B, C, D`
Discrete	$x[n + 1] = \mathbf{A}x[n] + \mathbf{B}u[n]$ $y[n] = \mathbf{C}x[n] + \mathbf{D}u[n]$
	MATLAB: `A, B, C, D`

$$\begin{bmatrix} y_1(s) \\ y_2(s) \end{bmatrix} = \begin{bmatrix} \dfrac{10}{s+10} & \dfrac{s+10}{s^2+6s+10} \\ \dfrac{-1}{s} & \dfrac{3s}{s^2+3s+3} \end{bmatrix} \begin{bmatrix} u_1(s) \\ u_2(s) \end{bmatrix}$$

That is, there is a natural one-to-one correspondence between the cell array indices and the corresponding transfer-function matrix indices.

MIMO zero-pole-gain models use cell arrays in the same way for the zero and pole arrays and a common numerical array for the gains. For example:

```
EDU» k=[1 3];

EDU» z={[],[−1]};

EDU» p={[0],[−10 −2]};
```

describes the system having two inputs and one output

$$y(s) = \begin{bmatrix} \dfrac{1}{s} & 3\dfrac{s+1}{(s+10)(s+2)} \end{bmatrix} \begin{bmatrix} u_1(s) \\ u_2(s) \end{bmatrix}$$

Note that an empty matrix [] is used to denote the absence of finite zeros in the first transfer function above.

21.2 LTI Objects

Rather than use system representations in terms of their corresponding data arrays as shown previously, MATLAB provides a way to encapsulate them into linear, time-invariant objects, or **LTI objects** for short. This approach makes it easier to keep track of them. For example:

```
EDU» my_sys=zpk(z,p,k)

Zero/pole/gain from input 1 to output:
1
-
s

Zero/pole/gain from input 2 to output:
  3 (s+1)
------------
(s+10) (s+2)
```

creates a zero-pole-gain LTI object called my_sys that contains the two-input, one-output system described by the zero-pole-gain model given earlier. Note that the system is displayed in an easy-to-understand manner. Likewise:

```
EDU»H=tf(num,den)

Transfer function from input 1 to output...
          10
#1:    ------
       s + 10

        −1
#2:    --
       s
```

Transfer function from input 2 to output...

```
          s + 10
#1:    --------------
       s^2 + 6 s + 10

          3 s + 1
#2:    -------------
       s^2 + 3 s + 3
```

creates a transfer function LTI object from the num and den cell arrays entered earlier. Once again, the display presents the system in an easy-to-understand format.

Finally, state-space LTI objects are created by

```
EDU» a=[0 1;−2 −4]; b=[0;1]; c=[1 1]; d=0;   % define state
                                             % space matrices

EDU» system2=ss(a,b,c,d)

a =
                        x1            x2
        x1               0       1.00000
        x2        −2.00000      −4.00000

b =
                        u1
        x1               0
        x2         1.00000

c =
                        x1            x2
        y1         1.00000       1.00000

d =
                        u1
        y1               0

Continuous-time system.
```

In this case, the display identifies the variable components associated with each element and identifies the system as being continuous-time.

To create discrete-time systems using the functions zpk, tf, and ss, you merely must specify a sampling period associated with the system as the last input argument. For example:

```
EDU» dt_sys=tf([1 0.2],[1 −1],0.01)

Transfer function:
z + 0.2
--------
 z − 1

Sampling time: 0.01
```

This discrete-time system has a sampling period of 0.01 seconds.

21.3   Data Retrieval

Once LTI objects are created, the data in them may be extracted using the functions tfdata, zpkdata, and ssdata, respectively. For example:

```
EDU» [nz,dz]=tfdata(dt_sys)  % extract tf parts as cell arrays
nz =
    [1x2 double]
dz =
    [1x2 double]
EDU» [nz,dz]=tfdata(dt_sys,'v')  % extract as vectors
nz =
    1                 0.2
dz =
    1     −1

EDU» [z,p,k]=zpkdata(dt_sys)  % can also extract in other forms!
z =
    [−0.2]
p =
    [1]
k =
    1

EDU» [z,p,k]=zpkdata(dt_sys,'v')  % extract as vectors
z =
    −0.2
p =
    1
```

```
k =
     1
EDU» [a,b,c,d]=ssdata(dt_sys)  % extract numeric state-space
                              % matrices too
a =
     1
b =
     1
c =
     1.2
d =
     1
```

Once an LTI object has been created, it may be extracted in any form. Moreover, all analysis commands apply, no matter what form was used to create an LTI object.

21.4   LTI Object Conversion

Besides extracting LTI objects in forms other than what they were originally created in, they may be converted to other forms by using the creation functions themselves. For example:

```
EDU» t=tf(100,[1 6 100])  % create transfer function
Transfer function:
      100
--------------
s^2 + 6 s + 100
EDU» sst=ss(t)
a =
                     x1          x2
          x1     -6.00000    -6.25000
          x2     16.00000           0

b =
                     u1
          x1     2.00000
          x2           0

c =
                     x1          x2
          y1           0     3.12500

d =
                     u1
          y1           0
```

```
Continuous-time system.
EDU» zpkt=zpk(t)

Zero/pole/gain:
      100
----------------
(s^2 + 6s + 100)
```

21.5   LTI Object Arithmetic

Using LTI objects also allows you to perform block-diagram arithmetic. For example, if the loop transfer function of a unity feedback system is $G(s)$, the closed-loop transfer function is $T(s) = G(s)/(1 + G(s))$. In MATLAB, this becomes

```
EDU» g=tf(100,[1 6 0])  % loop transfer function

Transfer function:
   100
---------
s^2 + 6 s

EDU» t=g/(1+g)  % closed loop transfer function—not simplified

Transfer function:
      100 s^2 + 600 s
-------------------------------
s^4 + 12 s^3 + 136 s^2 + 600 s

EDU» t=minreal(t)  % perform pole-zero cancellation

Transfer function:
      100
--------------
s^2 + 6 s + 100
```

LTI object arithmetic is done right in the *Command* window, using standard arithmetic expressions!

21.6   System Analysis

The *Control System Toolbox* offers numerous system analysis and design functions. For complete documentation, see the on-line help. To understand some of the features, consider the open-loop and closed-loop LTI objects

```
EDU» g=zpk([],[0,-5,-10],100)  % open-loop system

Zero/pole/gain:
      100
--------------
s (s+5) (s+10)
```

```
EDU» t=minreal(g/(1+g))  % closed-loop system

Zero/pole/gain:
                100
------------------------------------
(s+11.38) (s^2 + 3.622s + 8.789)
```

The poles of this system are

```
EDU» pole(t)
ans =
    -11.378
    -1.811 +      2.3472i
    -1.811 -      2.3472i
```

A Bode plot of the open-loop system with the gain and phase margins identified is given by

```
EDU» margin(g)
```

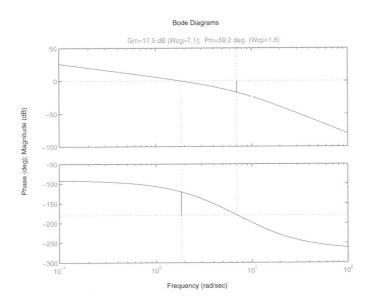

A simple Bode plot of the closed-loop system is

```
EDU» bode(t)
```

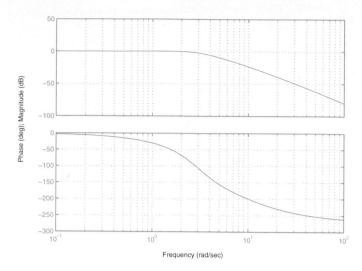

The unit step response of the system is

```
EDU» step(t)
```

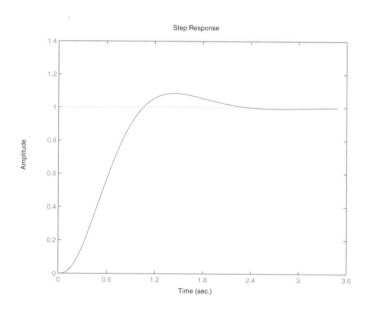

In addition to these and other analysis and design functions, the *Control System Toolbox* offers a GUI-based system response viewer, invoked with the `ltiview` command. This function allows you to select LTI objects from the *Command* window and view various responses based on selections with the mouse. A sample of the LTI Viewer GUI window is shown in the accompanying figure.

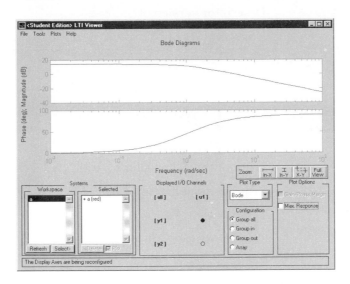

21.7   Control System Toolbox Function Listing

Creation of LTI Models	
ss	Create a state-space model
zpk	Create a zero-pole-gain model
tf	Create a transfer-function model
dss	Specify a descriptor state-space model
filt	Specify a digital filter
set	Set/modify properties of LTI models
ltiprops	Detailed help for available LTI properties

Data Extraction	
ssdata	Extract state-space matrices
zpkdata	Extract zero-pole-gain data
tfdata	Extract numerator(s) and denominator(s)
dssdata	Descriptor version of ssdata
get	Access values of LTI model properties

Model Characteristics	
class	Model type ('ss', 'zpk', or 'tf')
size	Input/output dimensions
isempty	True for empty LTI models
isct	True for continuous-time models
isdt	True for discrete-time models
isproper	True for proper LTI models
issiso	True for single-input/single-output systems
isa	Test if LTI model is of given type

Conversions	
ss	Conversion to state-space
zpk	Conversion to zero-pole-gain
tf	Conversion to transfer function
c2d	Continuous to discrete conversion
d2c	Discrete to continuous conversion
d2d	Resample discrete system or add input delay(s)

Overloaded Arithmetic Operations	
`+ and −`	Addition and subtraction LTI systems (parallel connection)
`*`	Multiplication of LTI systems (series connection)
`\`	Left divide: `sys1\sys2` means `inv(sys1)*sys2`
`/`	Right divide: `sys1/sys2` means `sys1*inv(sys2)`
`'`	Pertransposition
`.'`	Transposition of input/output map
`[...]`	Horizontal/vertical concatenation of LTI systems
`inv`	Inverse of an LTI system

Model Dynamics	
`pole, eig`	System poles
`tzero`	System transmission zeros
`pzmap`	Pole-zero map
`dcgain`	D.C. (low frequency) gain
`norm`	Norms of LTI systems
`covar`	Covariance of response to white noise
`damp`	Natural frequency and damping of system poles
`esort`	Sort continuous poles by real part
`dsort`	Sort discrete poles by magnitude
`pade`	Pade approximation of time delays

State-space Models	
rss, drss	Random stable state-space models
ss2ss	State coordinate transformation
canon	State-space canonical forms
ctrb, obsv	Controllability and observability matrices
gram	Controllability and observability gramians
ssbal	Diagonal balancing of state-space realizations
balreal	Gramian-based input/output balancing
modred	Model state reduction
minreal	Minimal realization and pole/zero cancellation
augstate	Augmentation of output by appending states

Time Response	
step	Step response
impulse	Impulse response
initial	Response of state-space system with given initial state
lsim	Response to arbitrary inputs
ltiview	Response analysis GUI
gensig	Generate input signal for lsim
stepfun	Generate unit-step input

Frequency Response	
bode	Bode plot of the frequency response
sigma	Singular value frequency plot
nyquist	Nyquist plot
nichols	Nichols chart
ltiview	Response analysis GUI
evalfr	Evaluate frequency response at a given frequency
freqresp	Frequency response over a frequency grid
margin	Gain and phase margins

System Interconnections	
append	Group LTI systems by appending inputs and outputs
parallel	Generalized parallel connection (see also overloaded +)
series	Generalized series connection (see also overloaded *)
feedback	Feedback connection of two systems
star	Redheffer star product (LFT interconnections)
connect	Derive state-space model from block diagram description

Classical Design Tools	
rlocus	Evans root locus
rlocfind	Interactive root locus gain determination
acker	SISO pole placement
place	MIMO pole placement
estim	Form estimator given estimator gain
reg	Form regulator given state-feedback and estimator gains

LQG Design Tools	
lqr, dlqr	Linear-quadratic (LQ) state-feedback regulator
lqry	LQ regulator with output weighting
lqrd	Discrete LQ regulator for continuous plant
kalman	Kalman estimator
kalmd	Discrete Kalman estimator for continuous plant
lqgreg	Form LQG regulator given LQ gain and Kalman estimator

Matrix Equation Solvers	
lyap	Solve continuous Lyapunov equations
dlyap	Solve discrete Lyapunov equations
care	Solve continuous algebraic Riccati equations
dare	Solve discrete algebraic Riccati equations

Demonstrations	
ctrldemo	Introduction to the Control System Toolbox
jetdemo	Classical design of jet transport yaw damper
diskdemo	Digital design of hard-disk-drive controller
milldemo	SISO and MIMO LQG control of steel rolling mill
kalmdemo	Kalman filter design and simulation

Signal Processing Toolbox

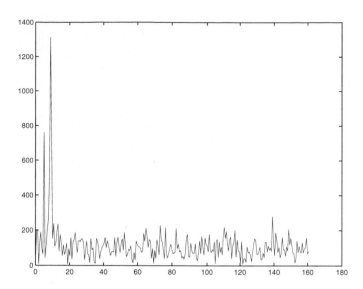

```
EDU» i=find(w<=20);  % pick out frequencies of interest
EDU» plot(w(i),Xp(i))  % plot restricted range only
EDU» grid
EDU» xlabel('Frequency, Rad/s')
EDU» title('Magnitude Spectrum of Noisy Signal')
```

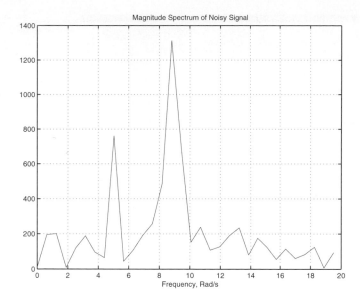

Note in this last plot how the original sinusoids at 5 and 9 radians per second appear in the spectrum, whereas they were hard to distinguish in the time-domain plot.

22.2 Filter Design

The *Signal Processing Toolbox* offers numerous digital filter design functions. The filter design demonstration function `filtdemo` provides a GUI-based introduction to these functions. Typing `EDU»` `filtdemo` brings up the GUI design window shown in the following figure.

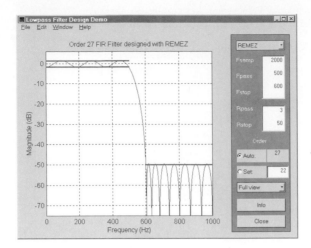

Explore this GUI by making selections from the menus on the right-hand side, and by dragging the horizontal response specifications that appear in the frequency-response window. The functions called by this GUI are documented in the accompanying function listing.

22.3   GUI Signal Analysis and Filter Design

In addition to the functions available in the *Command* window, the *Signal Processing Toolbox* offers a general-purpose GUI for signal analysis and filter design. This tool is created by typing `sptool` at the MATLAB prompt. Doing so produces the window given here.

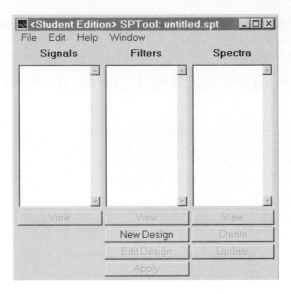

The **left** panel in this GUI shows all signals available for analysis, the **center** panel shows all filters, and the **right** panel shows all frequency spectra available. Using the **File**, **Edit**, **Help**, and **Window** menus, as well as the pushbuttons under each of the panels, allows you to import signals, filters, and spectra for consideration, and to save results to disk. The **Help** menu, in particular, offers context-sensitive help that explains how to use sptool.

MATLAB comes with a sample data file that can be imported into sptool. To open this file, choose **Import...** from the **File** menu. Click the **From Disk** radio button, then click the **Browse...** pushbutton. This opens a standard **File** dialog box for selecting a file. Using the dialog box, select the file mtlb.mat that resides within the signal subdirectory or folder of the Toolbox directory where MATLAB resides. Back in the *Import to SPTool* window, select Fs from the **file contents** panel, then click the arrow → pointing to the **Sampling Frequency** edit box in the **right** panel. This makes the value of the variable Fs be the sampling frequency of the input signal to be analyzed. Next, select mtlb from the center **file contents** panel, and click the arrow → pointing to the data edit box in the **right** panel. This makes the data named mtlb be the signal to be analyzed. Finally, click the **OK** button to place the signal in the **left** panel of the sptool GUI.

Select the signal sig1 that appear in the **Signals** panel on the left, and click the **View** button under the **Signals** panel to view the signal with a sophisticated GUI-based signal browser that is part of the *Signal Processing Toolbox*. Explore the various analysis features found in the signal browser. If you need help, click the **Help** button.

With this introduction, explore all the features of the signal processing tool `sptool`. Use context-sensitive help when needed, and consult on-line help and other documentation on the MATLAB CD for more thorough assistance.

22.4 Signal Processing Toolbox Function Listing

Waveform Generation	
chirp	Swept-frequency cosine generator
diric	Dirichlet (periodic sinc) function
gauspuls	Gaussian pulse generator
pulstran	Pulse train generator
rectpuls	Sampled aperiodic rectangle generator
sawtooth	Sawtooth function
sinc	Sinc or `sin(pi*x)/(pi*x)` function
square	Square wave function
tripuls	Sampled aperiodic triangle generator

Filter Analysis and Implementation	
abs	Magnitude
angle	Phase angle
casfilt	Cascade filter implementation
conv	Convolution
fftfilt	Overlap-add filter implementation
filter	Filter implementation
filtfilt	Zero-phase version of filter
filtic	Determine filter initial conditions
freqs	Laplace transform frequency response
freqspace	Frequency spacing for frequency response
freqz	Z-transform frequency response
grpdelay	Group delay
impz	Impulse response (discrete)
latcfilt	Lattice filter implementation
unwrap	Unwrap phase
upfirdn	Upsample, FIR filter, downsample
zplane	Discrete pole-zero plot

Linear System Transformations	
convmtx	Convolution matrix
latc2tf	Lattice or lattice ladder to transfer function conversion
poly2rc	Polynomial to reflection coefficients transformation
rc2poly	Reflection coefficients to polynomial transformation
residuez	Z-transform partial fraction expansion
sos2ss	Second-order sections to state-space conversion
sos2tf	Second-order sections to transfer function conversion
sos2zp	Second-order sections to zero-pole conversion
ss2sos	State-space to second-order sections conversion
ss2tf	State-space to transfer function conversion
ss2zp	State-space to zero-pole conversion
tf2latc	Transfer function to lattice or lattice-ladder conversion
tf2ss	Transfer function to state-space conversion
tf2zp	Transfer function to zero-pole conversion
zp2sos	Zero-pole to second-order sections conversion
zp2ss	Zero-pole to state-space conversion
zp2tf	Zero-pole to transfer-function conversion

IIR Digital Filter Design	
butter	Butterworth filter design.
cheby1	Chebyshev type I filter design
cheby2	Chebyshev type II filter design
ellip	Elliptic filter design
maxflat	Generalized Butterworth lowpass filter design
yulewalk	Yule-Walker filter design

IIR Filter Order Selection	
buttord	Butterworth filter order selection
cheb1ord	Chebyshev type I filter order selection
cheb2ord	Chebyshev type II filter order selection
ellipord	Elliptic filter order selection

FIR Filter Design	
cremez	Complex and nonlinear phase equiripple FIR filter design
fir1	Window-based FIR filter design—low, high, band, stop, multi
fir2	Window-based FIR filter design—arbitrary response
fircls	Constrained least squares filter design—arbitrary response
fircls1	Constrained least squares FIR filter design—lowpass and highpass
firls	FIR filter design—arbitrary response with transition bands
firrcos	Raised cosine FIR filter design
intfilt	Interpolation FIR filter design
kaiserord	Window-based filter order selection using Kaiser window
remez	Parks-McClellan optimal FIR filter design
remezord	Parks-McClellan filter order selection

Transforms	
czt	Chirp-z transform
dct	Discrete cosine transform
dftmtx	Discrete Fourier transform matrix
fft	Fast Fourier transform
fftshift	Swap vector halves
hilbert	Hilbert transform
idct	Inverse discrete cosine transform
ifft	Inverse fast Fourier transform

Statistical Signal Processing	
cohere	Coherence function estimate
corrcoef	Correlation coefficients
cov	Covariance matrix
csd	Cross spectral density
psd	Power spectral density
spectrum	psd, csd, cohere, and tfe combined
tfe	Transfer function estimate
xcorr	Cross-correlation function
xcov	Covariance function

Windows	
bartlett	Bartlett window
blackman	Blackman window
boxcar	Rectangular window
chebwin	Chebyshev window
hamming	Hamming window
hanning	Hanning window
kaiser	Kaiser window
triang	Triangular window

Parametric Modeling	
invfreqs	Analog filter fit to frequency response
invfreqz	Discrete filter fit to frequency response
levinson	Levinson-Durbin recursion
lpc	Linear predictive coefficients using autocorrelation method
prony	Prony's discrete filter fit to time response
stmcb	Steiglitz-McBride iteration for ARMA modeling

Specialized Operations	
cceps	Complex cepstrum
decimate	Resample data at a lower sample rate
deconv	Deconvolution
demod	Demodulation for communications simulation
interp	Resample data at a higher sample rate
interp1	General one-dimensional interpolation (MATLAB Toolbox)
medfilt1	One-dimensional median filtering
modulate	Modulation for communications simulation
rceps	Real cepstrum and minimum-phase reconstruction
resample	Resample sequence with new sampling rate
specgram	Spectrogram, for speech signals
spline	Cubic spline interpolation
vco	Voltage-controlled oscillator

Analog Lowpass Filter Prototypes	
besselap	Bessel filter prototype
buttap	Butterworth filter prototype
cheb1ap	Chebyshev type I filter prototype (passband ripple)
cheb2ap	Chebyshev type II filter prototype (stopband ripple)
ellipap	Elliptic filter prototype

Frequency Translation	
lp2bp	Lowpass to bandpass analog filter transformation
lp2bs	Lowpass to bandstop analog filter transformation
lp2hp	Lowpass to highpass analog filter transformation
lp2lp	Lowpass to lowpass analog filter transformation

Filter Discretization	
`bilinear`	Bilinear transformation with optional prewarping
`impinvar`	Impulse invariance analog to digital conversion

Other	
`besself`	Bessel analog filter design
`conv2`	Two-dimensional convolution
`cplxpair`	Order vector into complex conjugate pairs
`detrend`	Linear trend removal
`fft2`	Two-dimensional fast Fourier transform
`fftshift`	Swap quadrants of array
`ifft2`	Inverse two-dimensional fast Fourier transform
`polystab`	Polynomial stabilization
`sptool`	Signal processing tool interface
`stem`	Plot discrete data sequence
`strips`	Strip plot
`xcorr2`	Two-dimensional cross-correlation

Demonstrations	
`cztdemo`	Chirp-z transform and FFT demonstration
`filtdemo`	Filter design demonstration
`moddemo`	Modulation/demodulation demonstration
`sosdemo`	Second-order sections demonstration

23

Help!

You probably have the sense that MATLAB has many more commands than you could possibly remember. To help you find commands, MATLAB provides assistance through its extensive *online help* capabilities. These capabilities include MATLAB commands to get quick help in the *Command* window; a separate mouse-driven *Help* window; a browser-based help system; and access to more information, technical support, and user-contributed utilities using a network connection, if one is available.

23.1   *Command* Window Help

MATLAB offers a number of commands to help you get quick information about a MATLAB command or function within the *Command* window, including `help`, `lookfor`, `whatsnew`, and `info`.

23.1.1   The `help` Command

The MATLAB `help` command is the simplest way to get help if you know the topic on which you want help. Typing `help topic` displays help about that topic if it exists, e.g.,

```
EDU» help sqrt

 SQRT    Square root.
     SQRT(X) is the square root of the elements of X. Complex
     results are produced if X is not positive.

     See also SQRTM.
```

Here, we received help on MATLAB's square-root function. On the other hand,

```
EDU» help cows

cows not found.
```

says simply that MATLAB knows nothing about `cows`.

Note in the preceding `sqrt` example that `SQRT` is capitalized in the help text. When used, however, `sqrt` is never capitalized. In fact, because MATLAB is case sensitive, `SQRT` is unknown and produces an error:

```
EDU» SQRT(2)
??? SQRT(
        |
Missing operator, comma, or semicolon.
```

To summarize, function names are capitalized in help text solely to aid readability, but, in use, functions use lowercase characters.

The help command works well if you know the exact topic on which you want help. Since this often isn't so, help provides guidance to direct you to the exact topic you want when you simply type help with no topic:

```
EDU» help

HELP topics:

MATLAB :general    - General-purpose commands.
MATLAB :ops        - Operators and special characters.
MATLAB :lang       - Programming language constructs.
MATLAB :elmat      - Elementary matrices and matrix
                     manipulation.
MATLAB :elfun      - Elementary math functions.
MATLAB :specfun    - Specialized math functions.
MATLAB :matfun     - Matrix functions - numerical linear algebra.
MATLAB :datafun    - Data analysis and Fourier transform
                     functions.
MATLAB :polyfun    - Interpolation and polynomials.
MATLAB :funfun     - Function functions and ODE solvers.
MATLAB :sparfun    - Sparse matrices.
MATLAB :graph2d    - Two-dimensional graphs.
MATLAB :graph3d    - Three-dimensional graphs.
MATLAB :specgraph  - Specialized graphs.
MATLAB :graphics   - Handle Graphics.
MATLAB :uitools    - Graphical user interface tools.
MATLAB :strfun     - Character strings.
MATLAB :iofun      - File input/output.
MATLAB :timefun    - Time and dates.
MATLAB :datatypes  - Data types and structures.
MATLAB :MacOS      - Macintosh specific functions.
MATLAB :demos      - Examples and demonstrations.
MATLAB :specmat    - Specialized matrices.
Toolbox:local      - Preferences.
Toolbox:control    - Control System Toolbox.
Toolbox:signal     - Signal Processing Toolbox.
Toolbox:symbolic   - Symbolic Math Toolbox.

For more help on directory:topic, type "help topic".
```

Your display may differ slightly from this one. This display describes primary topics or categories from which you can ask for additional help. Each of these primary topics corresponds to a directory name on the MATLAB search path. For example, help general returns a list (too long to show here) of general MATLAB topics that you can use the help topic command to get help on.

While the `help` command allows you to access help quickly, it is not the most convenient way to do so unless you know the exact topic you are seeking help on. When you are uncertain about the spelling or the existence of a topic, other approaches to obtaining help often are more productive.

23.1.2 The `lookfor` Command

The `lookfor` command provides help by searching through all the *first* lines of MATLAB help topics and M-files on the MATLAB search path, and returning a list of those that contain the key word you specify. *Most important is that the key word need not be a MATLAB command.* For example:

```
EDU» lookfor complex

CONJ     Complex conjugate.
IMAG     Complex imaginary part.
REAL     Complex real part.
CDF2RDF  Complex diagonal form to real block diagonal form.
RSF2CSF  Real block diagonal form to complex diagonal form.
CPLXPAIR Sort numbers into complex conjugate pairs.
```

The key word `complex` is not a MATLAB command, but it was found in the help descriptions of six MATLAB commands. Given this information, the `help` command may be used to display help about a specific command, e.g.:

```
EDU» help conj

 CONJ     Complex conjugate.
     CONJ(X) is the complex conjugate of X.
     For a complex X, CONJ(X) = REAL(X) — i*IMAG(X).

     See also: REAL, IMAG, I, J.
```

Adding the qualifier `-all` to the lookfor command, e.g., `lookfor complex -all`, searches the entire help text of all M-files, not just the first line, and lists the functions containing keyword matches. The search will take a little longer, but it will return many more matches. In summary, the `lookfor` command provides a way to find MATLAB commands and help topics, given a general keyword.

23.1.3 The `whatsnew` and `info` Commands

As the names suggest, the `whatsnew` and `info` commands display information about changes and improvements to MATLAB and the toolboxes. If used without an argument, `info` displays general information about MATLAB, how to contact The MathWorks, and how to become a subscribing user. If used with arguments, e.g., `whatsnew matlab` or `info signal`, the Readme file for the specified toolbox is displayed, if it exists.

23.2 The *Help* Window

A major enhancement to the MATLAB help system in MATLAB 5 is the new *Help* window. The `helpwin` command opens a new window on your computer screen that can be used to view the help text for MATLAB commands in an interactive *Help* window that uses a mouse for navigation. This is in addition to the *Command* window and any *Figure* windows you have open. If `helpwin` is used without arguments, the *Help* window initially contains the list of primary help topics as shown:

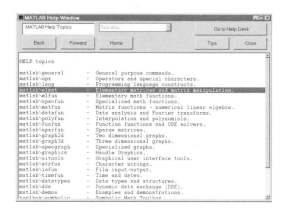

Double-click any of the help topics displayed in the central text window to list the associated functions or subtopics.

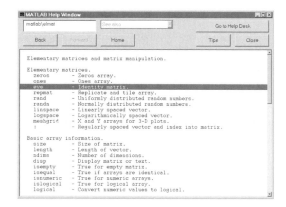

Double-click any function to visit the help text for that function.

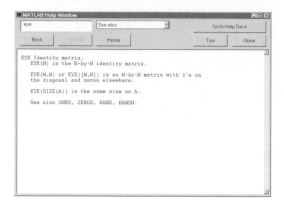

If invoked with an argument, e.g., helpwin plot, the *Help* window will appear with the help text for the argument (the plot command, in this case) in the central text window.

Scroll bars at the right and bottom of the central text window are available to move through the text. The **Back** and **Forward** buttons help you navigate between the help screens you have visited, and the **Home** button returns to the primary help topics, as previously shown. The **Tips** button on the right of the *Help* window displays general information about help and helpwin, as well as the helpdesk command to be discussed later. The **Close** button makes the *Help* window disappear.

The **See also** popup lists related functions; they can be visited by selecting a function name from the **See also** popup. You can also enter a command or topic in the text box at the top left of the *Help* window to jump to that command or topic.

The *Help* window may also be accessed from the **Help** menu on the *Command* and *Figure* windows, in the PC version. Macintosh users can get help by selecting **MATLAB Help** from the **Balloon Help** menu. You can also click the question-mark button icon on the *Command* window toolbar on either platform to open the *Help* window.

23.3   Browsing for Help

Your Netscape or Internet Explorer Web browser can also be used to display a wide range of help and reference information. All of this information is stored on disk or CD-ROM on your local system, so a network connection is optional.

Many of the documents use HyperText Markup Language (HTML) to take advantage of graphics and the "hot links" used in HTML documents for navigation between pages. All of MATLAB's operators and functions have on-line reference pages in HTML format, and many provide more details and examples than the basic `help` entries do. The reference index may be searched for a keyword, as well.

Browser-based help may be accessed by using the `helpdesk` or `doc` commands from the *Command* window, or by selecting the **Help Desk (HTML)** option from the **Help** menu, as just described. The **Go To Help Desk** button on the *Help* window, and the **See also** popup item beginning with the word **More**, e.g., **More** `helpwin` **help (HTML)**, also launch your favorite Web browser. You can specify the Web browser to use in MATLAB preferences.

Your browser will open on a page similar to the following:

All of the highlighted links (underlined text) may be used to access more information on various topics. The MATLAB **Topics** section of the page contains links to tutorials, a function index, and a subject index. A search engine running on your own computer can query an index of the on-line reference material. Simply enter the desired keyword in the text box, and click the **Return** or **Enter** key. The **New in MATLAB 5** section contains links to information on new features, release notes, and help for updating your MATLAB code or M-files to work with version 5. The **SIMULINK Topics** section does not apply to the Student Edition of MATLAB, but it will apply if you have the Student Edition of **SIMULINK,** also published by Prentice Hall.

At the bottom of the page is a link to the **Full Documentation Set** of on-line reference pages in the Portable Document Format (PDF) used by Adobe's Acrobat reader. These pages reproduce the look and feel of the printed page, complete with fonts, graphics, formatting, and images. This is the best way to get printed copies of the reference material.

Please note that although Web browsers and PDF viewers may present useful information in familiar formats, they are large programs, and consequently use significant amounts of computer memory and other resources. If you are running MATLAB on a computer with limited memory or a slow processor, starting a Web browser or PDF viewer while MATLAB is running may result in very slow response time. The `help` and `lookfor` commands and the *Help* window are recommended in these situations.

23.4 Internet Resources

If your computer is connected to the Internet, the Help Desk provides a connection to **The MathWorks Web Site**, the Internet home of MATLAB. You can use e-mail to ask questions, make suggestions, and report possible bugs. You can get product information or register to become a subscribing user. You can also use the *Solution Search Engine* at the MathWorks Web site to query an up-to-date data base of technical support information. Clicking the image of a globe will take you to the MathWorks Web site.

You can also access the MathWorks Web site directly by pointing your browser at `http://education.mathworks.com` for the MathWorks Web site for education. The general MathWorks Web site is also available at `http://www.mathworks.com`. Both of these sites have links to product information, books, support resources, the MATLAB newsgroup, and user-contributed software and M-files. The education site has additional resources for students and teachers. Here is a view of the education site:

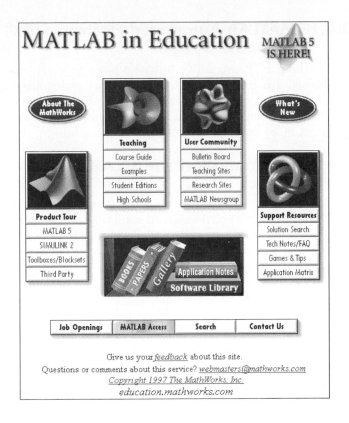

Anonymous FTP sites are repositories of files and software on the Internet that allow users to connect to them and transfer files without requiring a user account and password on the host computer. The MathWorks has an extensive anonymous FTP site containing many thousands of files you can access from its Web site. If you prefer to access the MathWorks FTP site directly using an FTP program such as WinFTP, Fetch, or command-line `ftp`, simply connect to `ftp.mathworks.com`, log in as *anonymous*, and use your electronic mail address as a password.

Additional help for specific questions or problems may be available on the Internet News bulletin boards. Questions and comments about using MATLAB may be posted to a newsgroup read by many MATLAB users, as well as the MathWorks technical support people. Someone already may have solved your problem. Point your Internet News reader at the `comp.soft-sys.matlab` newsgroup to join the discussions.

23.4.1 MATLAB Automated Electronic Mail Response System

Those without FTP capability, but who have an electronic mail connection to the Internet, are not left out. The MathWorks maintains an automated file-by-mail service that will send files from the FTP site by e-mail. Send e-mail to `matlib@mathworks.com` with the single word `help` in the *body* of the message to get more detailed instructions about accessing the server.

23.4.2 The MathWorks MATLAB Digest

The MATLAB *Digest* is a monthly electronic newsletter sent to subscribers by e-mail. This newsletter contains MATLAB news, articles contributed by MATLAB developers and users, hints and tips, and responses to user questions. To subscribe to the Digest, send e-mail to `subscribe@mathworks.com` with a request to be added to the mailing list, or type `subscribe` at the MATLAB prompt. The `subscribe` command asks questions and uses your answers to generate an e-mail message or a printed request form that can be mailed or faxed to The MathWorks. Back issues of the Digest are available at the MATLAB FTP site in the directory `/pub/doc/tmw-digest`.

23.4.3 The MATLAB Newsletter

The quarterly hardcopy publication, MATLAB *News & Notes*, is available to anyone who uses MATLAB. If you become a subscribing user, you will receive the Digest and the quarterly newsletter. You do not have to be a registered user to become a subscribing user, and it is a free service. Use the form on the World Wide Web site, type `subscribe` at the MATLAB prompt, or send e-mail to `subscribe@mathworks.com` with your request. The newsletter usually has news, tips, articles by Cleve Moler and others, and a calendar of events.

E-mail Addresses at The MathWorks

`subscribe@mathworks.com`	Subscribing user information
`matlib@mathworks.com`	File-by-mail server
`digest@mathworks.com`	MATLAB Digest submissions

MATLAB Network Resources

`education.mathworks.com`	MATLAB for Education Web site
`ftp.mathworks.com`	Anonymous FTP site
`144.212.100.10`	WWW and FTP Internet address
`144.212.100.21`	Education Web site address

Other Network Resources

`home.netscape.com`	Netscape Web browser for PC, Mac, and Unix
`www.microsoft.com`	Internet Explorer Web browser for PC and Mac
`www.ncsa.uiuc.edu`	Mosaic Web browser for PC, Mac, and Unix
`www.adobe.com`	Adobe Acrobat PDF viewer for PC, Mac, and Unix
`comp.soft-sys.matlab`	MATLAB newsgroup on Internet News

M-File List of Student Edition

HELP Topics

Preferences

General Purpose Commands

Operators and Special Characters

Programming Language Constructs

Elementary Matrices and Matrix Manipulation

Elementary Math Functions

Specialized Math Functions

Matrix Functions and Numerical Linear Algebra

Data Analysis and Fourier Transforms

Interpolation and Polynomials

Function Functions and ODE Solvers

Sparse Matrices

Two-dimensional Graphs

Three-dimensional Graphs

Specialized Graphs

Handle Graphics

Graphical User Interface Tools

Character Strings

File Input/Output

Time and Dates

Data Types and Structures

Dynamic Data Exchange (DDE)

Examples and Demonstrations

HELP Topics

MATLAB Directories	
toolbox/local	Preferences
matlab/general	General-purpose commands
matlab/ops	Operators and special characters
matlab/lang	Programming language constructs
matlab/elmat	Elementary matrices and matrix manipulation
matlab/elfun	Elementary math functions
matlab/specfun	Specialized math functions
matlab/matfun	Matrix functions—numerical linear algebra
matlab/datafun	Data analysis and Fourier transforms
matlab/polyfun	Interpolation and polynomials
matlab/funfun	Function functions and ODE solvers
matlab/sparfun	Sparse matrices
matlab/graph2d	Two-dimensional graphs
matlab/graph3d	Three-dimensional graphs
matlab/specgraph	Specialized graphs
matlab/graphics	Handle Graphics
matlab/uitools	Graphical user interface (GUI) tools
matlab/strfun	Character strings
matlab/iofun	File input/output
matlab/timefun	Time and dates
matlab/datatypes	Data types and structures
matlab/dde	Dynamic data exchange (DDE) - PC only
matlab/MacOS	Macintosh specific - Mac only
matlab/demos	Examples and demonstrations
toolbox/control	Control System Toolbox
toolbox/signal	Signal Processing Toolbox
toolbox/symbolic	Symbolic Math Toolbox

Preferences

Saved Preferences Files	
startup	User startup M-file
finish	User finish M-file
matlabrc	Master startup M-file
pathdef	Search path defaults
docopt	Web browser defaults
printopt	Printer defaults

Preference Commands	
cedit	Set command line editor keys
terminal	Set graphics terminal type
colordef	Set color defaults
graymon	Set graphics window defaults for gray-scale monitors
whitebg	Change axes' background color

Configuration Information	
hostid	MATLAB server host identification number
license	License number
version	MATLAB version number

General Purpose Commands

General Information	
help	On-line help, display text at command line
helpwin	On-line help, separate window for navigation
helpdesk	Comprehensive hypertext documentation and troubleshooting
demo	Run demonstrations
ver	MATLAB, SIMULINK, and toolbox version information
whatsnew	Display Readme files
Readme	What's new in MATLAB 5

Managing the Workspace	
who	List current variables
whos	List current variables, long form
clear	Clear variables and functions from memory
pack	Consolidate workspace memory
load	Load workspace variables from disk
save	Save workspace variables to disk
quit	Quit MATLAB session

Managing Commands and Functions	
what	List MATLAB-specific files in directory
type	List M-file
edit	Edit M-file
lookfor	Search all M-files for keyword
which	Locate functions and files
pcode	Create pre-parsed pseudo-code file (P-file)
inmem	List functions in memory
mex	Compile MEX-function

Managing the Search Path	
path	Get/set search path
addpath	Add directory to search path
rmpath	Remove directory from search path
editpath	Modify search path

Controlling the Command Window	
echo	Echo commands in M-files
more	Control paged output in command window
diary	Save text of MATLAB session
format	Set output format

Operating System Commands	
cd	Change current working directory
pwd	Show (print) current working directory
dir	List directory
delete	Delete file
getenv	Get environment variable
!	Execute operating system command
dos	Execute DOS command and return result
unix	Execute UNIX command and return result
vms	Execute VMS DCL command and return result
web	Open Web browser on site or files
computer	Computer type

Profiling M-files	
profile	Profile M-file execution time

Debugging M-files	
debug	List debugging commands
dbstop	Set breakpoint
dbclear	Remove breakpoint
dbcont	Continue execution
dbdown	Change local workspace context
dbstack	Display function call stack
dbstatus	List all breakpoints
dbstep	Execute one or more lines
dbtype	List M-file with line numbers
dbup	Change local workspace context
dbquit	Quit debug mode
dbmex	Debug MEX-files (UNIX only)

Operators and Special Characters

Arithmetic Operators	
plus (+)	Plus
uplus (+)	Unary plus
minus (−)	Minus
uminus (−)	Unary minus
mtimes (.*)	Matrix multiply
times (*)	Array multiply
mpower (^)	Matrix power
power (.^)	Array power
mldivide (\)	Backslash or left matrix divide
mrdivide (/)	Slash or right matrix divide
ldivide (.\)	Left array divide
rdivide (./)	Right array divide
kron	Kronecker tensor product

Relational Operators	
eq (==)	Equal
ne (~=)	Not equal
lt (<)	Less than
gt (>)	Greater than
le (<=)	Less than or equal
ge (>=)	Greater than or equal

Logical Operators	
`and (&)`	Logical AND
`or (|)`	Logical OR
`not (~)`	Logical NOT
`xor`	Logical EXCLUSIVE OR
`any`	True if any element of vector is nonzero
`all`	True if all elements of vector are nonzero

Special Characters	
`colon`	Colon :
`( )`	Parentheses and subscripting
`[ ]`	Brackets
`{ }`	Braces and subscripting
`.`	Decimal point
`.`	Structure field access
`. .`	Parent directory
`. . .`	Continuation
`,`	Separator
`;`	Semicolon
`%`	Comment
`!`	Invoke operating-system command
`=`	Assignment
`'`	Quote
`transpose (.')`	Transpose
`ctranspose (')`	Complex conjugate transpose
`horzcat [,]`	Horizontal concatenation
`vertcat [;]`	Vertical concatenation
`subsasgn`	Subscripted assignment ( ),{ },.
`subsref`	Subscripted reference ( ),{ },.
`subsindex`	Subscript index

Bitwise Operators	
bitand	Bitwise AND
bitcmp	Complement bits
bitor	Bitwise OR
bitmax	Maximum floating point integer
bitxor	Bitwise XOR
bitset	Set bit
bitget	Get bit
bitshift	Bitwise shift

Set Operators	
union	Set union
unique	Set unique
intersect	Set intersection
setdiff	Set difference
setxor	Set EXCLUSIVE OR
ismember	True for set member

Programming Language Constructs

Control Flow	
if	Conditionally execute statements
else	if statement condition
elseif	if statement condition
end	Terminate scope of for, while, switch, and if statements
for	Repeat statements a specific number of times
while	Repeat statements an indefinite number of times
break	Terminate execution of while or for loop
switch	Switch among several cases based on expression
case	switch statement case
otherwise	Default switch statement case
return	Return to invoking function

Evaluation and Execution	
eval	Execute string with MATLAB expression
feval	Execute function specified by string
evalin	Evaluate expression in workspace
builtin	Execute built-in function from overloaded method
assignin	Assign variable in workspace
run	Run script

Scripts, Functions, and Variables	
script	About MATLAB scripts and M-files
function	Add new function
global	Define global variable
mfilename	Name of currently executing M-file
lists	Comma separated lists
exist	Check if variables or functions are defined
isglobal	True for global variables

Argument Handling	
nargchk	Validate number of input arguments
nargin	Number of function input arguments
nargout	Number of function output arguments
varargin	Variable length input argument list
varargout	Variable length output argument list
inputname	Input argument name

Message Display	
error	Display error message and abort function
warning	Display warning message
lasterr	Last error message
errortrap	Skip error during testing
disp	Display an array
fprintf	Display formatted message
sprintf	Write formatted data to a string

Interactive Input	
input	Prompt for user input
keyboard	Invoke keyboard from M-file
pause	Wait for user response
uimenu	Create user interface menu
uicontrol	Create user interface control

Elementary Matrices and Matrix Manipulation

Elementary Matrices	
zeros	Zeros array
ones	Ones array
eye	Identity matrix
repmat	Replicate and tile array
rand	Uniformly distributed random numbers
randn	Normally distributed random numbers
linspace	Linearly spaced vector
logspace	Logarithmically spaced vector
meshgrid	X and Y arrays for three-dimensional plots
:	Regularly spaced vector and index into matrix

Basic Array Information	
`size`	Size of matrix
`length`	Length of vector
`ndims`	Number of dimensions
`disp`	Display matrix or text
`isempty`	True for empty matrix
`isequal`	True if arrays are identical
`isnumeric`	True for numeric arrays
`islogical`	True for logical array
`logical`	Convert numeric values to logical

Matrix Manipulation	
`reshape`	Change size
`diag`	Diagonal matrices and diagonals of matrix
`tril`	Extract lower triangular part
`triu`	Extract upper triangular part
`fliplr`	Flip matrix in left/right direction
`flipud`	Flip matrix in up/down direction
`flipdim`	Flip matrix along specified dimension
`rot90`	Rotate matrix 90 degrees
`:`	Regularly spaced vector and index into matrix
`find`	Find indices of nonzero elements
`end`	Last index
`sub2ind`	Linear index from multiple subscripts
`ind2sub`	Multiple subscripts from linear index

Special Variables and Constants	
ans	Most recent answer
eps	Floating-point relative accuracy
realmax	Largest positive floating-point number
realmin	Smallest positive floating-point number
pi	3.1415926535897....
i, j	Imaginary unit
inf	Infinity
NaN	Not-a-Number
isnan	True for Not-a-Number
isinf	True for infinite elements
isfinite	True for finite elements
flops	Floating-point operation count
why	Succinct answer

Specialized Matrices	
compan	Companion matrix
gallery	Higham test matrices
hadamard	Hadamard matrix
hankel	Hankel matrix
hilb	Hilbert matrix
invhilb	Inverse Hilbert matrix
magic	Magic square
pascal	Pascal matrix
rosser	Classic symmetric eigenvalue test problem
toeplitz	Toeplitz matrix
vander	Vandermonde matrix
wilkinson	Wilkinson's eigenvalue test matrix

Elementary Math Functions

Trigonometric	
sin	Sine
sinh	Hyperbolic sine
asin	Inverse sine
asinh	Inverse hyperbolic sine
cos	Cosine
cosh	Hyperbolic cosine
acos	Inverse cosine
acosh	Inverse hyperbolic cosine
tan	Tangent
tanh	Hyperbolic tangent
atan	Inverse tangent
atan2	Four-quadrant inverse tangent
atanh	Inverse hyperbolic tangent
sec	Secant
sech	Hyperbolic secant
asec	Inverse secant
asech	Inverse hyperbolic secant
csc	Cosecant
csch	Hyperbolic cosecant
acsc	Inverse cosecant
acsch	Inverse hyperbolic cosecant
cot	Cotangent
coth	Hyperbolic cotangent
acot	Inverse cotangent
acoth	Inverse hyperbolic cotangent

Exponential	
exp	Exponential
log	Natural logarithm
log10	Common (base 10) logarithm
log2	Base 2 logarithm and dissect floating-point number
pow2	Base 2 power and scale floating-point number
sqrt	Square root
nextpow2	Next higher power of 2

Complex	
abs	Absolute value
angle	Phase angle
conj	Complex conjugate
imag	Complex imaginary part
real	Complex real part
unwrap	Unwrap phase angle
isreal	True for real array
cplxpair	Sort numbers into complex conjugate pairs

Rounding and Remainder	
fix	Round toward zero
floor	Round toward minus infinity
ceil	Round toward plus infinity
round	Round toward nearest integer
mod	Modulus (signed remainder after division)
rem	Remainder after division
sign	Signum

Specialized Math Functions

Specialized Math Functions	
airy	Airy functions
besselj	Bessel function of the first kind
bessely	Bessel function of the second kind
besselh	Bessel function of the third kind (Hankel function)
besseli	Modified Bessel function of the first kind
besselk	Modified Bessel function of the second kind
beta	Beta function
betainc	Incomplete beta function
betaln	Logarithm of beta function
ellipj	Jacobi elliptic functions
ellipke	Complete elliptic integral
erf	Error function
erfc	Complementary error function
erfcx	Scaled complementary error function
erfinv	Inverse error function
expint	Exponential integral function
gamma	Gamma function
gammainc	Incomplete gamma function
gammaln	Logarithm of gamma function
legendre	Associated Legendre function
cross	Vector cross product

Number Theoretic Functions	
factor	Prime factors
isprime	True for prime numbers
primes	Generate list of prime numbers
gcd	Greatest common divisor
lcm	Least common multiple
rat	Rational approximation
rats	Rational output
perms	All possible permutations
nchoosek	All combinations of N elements taken K at a time

Coordinate Transforms	
cart2sph	Transform Cartesian to spherical coordinates
cart2pol	Transform Cartesian to polar coordinates
pol2cart	Transform polar to Cartesian coordinates
sph2cart	Transform spherical to Cartesian coordinates
hsv2rgb	Convert hue-saturation-value colors to red-green-blue
rgb2hsv	Convert red-green-blue colors to hue-saturation-value

Matrix Functions and Numerical Linear Algebra

Matrix Analysis	
norm	Matrix or vector norm
normest	Estimate the matrix 2-norm
rank	Matrix rank
det	Determinant
trace	Sum of diagonal elements
null	Null space
orth	Orthogonalization
rref	Reduced row echelon form
subspace	Angle between two subspaces

Linear Equations	
\ and /	Linear equation solution; use help slash
inv	Matrix inverse
cond	Condition number with respect to inversion
condest	1-norm condition number estimate
chol	Cholesky factorization
cholinc	Incomplete Cholesky factorization
lu	LU factorization
luinc	Incomplete LU factorization
qr	Orthogonal-triangular decomposition
nnls	Non-negative least squares
pinv	Pseudoinverse
lscov	Least squares with known covariance

Eigenvalues and Singular Values	
eig	Eigenvalues and eigenvectors
svd	Singular-value decomposition
eigs	A few eigenvalues
svds	A few singular values
poly	Characteristic polynomial
polyeig	Polynomial eigenvalue problem
condeig	Condition number with respect to eigenvalues
hess	Hessenberg form
qz	QZ factorization for generalized eigenvalues
schur	Schur decomposition

Matrix Functions	
expm	Matrix exponential
logm	Matrix logarithm
sqrtm	Matrix square root
funm	Evaluate general matrix function

Factorization Utilities	
qrdelete	Delete column from QR factorization
qrinsert	Insert column in QR factorization
rsf2csf	Real block diagonal form to complex diagonal form
cdf2rdf	Complex diagonal form to real block diagonal form
balance	Diagonal scaling to improve eigenvalue accuracy
planerot	Given's plane rotation

Data Analysis and Fourier Transforms

Basic Operations	
max	Largest component
min	Smallest component
mean	Average or mean value
median	Median value
std	Standard deviation
sort	Sort in ascending order
sortrows	Sort rows in ascending order
sum	Sum of elements
prod	Product of elements
hist	Histogram
trapz	Trapezoidal numerical integration
cumsum	Cumulative sum of elements
cumprod	Cumulative product of elements
cumtrapz	Cumulative trapezoidal numerical integration

Finite Differences	
diff	Difference and approximate derivative
gradient	Approximate gradient
del2	Discrete Laplacian

Correlation	
corrcoef	Correlation coefficients
cov	Covariance matrix
subspace	Angle between subspaces

Filtering and Convolution	
`filter`	One-dimensional digital filter
`filter2`	Two-dimensional digital filter
`conv`	Convolution and polynomial multiplication
`conv2`	Two-dimensional convolution
`convn`	N-dimensional convolution
`deconv`	Deconvolution and polynomial division

Fourier Transforms	
`fft`	Discrete Fourier transform
`fft2`	Two-dimensional discrete Fourier transform
`fftn`	N-dimensional discrete Fourier transform
`ifft`	Inverse discrete Fourier transform
`ifft2`	Two-dimensional inverse discrete Fourier transform
`ifftn`	N-dimensional inverse discrete Fourier transform
`fftshift`	Move zeroth lag to center of spectrum

Sound and Audio	
`sound`	Play vector as sound
`soundsc`	Autoscale and play vector as sound
`speak`	Convert input string to speech (Macintosh only)
`recordsound`	Record sound (Macintosh only)
`soundcap`	Sound capabilities (Macintosh only)
`mu2lin`	Convert mu-law encoding to linear signal
`lin2mu`	Convert linear signal to mu-law encoding

Audio File Inport/export	
auwrite	Write NeXT/SUN (".au") sound file
auread	Read NeXT/SUN (".au") sound file
wavwrite	Write Microsoft WAVE (".wav") sound file
wavread	Read Microsoft WAVE (".wav") sound file
readsnd	Read SND resources and files (Macintosh only)
writesnd	Write SND resources and files (Macintosh only)

Interpolation and Polynomials

Data Interpolation	
interp1	One-dimensional interpolation (table lookup)
interp1q	Quick one-dimensional linear interpolation
interpft	One-dimensional interpolation using FFT method
interp2	Two-dimensional interpolation (table lookup)
interp3	Three-dimensional interpolation (table lookup)
interpn	N-dimensional interpolation (table lookup)
griddata	Data gridding and surface fitting

Spline Interpolation	
spline	Cubic spline interpolation
ppval	Evaluate piecewise polynomial

Geometric Analysis	
delaunay	Delaunay triangulation
dsearch	Search Delaunay triangulation for nearest point
tsearch	Closest triangle search
convhull	Convex hull
voronoi	Voronoi diagram
inpolygon	True for points inside polygonal region
rectint	Rectangle intersection area
polyarea	Area of polygon

Polynomials	
roots	Find polynomial roots
poly	Convert roots to polynomial
polyval	Evaluate polynomial
polyvalm	Evaluate polynomial with matrix argument
residue	Partial-fraction expansion (residues)
polyfit	Fit polynomial to data
polyder	Differentiate polynomial
conv	Multiply polynomials
deconv	Divide polynomials

Function Functions and ODE Solvers

Optimization and Root Finding	
fmin	Minimize function of one variable
fmins	Minimize function of several variables
fzero	Find zero of function of one variable

M-File List of Student Edition

Numerical Integration (Quadrature)	
quad	Numerically evaluate integral, low-order method
quad8	Numerically evaluate integral, higher-order method
dblquad	Numerically evaluate double integral

Plotting	
ezplot	Easy-to-use function plotter
fplot	Plot function

Inline Function Object	
inline	Construct INLINE object
argnames	Argument names
formula	Function formula
char	Convert INLINE object to character array

Ordinary Differential Equation Solvers	
ode45	Solve non-stiff differential equations, medium-order method
ode23	Solve non-stiff differential equations, low-order method
ode113	Solve non-stiff differential equations, variable-order method
ode15s	Solve stiff differential equations, variable-order method
ode23s	Solve stiff differential equations, low-order method
odefile	ODE file syntax

ODE Option Handling	
odeset	Create/alter ODE OPTIONS structure
odeget	Get ODE OPTIONS parameters

ODE Output Functions	
odeplot	Time series ODE output function
odephas2	Two-dimensional phase plane ODE output function
odephas3	Three-dimensional phase plane ODE output function
odeprint	Command window printing ODE output function

Sparse Matrices

Elementary Sparse Matrices	
speye	Sparse identity matrix
sprand	Sparse uniformly distributed random matrix
sprandn	Sparse normally distributed random matrix
sprandsym	Sparse random symmetric matrix
spdiags	Sparse matrix formed from diagonals

Full to Sparse Conversion	
sparse	Create sparse matrix
full	Convert sparse matrix to full matrix
find	Find indices of nonzero elements
spconvert	Import from sparse matrix external format

M-File List of Student Edition

Working with Sparse Matrices	
nnz	Number of nonzero matrix elements
nonzeros	Nonzero matrix elements
nzmax	Amount of storage allocated for nonzero matrix elements
spones	Replace nonzero sparse matrix elements with ones
spalloc	Allocate space for sparse matrix
issparse	True for sparse matrix
spfun	Apply function to nonzero matrix elements
spy	Visualize sparsity pattern

Reordering Algorithms	
colmmd	Column minimum degree permutation
symmmd	Symmetric minimum degree permutation
symrcm	Symmetric reverse Cuthill-McKee permutation
colperm	Column permutation
randperm	Random permutation
dmperm	Dulmage-Mendelsohn permutation

Linear Algebra	
eigs	A few eigenvalues
svds	A few singular values
luinc	Incomplete LU factorization
cholinc	Incomplete Cholesky factorization
normest	Estimate the matrix 2-norm
condest	1-norm condition number estimate
sprank	Structural rank

Linear Equations (Iterative Methods)	
pcg	Preconditioned conjugate gradients method
bicg	Biconjugate gradients method
bicgstab	Biconjugate gradients stabilized method
cgs	Conjugate gradients squared method
gmres	Generalized minimum residual method
qmr	Quasi-minimal residual method

Operations on Graphs (Trees)	
treelayout	Lay out tree or forest
treeplot	Plot picture of tree
etree	Elimination tree
etreeplot	Plot elimination tree
gplot	Plot graph, as in "graph theory"

Miscellaneous	
symbfact	Symbolic factorization analysis
spparms	Set parameters for sparse matrix routines
spaugment	Form least squares augmented system

Two-dimensional Graphs

Elementary X–Y Graphs	
plot	Linear plot
loglog	Log-log scale plot
semilogx	Semi-log scale plot
semilogy	Semi-log scale plot
polar	Polar coordinate plot
plotyy	Graphs with y tick labels on the left and right

Axis Control	
axis	Control axis scaling and appearance
zoom	Zoom in and out on a two-dimensional plot
grid	Grid lines
box	Axis box
hold	Hold current graph
axes	Create axes in arbitrary positions
subplot	Create axes in tiled positions

Graph Annotation	
legend	Graph legend
title	Graph title
xlabel	x-axis label
ylabel	y-axis label
text	Text annotation
gtext	Place text with mouse

Hardcopy and Printing	
print	Print graph or SIMULINK system; or save graph to M-file
printopt	Printer defaults
orient	Set paper orientation

Three-dimensional Graphs

Elementary Three-dimensional Plots	
plot3	Plot lines and points in three-dimensional space
mesh	Three-dimensional mesh surface
surf	Three-dimensional colored surface
fill3	Filled three-dimensional polygons

Color Control	
colormap	Color look-up table
caxis	Pseudocolor axis scaling
shading	Color shading mode
hidden	Mesh hidden line removal mode
brighten	Brighten or darken colormap

Lighting	
surfl	Three-dimensional shaded surface with lighting
lighting	Lighting mode
material	Material reflectance mode
specular	Specular reflectance
diffuse	Diffuse reflectance
surfnorm	Surface normals

Colormaps	
hsv	Hue-saturation-value colormap
hot	Black-red-yellow-white colormap
gray	Linear gray-scale colormap
bone	Gray-scale with tinge of blue colormap
copper	Linear copper-tone colormap
pink	Pastel shades of pink colormap
white	All-white colormap
flag	Alternating red, white, blue, and black colormap
lines	Colormap with the line colors
colorcube	Enhanced color-cube colormap
jet	Variant of HSV
prism	Prism colormap
cool	Shades of cyan and magenta colormap
autumn	Shades of red and yellow colormap
spring	Shades of magenta and yellow colormap
winter	Shades of blue and green colormap
summer	Shades of green and yellow colormap

Axis Control	
axis	Control axis scaling and appearance
zoom	Zoom in and out on a two-dimensional plot
grid	Grid lines
box	Axis box
hold	Hold current graph
axes	Create axes in arbitrary positions
subplot	Create axes in tiled positions

Three-dimensional Graphs

Viewpoint Control	
view	Three-dimensional graph viewpoint specification
viewmtx	View transformation matrix
rotate3d	Interactively rotate view of three-dimensional plot

Graph Annotation	
title	Graph title
xlabel	x-axis label
ylabel	y-axis label
zlabel	z-axis label
colorbar	Display colorbar (color scale)
text	Text annotation
gtext	Mouse placement of text

Hardcopy and Printing	
print	Print graph or SIMULINK system; or save graph to M-file
printopt	Printer defaults
orient	Set paper orientation

Specialized Graphs

Specialized Two-dimensional Graphs	
area	Filled area plot
bar	Bar graph
barh	Horizontal bar graph
bar3	Three-dimensional bar graph
bar3h	Horizontal three-dimensional bar graph
comet	Comet-like trajectory
errorbar	Error bar plot
ezplot	Easy-to-use function plotter
feather	Feather plot
fill	Filled two-dimensional polygons
fplot	Plot function
hist	Histogram
pareto	Pareto chart
pie	Pie chart
pie3	Three-dimensional pie chart
plotmatrix	Scatter plot matrix
ribbon	Draw two-dimenionsal lines as ribbons in three-dimensional
stem	Discrete sequence or "stem" plot
stairs	Stairstep plot

Contour and Two-and-a-half-dimensional Graphs	
contour	Contour plot
contourf	Filled contour plot
contour3	Three-dimensional contour plot
clabel	Contour plot elevation labels
pcolor	Pseudocolor (checkerboard) plot
quiver	Quiver plot
voronoi	Voronoi diagram

Specialized Three-dimensional Graphs	
comet3	Three-dimensional comet-like trajectories
meshc	Combination mesh/contour plot
meshz	Three-dimensional mesh with curtain
stem3	Three-dimensional stem plot
quiver3	Three-dimensional quiver plot
slice	Volumetric slice plot
surfc	Combination surf/contour plot
trisurf	Triangular surface plot
trimesh	Triangular mesh plot
waterfall	Waterfall plot

Images Display and File I/O	
image	Display image
imagesc	Scale data and display as image
colormap	Color look-up table
gray	Linear gray-scale colormap
contrast	Gray-scale colormap to enhance image contrast
brighten	Brighten or darken colormap
colorbar	Display colorbar (color scale)
imread	Read image from graphics file
imwrite	Write image to graphics file
imfinfo	Information about graphics file

Movies and Animation	
capture	Screen capture of current figure
moviein	Initialize movie-frame memory
getframe	Get movie frame
movie	Play recorded movie frames
qtwrite	Translate movie into QuickTime format (Macintosh only)
rotate	Rotate object about specified orgin and direction
frame2im	Convert movie frame to indexcd image
im2frame	Convert index image into movie format

Color-related Functions	
spinmap	Spin colormap
rgbplot	Plot colormap
colstyle	Parse color and style from string

Solid Modeling	
cylinder	Generate cylinder
sphere	Generate sphere
patch	Create patch

Handle Graphics

Figure Window Creation and Control	
figure	Create *Figure* window
gcf	Get handle to current figure
clf	Clear current figure
shg	Show *Graph* window
close	Close figure
refresh	Refresh figure

Axis Creation and Control	
subplot	Create axes in tiled positions
axes	Create axes in arbitrary positions
gca	Get handle to current axes
cla	Clear current axes
axis	Control axis scaling and appearance
box	Axis box
caxis	Control pseudocolor axis scaling
hold	Hold current graph
ishold	Return hold state

Handle Graphics Objects	
figure	Create figure window
axes	Create axes
line	Create line
text	Create text
patch	Create patch
surface	Create surface
image	Create image
light	Create light
uicontrol	Create user interface control
uimenu	Create user interface menu

Handle Graphics Operations	
set	Set object properties
get	Get object properties
reset	Reset object properties
delete	Delete object
gco	Get handle to current object
gcbo	Get handle to current callback object
gcbf	Get handle to current callback figure
drawnow	Flush pending graphics events
findobj	Find objects with specified property values
copyobj	Make copy of graphics object and its children

Hardcopy and Printing	
print	Print graph or SIMULINK system; or save graph to M-file
printopt	Printer defaults
orient	Set paper orientation

Utilities	
closereq	Figure close request function
newplot	M-file preamble for NextPlot property
ishandle	True for graphics handles

Graphical User Interface Tools

GUI Functions	
uicontrol	Create user interface control
uimenu	Create user interface menu
ginput	Graphical input from mouse
dragrect	Drag XOR rectangles with mouse
rbbox	Rubberband box
selectmoveresize	Interactively select, move, resize, or copy objects
waitforbuttonpress	Wait for key/buttonpress over figure
waitfor	Block execution and wait for event
uiwait	Block execution and wait for resume
uiresume	Resume execution of blocked M-file

GUI Design Tools	
guide	Design GUI
align	Align user interface controls and axes
cbedit	Edit callback
menuedit	Edit menu
propedit	Edit property

Dialog Boxes	
dialog	Create dialog figure
axlimdlg	Axes limits dialog box
errordlg	Error dialog box
helpdlg	Help dialog box
inputdlg	Input dialog box
listdlg	List selection dialog box
menu	Generate menu of choices for user input
msgbox	Message box
questdlg	Question dialog box
warndlg	Warning dialog box
uigetfile	Standard open file dialog box
uiputfile	Standard save file dialog box
uisetcolor	Color selection dialog box
uisetfont	Font selection dialog box
pagedlg	Page position dialog box
printdlg	Print dialog box
waitbar	Display wait bar

Menu Utilities	
makemenu	Create menu structure
menubar	Computer dependent default setting for MenuBar property
umtoggle	Toggle "checked" status of uimenu object
winmenu	Create submenu for "Window" menu item

Toolbar Button Group Utilities	
btngroup	Create toolbar button group
btnstate	Query state of toolbar button group
btnpress	Button press manager for toolbar button group
btndown	Depress button in toolbar button group
btnup	Raise button in toolbar button group

User-defined Figure/axes Property Utilities	
clruprop	Clear user-defined property
getuprop	Get value of user-defined property
setuprop	Set user-defined property

Miscellaneous Utilities	
allchild	Get all object children
hidegui	Hide/unhide GUI
edtext	Interactive editing of axes text objects
getstatus	Get status text string in figure
setstatus	Set status text string in figure
popupstr	Get popup menu selection string
remapfig	Transform figure objects' positions
setptr	Set figure pointer
getptr	Get figure pointer
overobj	Get handle of object the pointer is over

Character Strings

General	
char	Create character array (string)
double	Convert string to numeric character codes
cellstr	Create cell array of strings from character array
blanks	String of blanks
deblank	Remove trailing blanks
eval	Execute string with MATLAB expression

String Tests	
ischar	True for character array (string)
iscellstr	True for cell array of strings
isletter	True for letters of the alphabet
isspace	True for white-space characters

String Operations	
strcat	Concatenate strings
strvcat	Vertically concatenate strings
strcmp	Compare strings
strncmp	Compare first N characters of strings
findstr	Find one string within another
strjust	Justify character array
strmatch	Find possible matches for string
strrep	Replace string with another
strtok	Find token in string
upper	Convert string to uppercase
lower	Convert string to lowercase

String to Number Conversion	
num2str	Convert number to string
int2str	Convert integer to string
mat2str	Convert matrix to evaluable string
str2num	Convert string to number
sprintf	Write formatted data to string
sscanf	Read string under format control

Base Number Conversion	
hex2num	Convert IEEE hexadecimal to double precision number
hex2dec	Convert hexadecimal string to decimal integer
dec2hex	Convert decimal integer to hexadecimal string
bin2dec	Convert binary string to decimal integer
dec2bin	Convert decimal integer to binary string
base2dec	Convert base B string to decimal integer
dec2base	Convert decimal integer to base B string

File Input/Output

File Opening and Closing	
fopen	Open file
fclose	Close file

Binary File I/O	
fread	Read binary data from file
fwrite	Write binary data to file

Formatted File I/O	
fscanf	Read formatted data from file
fprintf	Write formatted data to file
fgetl	Read line from file, discard newline character
fgets	Read line from file, keep newline character
input	Prompt for user input

String Conversion	
sprintf	Write formatted data to string
sscanf	Read string under format control

File Positioning	
ferror	Inquire file error status
feof	Test for end-of-file
fseek	Set file position indicator
ftell	Get file position indicator
frewind	Rewind file

Filename Handling	
matlabroot	Root directory of MATLAB installation
filesep	Directory separator for this platform
pathsep	Path separator for this platform
mexext	MEX filename extension for this platform
fullfile	Build full filename from parts
partialpath	Partial pathnames
tempdir	Get temporary directory
tempname	Get temporary file

File Import/export Functions	
load	Load workspace from MAT-file
save	Save workspace to MAT-file
dlmread	Read ASCII delimited file
dlmwrite	Write ASCII delimited file
wk1read	Read spreadsheet (WK1) file
wk1write	Write spreadsheet (WK1) file

Image File Import/export	
imread	Read image from graphics file
imwrite	Write image to graphics file
imfinfo	Return information about graphics file

Audio File Import/export	
auwrite	Write NeXT/SUN (".au") sound file
auread	Read NeXT/SUN (".au") sound file
wavwrite	Write Microsoft WAVE (".wav") sound file
wavread	Read Microsoft WAVE (".wav") sound file

Command Window I/O	
clc	Clear *Command* window
home	Send cursor home
disp	Display array
input	Prompt for user input
pause	Wait for user response

Time and Dates

Current Date and Time	
now	Current date and time as date number
date	Current date as date string
clock	Current date and time as date vector

Basic Functions	
datenum	Serial date number
datestr	String representation of date
datevec	Date components

Date Functions	
calendar	Calendar
weekday	Day of week
eomday	End of month
datetick	Date formatted tick labels

Timing Functions	
cputime	CPU time in seconds
tic, toc	Stopwatch timer
etime	Elapsed time
pause	Wait in seconds

Data Types and Structures

Data Types (Classes)	
double	Convert to double precision
sparse	Create sparse matrix
char	Create character array (string)
cell	Create cell array
struct	Create or convert to structure array
uint8	Convert to unsigned 8-bit integer
inline	Construct INLINE object

Multi-dimensional Array Functions	
cat	Concatenate arrays
ndims	Number of dimensions
ndgrid	Generate arrays for N–D functions and interpolation
permute	Permute array dimensions
ipermute	Inverse permute array dimensions
shiftdim	Shift dimensions
squeeze	Remove singleton dimensions

Cell-Array Functions	
`cell`	Create cell-array
`celldisp`	Display cell-array contents
`cellplot`	Display graphical depiction of cell array
`num2cell`	Convert numeric array into cell array
`deal`	Deal inputs to outputs
`cell2struct`	Convert cell array into structure array
`struct2cell`	Convert structure array into cell array
`iscell`	True for cell array

Structure Functions	
`struct`	Create or convert to structure array
`fieldnames`	Get structure field names
`getfield`	Get structure field contents
`setfield`	Set structure field contents
`rmfield`	Remove structure field
`isfield`	True if field is in structure array
`isstruct`	True for structures

Object-oriented Programming Functions	
`class`	Create object or return object class
`struct`	Convert object to structure array
`methods`	Display class method names
`isa`	True if object is a given class
`isobject`	True for objects
`inferiorto`	Inferior class relationship
`superiorto`	Superior class relationship

Overloadable Operators	
minus	Overloadable method for $a - b$
plus	Overloadable method for $a + b$
times	Overloadable method for $a .* b$
mtimes	Overloadable method for $a * b$
mldivide	Overloadable method for $a \setminus b$
mrdivide	Overloadable method for a / b
rdivide	Overloadable method for $a ./ b$
ldivide	Overloadable method for $a .\setminus b$
power	Overloadable method for $a .^\wedge b$
mpower	Overloadable method for $a ^\wedge b$
uminus	Overloadable method for $-a$
uplus	Overloadable method for $+a$
horzcat	Overloadable method for $[a\ b]$
vertcat	Overloadable method for $[a;b]$
le	Overloadable method for $a <\ = b$
lt	Overloadable method for $a < b$
gt	Overloadable method for $a > b$
ge	Overloadable method for $a >\ = b$
eq	Overloadable method for $a == b$
ne	Overloadable method for $a \sim\ = b$
not	Overloadable method for $\sim a$
and	Overloadable method for $a\ \&\ b$
or	Overloadable method for $a\ |\ b$
subsasgn	Overloadable method for $a(i) = b$, $a\{i\} = b$, and a.field $= b$
subsref	Overloadable method for $a(i)$, $a\{i\}$, and a.field
colon	Overloadable method for $a : b$
transpose	Overloadable method for $a.'$
ctranspose	Overloadable method for a'
subsindex	Overloadable method for $x(a)$

Dynamic Data Exchange (DDE)

DDE Client Functions	
ddeadv	Set up advisory link
ddeexec	Send string for execution
ddeinit	Initiate DDE conversation
ddepoke	Send data to application
ddereq	Request data from application
ddeterm	Terminate DDE conversation
ddeunadv	Release advisory link

Examples and Demonstrations

MATLAB/introduction	
demo	Browse demos for MATLAB, Toolboxes, and SIMULINK

MATLAB/matrices	
intro	Introduction to basic matrix operations in MATLAB
inverter	Demonstrate the inversion of a matrix
buckydem	Connectivity graph of the Buckminster Fuller geodesic dome
sparsity	Demonstrate effect of sparsity orderings
matmanip	Introduction to matrix manipulation
eigmovie	Symmetric eigenvalue movie
rrefmovie	Computation of reduced row echelon form
delsqdemo	Finite difference Laplacian on various domains
sepdemo	Separators for a finite element mesh
airfoil	Display sparse matrix from NASA airfoil

MATLAB/numerics	
funfuns	Demonstrate functions that operate on other functions
fitdemo	Nonlinear curve fit with simplex algorithm
sunspots	FFT: The answer is 1108; what is the question?
e2pi	Two-dimensional visual solutions: Which is greater, e ^ pi or pi ^ e?
bench	MATLAB benchmark
fftdemo	Use of the fast finite Fourier transform
census	Try to predict the U.S. population in the year 2000
spline2d	Demonstrate GINPUT and SPLINE in two dimensions
lotkademo	An example of ordinary differential equation solution
quaddemo	Adaptive quadrature
zerodemo	Zerofinding with fzero
fplotdemo	Plot a function
quake	Loma Prieta earthquake

MATLAB/visualization	
graf2d	Demonstrate two-dimensional plots
graf2d2	Demonstrate three-dimensional plots
grafcplx	Demonstrate complex function plots in MATLAB
lorenz	Plot the orbit around the Lorenz chaotic attractor
imageext	Image colormaps: changing and rotating colormaps
xpklein	Klein bottle demo
vibes	Vibration movie: vibrating L-shaped membrane
xpsound	Visualizing sound: Demonstrate MATLAB's sound capability
imagedemo	Demonstrate MATLAB's image capability
penny	Several views of the penny data
earthmap	View Earth's topography
xfourier	Graphic demo of Fourier series expansion
colormenu	Select colormap
cplxdemo	Maps of functions of a complex variable

MATLAB/language	
xplang	Introduction to the MATLAB language
hndlgraf	Demonstrate Handle Graphics for line plots
graf3d	Demonstrate Handle Graphics for surface plots
hndlaxis	Demonstrate Handle Graphics for axes

General Demo/helper Functions	
`cmdlnwin`	A Demo gateway routine for playing command line demos
`cmdlnbgn`	Set up for command line demos
`cmdlnend`	Clean up after command line demos
`finddemo`	Finds demos available for individual toolboxes
`helpfun`	Utility function for displaying help text conveniently
`pltmat`	Display a matrix in a *Figure* window

MATLAB/helper Functions	
`bucky`	Graph of the Buckminster Fuller geodesic dome
`peaks`	A sample function of two variables
`membrane`	Generate The MathWorks' logo

Index

M

Workspace Browser button, *Command window*, 24